Arnold Toynbee
Arthur Koestler
and others

•

LIFE AFTER DEATH

McGraw-Hill Book Company
New York   St. Louis   San Francisco

123456789   BPBP   79876

Library of Congress Cataloging in Publication Data

Toynbee, Arnold Joseph, 1889-1975.
    Life after death.

    Includes index.
    1. Future life—Addresses, essays, lectures.
I. Koestler, Arthur, 1905-   joint author. II. Title.
BL535.T69 1976   236'.2   76-16175
ISBN 0-07-065124-8

Contents

●

Part I

I

Man's concern with life after death

Arnold Toynbee

•

Concepts of the Sequel to Death

Death is the price paid by life for an enhancement of the complexity of a live organism's structure. Biological research has demonstrated that even the simplest live organisms are complex to a degree that astonishes a layman. However, relatively simple species perpetuate themselves without either dying or begetting progeny; instead, they divide periodically into separate specimens of the species, and then each separated specimen redivides in its turn. But life has not succeeded in attaining higher degrees of complexity without having to discard each specimen of a higher species and to replace it by a new one which is produced by sexual intercourse and procreation. A specimen that has ripened for mating with a specimen of the opposite sex to reproduce their kind and that has then duly performed this function becomes expendable. The formula in the genealogical verses of Chapter 12 of the *Book of Genesis* implies that an individual human being lives, not for his own sake, but for the sake of perpetuating his race by begetting children.

Nevertheless, every living being that is subject to death exerts itself to stay alive, whether or not it has produced progeny. Some non-human species grieve, as human beings grieve, at the loss of their mates, and also at the loss of other members of their community in the case of some social, non-human animals. But human beings appear to be unique among the fauna inhabiting the 'biosphere' that coats the planet earth in being aware that they themselves and all their living contemporaries are going to die, and that death has already overtaken countless earlier generations. The Greek historian Herodotus reports that the Persian emperor Xerxes wept after he had reviewed his immense expeditionary force, because he realized that not a single member of it would still be alive one hundred years later. This human awareness of the inevitability of death is accompanied by a concern with death, and Man's concern with death makes him also feel concern about the sequel to death.

The physical sequel to death is no mystery. After death, the dead person's material body disintegrates. It is re-absorbed into the inanimate component of the biosphere. Between the biosphere's inanimate and animate components there is a constant interchange of matter. Every specimen of a species is taking in fresh supplies of matter and is discarding waste matter so long as it remains alive; every species is producing new live specimens and is discarding corpses so long as the species survives. But a live organism does not consist solely of the matter that constitutes its body; it is a specimen of animate matter; and a human being is not only animate; he is also conscious, and his consciousness enables him to make choices, to remember past events, and to foresee some future events – among others, his own inevitable eventual death.

The corpse of a once live human being or non-human animal is a familiar sight, but no one has ever seen, or had the impression that he has seen, an unembodied live being. When someone sees a ghost, the ghost appears visually in the familiar form of one of the embodied human beings whom the seer of the ghost encounters in normal life. Moreover, ghosts appear not naked, but clothed, and this sometimes in the dress of an earlier age than the ghost-seer's own. A ghost that did not appear in human form would be invisible; in fact, an unembodied live human being has never been seen, except on the hypothesis that a ghost is alive but is incorporeal.

This hypothesis is unconvincing. It seems more likely that the apparent visibility of a ghost is an hallucination. Visibility and audibility are properties of matter. But material media such as sight, sound, and touch are not the only possible means of communication between conscious personalities, and it is conceivable that, in some cases, the appearance of a ghost may be an incidental accompaniment of a real, non-visual communication between the person who sees the ghost and another person who may be either dead or else still incarnate but not physically present. In Rosalind Heywood's contribution to the present book (see pp. 203–37) the reader will find accounts of instances of communication between two human beings who are both still incarnate in the biosphere; between one human being who is still incarnate and one who was once incarnate, but has ceased to be incarnate as a result of his having died; and between a human being and a spiritual presence which is not incarnate and which presumably never has been and never will be. These instances are first-hand experiences of Mrs Heywood's. Since they are, by their very nature, the personal experiences of an individual human being, and not the identical common experiences of a number of people, it is impossible, as Mrs Heywood points out, to demonstrate that they are experiences of communications that have really occurred. However, I should be surprised if readers of Mrs Heywood's chapter do not conclude, as I do, that her experiences are more likely to be valid than to be explicable as accidental coincidences or as illusions.

There is now a widespread recognition of the reality of extrasensory perception as a medium of communication between two or more incarnate persons. I have witnessed a number of instances of communication by this means, and the evidence for its reality is, to my mind, cogent. However, the reality of extrasensory communication between the living is contested; and the reality of extrasensory communications with the dead, or with conscious personalities that have never been incarnate, is disputed still more vehemently. All the same, the wise course for inquirers into the destiny of a personality after death is surely to keep their minds open for entertaining the possibility that in some cases the dead may have indicated the reality of the survival of their personalities by really entering into communication with persons who are still incarnate.

In infancy, human consciousness is only nascent; in old age it becomes dim or extinct in some cases. A human being may also be born mentally defective, and he may become mentally deranged at any stage of life, but these maladies are exceptional. A normal live human being is not only alive; he is also conscious. At death, if not before death, his consciousness, as well as his life, disappears – in contrast to his corpse. A corpse does not disappear. The matter of which it is composed is not annihilated; the corpse disintegrates, yet its physical components manifestly continue to exist. Unlike a body, however, life and consciousness are invisible and impalpable. What, then, has happened to the life that formerly animated the now dead body? And, if it is a human dead body, what has happened to the consciousness that formerly accompanied that person's life? In other words, what has happened to his personality?

We do not know what happens to a human being's personality after death. We have no conclusive and indisputable evidence about the sequel for the personality, as we have about the sequel for the body. The question presents itself insistently, and it has been answered in a number of different guesses. These guesses may be based on personal experiences, but these experiences are not verifiable. Some of the guesses are incompatible with others, and some people in some societies have given credence simultaneously to two or more incompatible guesses. In this field there is room for variety and for incongruity, because here we are in the realm of guesswork, not of demonstration based on observation. However, the traditional contrast between the uncertainty of guesswork and the certainty of demonstration has now been called in question by the findings of recent scientific observation of matter. When 'matter' is observed in minute quantities moving at high speeds, it presents itself *either* as material particles *or* as non-material waves of energy. These two equally well-attested appearances are incompatible with each other. They are each observed, but this never simultaneously. Thus the nature of 'matter' has become enigmatic as a consequence of the scientific observer's improvement of his means of observation. This paradox was unforeseen. It has taken its discoverers by surprise.

The most logical guess about the fate of a human personality after death is to suppose that it is analogous to the fate of a corpse. At death the corpse begins to disintegrate, and, if we assume that the analogy is valid, we should conclude that, at death, a human being's personality becomes extinct. This guess has had adherents. It was held to be the truth by the Epicurean school of Greek philosophers. Its most earnest, and most distinguished, spokesman is the Roman Epicurean poet Lucretius; Lucretius's doctrine has had an echo in the poetry of a modern English poet, A. E. Housman. This Epicurean answer to the question of the sequel to death for a human personality may look like the obvious answer. It is, indeed, a 'commonsense' inference from the known to the unknown, or, it would now seem to be nearer to the truth to say: to the unknown from what was believed to be known for certain till recently. No one has ever met an unincarnate live human being, unless a ghost that appears in human form is deemed to be both unincarnate and alive. Every human personality that any human being has encountered, apart from the infrequent phenomenon of the appearance of ghosts and the unverifiable experience of extra-sensory communication with the dead, has been associated unquestionably with a live human body. It seems reasonable to infer that, when the body dies and disintegrates, the personality, which instantly disappears, is annihilated simultaneously.

Lucretius makes much of the fact, already mentioned in the present essay, that a human being's personality is sometimes deranged, and sometimes fades out into senility, before this human being's body is overtaken by physical death. Lucretius also observes that a considerable part of a human being's lifetime is spent in sleep, and he suggests that the suspension of consciousness in sleep is comparable with the annihilation of consciousness which, according to Epicurean doctrine, is the sequel to physical death. However, a psychologist might point out that a sleeper dreams; that his dreams are probably much more copious than his memory of them when he re-awakes; and that while, in sleep, the consciousness temporarily abdicates, the subconscious layer of the psyche then regains a temporary freedom and makes the most of this. The subconscious layer of the psyche, as well as the conscious layer, is a genuine and an integral part of a human being's personality; and consequently the Epicurean comparison of sleep with death is an imperfect analogy.

In any case, it is remarkable that this Epicurean view of the personality's fate after death has not been the prevalent view, in spite of its being obviously the 'commonsense' view. Possibly it is now the prevalent view in Western countries and also among a minority in non-Western countries in which the modern Western scientists' recent *Weltanschauung* has been accepted by the intelligentsia. This, however, is doubtful, whereas it is certain that an overwhelming majority of mankind, in all places and at all times since our ancestors awakened to consciousness, has held that a human being's personality is not annihilated at death. There has been a consensus in favour of this negative guess, though there has not been any unanimity in the positive answers to the question of the personality's destiny after death – a question that arises for anyone who rejects the guess that, at death, a human being's personality is extinguished. This general rejection of the hypothesis of extinction might be discounted as being inspired by self-conceit or by an unwillingness to face an unpalatable truth. All the same, the consensus of a majority of mankind in rejecting the hypothesis of annihilation requires a serious consideration of the alternative guesses – bearing in mind such experiences as those described by Mrs Heywood.

One alternative guess is still more logical than the hypothesis that, at death, the personality is extinguished. A corpse is not extinguished; it is re-absorbed into the inanimate component of the biosphere. Since the biosphere manifestly does have an inanimate component, presumably it also has a live component and a conscious component. The inanimate component of the biosphere is not found only in the biosphere. Other stars have been proved, by analysis of the spectrum of the light that they emit, to have material components that are identical with elements present in the physical composition of the planet earth. Actual specimens of matter have now been brought to earth from the earth's moon, which is the nearest star to earth. On this analogy it might be guessed that the life and consciousness which exist in the biosphere that coats the planet earth are not confined to this infinitesimally small fraction of the stellar cosmos, and may also exist, unassociated with matter, in some incorporeal order of reality. This guess suggests the further guess that when, at death, a human body is reabsorbed into the inanimate material component of the cosmos, the life and the personality of the human being who has died, are likewise reabsorbed respectively into a hypothetical, but logically credible non-material, live mode and conscious mode of being.

The material component of a living organism in the biosphere is a portion of the biosphere's matter that is temporarily separated from the rest – both from the inanimate portion and from portions temporarily embodied in other live organisms. This segregation of a portion of matter in a living organism is not only temporary; it is also contingent. It depends on the organism's ability to obtain air, water, food, and replacements of its chemical components from the rest of the biosphere. As Lucretius puts it, 'life is not given to anyone in absolute ownership; it is given to all of us for [temporary] usufruct [only]'. It would be logical to guess that this is also true for a human personality (i.e. for the sum total of the conscious and the subconscious 'layers' of a human psyche). It might be guessed that there is a non-material non-personal or suprapersonal spiritual reality; that this, like the material aspect of reality, exists (in metaphorical terms taken from our spatial vocabulary) 'beyond' as well as 'within', the biosphere that coats our planet; that a human personality is a temporarily detached splinter of this unconfined spiritual reality; and that, at death, the personality is reabsorbed into the spiritual reality that is its source. A few people have had experiences which suggest that this is the truth; many people have had intuitions that it is the truth, and some people, especially poets, have expressed these intuitions (perhaps derived, in their case, from experiences) in memorable words.

Examples are the English poet, Henry Vaughan's, poem *The Retreat*, and another English poet, William Wordsworth's better-known poem *Intimations of Immortality from Recollections of Early Childhood*. Though Vaughan lived a century and a half earlier than Wordsworth, there is no evidence, so far as I know, that Wordsworth's poem was consciously inspired by his predecessor's; yet the two poems agree in recording an identical memory and in drawing an identical inference from it. Each poet remembers that, in infancy, he was conscious of having formerly been the denizen of a world that is not the planet Earth's biosphere, and that the child's life in the afterglow of this 'Heaven' was blissful, in contrast to the adult's life on earth when the spiritual light that illuminated his infancy has faded out. 'Happy those early days when I/Shin'd

in my Angel-infancy' (Vaughan); 'Heaven lies about us in our infancy'
(Wordsworth). Each poet infers that, at death, he is going to return to
the blissful state of existence from which he was estranged at birth.
'Some men a forward motion love,/But I by backward steps would
move;/and when this dust falls to the urn,/In that state I came, return'
(Vaughan); 'Our noisy years seem moments in the being/Of the eternal
silence' (Wordsworth). A human life in the biosphere appears to each
poet to be an interlude which is not only brief, but is also abnormal and
unhappy. Life in the biosphere was likewise judged to be unhappy, and
therefore undesirable, by the pre-Christian Greeks (for instance, by
Sophocles, in a famous passage, as well as by Herodotus in his tale of a
dialogue between the Greek philosopher Solon and the Lydian king
Croesus).

The happy normal condition, which life on earth temporarily inter-
rupts, is called 'eternity' by Vaughan, and 'immortality' by Wordsworth.
Vaughan's image of it is 'that shady city of palm-trees'; Wordsworth's
is 'that immortal sea'. These two poets, being Christians, imagine
the eternal spiritual reality as being associated with a person in the
sense in which a human being is one. For Vaughan, the state from
which he came, and to which he will return, is illuminated by the light
of God's countenance; for Wordsworth, God himself is 'our home'.
But a person can only be a neighbour or a companion; he cannot be a
home, and, if a human being's first and last state is an 'eternal silence'
or an 'immortal sea', his personality, which is his distinctive characteristic during his life on earth, must be a peculiar feature of his existence
during this interlude. The 'eternal silence' and the 'immortal sea' from
which he has come, and to which he is going to return, are images of
a non-personal mode of spiritual being. If this eternal reality were a
divine person, and if a human being were an immortal person, the
human being in his pre-natal and post-mortem state could commune
with God, but a divine and a human person could never be absorbed
into each other. They could not, because the essence of personality is
separateness. The blissful state to which the poet looks back wistfully
and looks forward longingly is a condition in which he is not separate
from the rest of spiritual reality. A temporary alienation is the price of
personality; reabsorption into a timeless non-personal sea of spiritual
life is the sequel to the sloughing off of the separate personality that is a
feature of life on earth.

This incompatibility between psychic individuality and psyche union
is as logical as the incompatibility between particles of matter and waves
of energy. However, it has already been noted that, at a certain level of

scientific observation, identical physical phenomena present themselves, incongruously but equally cogently, now as particles and now as waves. This calls to mind the information given to Mrs Heywood by the sage who appeared to lean out of his picture to enlighten her. As between personalities incarnate in the biosphere, separateness and coalescence may be incompatible; at this spiritual level, they are logically incongruous; but, at a higher level, mundane logic may be transcended. In the words of the message that Mrs Heywood appeared to receive from the sage: 'If those two were to meet in the sense you want them to on your level, they would lose their identity. But they will be able to do so and yet retain it, when they reach ours.'

If Wordsworth had been brought up, not as a Christian, but as a Buddhist, he would have called his ode 'Intimations of Nirvana'. This Sanskrit word means 'extinguishedness', but the condition which it denotes is difficult to apprehend; for, on this subject, the Buddhist scriptures are deliberately uncommunicative. In so far as they describe Nirvana, they do this in negative terms. The positive reality may be a state in which the incompatibility between separateness and coalescence is transcended. The word Nirvana does not imply the extinction of life or of consciousness; for it is possible to reach the threshold of Nirvana before death. The Buddha himself is said to have reached this point at the moment of his enlightenment, but then to have retained his incarnate personality voluntarily, in order to teach to other sentient beings the way of release from suffering which he had discovered for himself by his own unaided spiritual efforts.

The thing that is extinguished through the attainment of Nirvana is not life and is not consciousness; it is desire, acquisitiveness, greed, grasping – impulses that are characteristic of a personality's condition while incarnate in the biosphere. Some of the Buddha's Indian contemporaries held that the core of a human being's personality – his soul – is identical with the ultimate spiritual reality and is consequently eternal in the ultimate spiritual reality's non-personal mode of being. The Buddha denied the existence of a soul. He held that a human being's consciousness is merely a stream of disparate ephemeral psychological states; but he also held that cupidity compacts these transitory psychic phenomena into a bundle that is so close-knit and so tenacious that it condemns a living being to be reborn any number of times unless and until, in the course of successive lives, the sufferer succeeds in ridding himself of the cupidity that has prevented him from making a final exit from the suffering that is inherent in life, as life is experienced by all sentient living beings that are incarnate in the biosphere. This bundle of psychological states that is an obstacle to an escape from rebirth is *karma* – an ethical current account which runs on from one incarnation to another and which is being modified by fresh debit and credit entries in each successive life. This account cannot be closed unless and until all the debit has been cleared.

According to Buddhist doctrine in all schools of Buddhism, every living being's paramount concern should be to attain Nirvana, as the Buddha attained it, by his own spiritual exertions. The Buddha has shown his followers the way, and they can draw inspiration from his example. The Buddha was not only enlightened, he was compassionate. However, since his death, he cannot help his followers directly and personally. He cannot do this because, since his death, he is in the state of Nirvana; and a being who has made his exit into Nirvana is deemed to have become inaccessible. For any aspirant to Nirvana who is not endowed with the Buddha's extraordinary spiritual power, the spiritual demand is so severe, and the way is so bleak, that the Northern School of Buddhism – called by its adherents the Mahayana ('Great Way' or 'Great Vehicle') – has conjured up a pantheon of potent accessible saviours. These are *bodhisattvas* – potential Buddhas who like the historical Buddha Siddhartha Gautama, have reached the threshold of Nirvana but have then refrained from making their exit, as the Buddha refrained till he was overtaken by death. Like the Buddha, the *bodhisattvas* have been moved by compassion for their fellow sentient beings, and they have remained accessible for aeons, and not, like the Buddha, only for the remainder of a single lifetime on earth.

In theory, Nirvana is the objective that a *bodhisattva* helps his devotees to pursue. Actually one of the *bodhisattvas*, Amitabha, offers to his devotees a nearer goal that they can reach with less strenuous spiritual effort. This nearer goal is a sojourn in a paradise before the devotee's next incarnation; and this paradise can be gained by faith in Amitabha's saving grace. For Buddhists of the Mahayana school who are devotees of Amitabha, the ultimate goal, Nirvana, has become remote. The *bodhisattva* Amitabha is a saviour, like the Hindu god Vishnu and like Christ, the Second Person of the triune god of Christianity. The pursuit of Nirvana, which *prima facie*, is a non-personal mode of being, has been replaced by an emotional relation between two persons: a superhuman saviour and a human devotee. A sojourn in a paradise, in personal communication with Amitabha, has become the sequel to death to which the devotee looks forward.

Nirvana is a post-personal state of being. A sojourner in Amitabha's paradise retains his personality when he goes there after death, and this paradise is an earthly paradise. It is located in the west; it is presumably a part of the material world; and, if it is, a sojourner in it must be embodied in some form. Thus the Mahayanian Buddhist devotee of the *bodhisattva* Amitabha has lapsed into the belief that the immediate sequel to death is re-embodiment. However, there is also a very widespread belief that the world is full of spirits who are unembodied and are therefore invisible, but who nevertheless have power to influence the course of events in the visible tangible world. In some cultures, some of these unembodied but potent spirits have been held to be the disembodied souls of the dead. These are believed to retain their personality after having become disengaged, at death, from the bodies with which they were associated during their lifetime. For instance, the Greek poet Hesiod, in his catalogue of the successive races of human beings, declares that the members of the earliest and best race, namely the golden race, have become, after death, invisible beneficent spirits. Unembodied conscious personalities are not frequent data of human experience, though Mrs Heywood has had an intimation of the presence of one or more of these. It has been noted already in this chapter that ghosts appear in at least the semblance of live incarnate persons. The wide currency of the belief in the survival, and in the invisible presence, of disembodied souls of dead persons, is therefore remarkable.

The disembodied spirits of dead representatives of the golden race are credited by Hesiod with being altruistically beneficent. A more usual belief is that the behaviour of the disembodied souls of the dead is influenced by the conduct of the living generation. If the souls of the dead are propitiated, they will behave beneficently; if they are neglected or spurned, they will react maleficently. They are believed to be potent for doing either good or evil, and therefore it is held to be advisable to try to induce them to do good by gratifying them with pious attentions: a ritually correct burial or cremation; costly grave-gifts; and periodical offerings of food and drink.

According to Zoroastrian, Pharisaic Jewish, Christian, and Islamic doctrine, the souls of the dead survive, disembodied, from the respective dates of their deaths until the unknown future date of a general bodily resurrection of the dead. According to the Buddha's teaching, as this is described in the scriptures of the Southern School of Buddhism, the undissipated bundle of psychological states that causes reincarnation persists in an unincarnate state during the interval between one birth and another. But, even in this intermediate period, it is difficult to imagine the spiritual relics of dead people in a non-corporeal form. Dante's Hell and Purgatory are located, like Amitabha's paradise, on the planet earth – his Hell in the planet's interior and his Purgatory in the Antipodes of the planet's biospherical envelope. The physical location of Dante's Heaven would be 'outer space' in terms of present-day science; and, in these terms, Heaven would be difficult to locate, since present-day scientists recognize that they do not know whether space-time (space and time are now held by physicists to be inseparable) is infinite or whether it has limits.

Amitabha's luscious paradise in the west has counterparts in a pre-Columbian Mexican fresco at Teotihuacan, in the Pharaonic Egyptian Kentamentiu and in the Homeric Greek Elysium; but the Homeric-Age Greeks believed that admission to Elysium was reserved for a privileged minority, and the qualification for admission was not good conduct in a previous life; it was aristocratic birth or marriage. The destiny of all commoners, and of most aristocrats too, was an enfeebled form of physical survival in an underworld to which the dead were consigned indiscriminately, without regard to the record of a dead person's conduct during his lifetime. This Homeric Greek concept of a dim and dismal after-life in the realm of Hades had its parallel in the Israelites' concept of Sheol, and both the Israelite and the Greek belief had been anticipated in the Sumerian concept of the underworld to which the dead were consigned.

In the *Odyssey* there is an account of Odysseus's voyage to the realm of Hades and his evocation of the 'souls' or 'corpses' (the two words are used as synonyms in this context) of a number of dead people. Odysseus's ship is wafted by the north wind to the far side of the ocean, which is thought to be a river encircling the land of the living. However, one live people, the Cimmerians, inhabit the foggy far bank (actually the Cimmerians occupied the steppe to the north of the Black Sea in the eighth century BC, which is the date at which the *Odyssey* is believed to have been composed). The realm of Hades is in the neighbourhood, and it is both above-ground and below-ground. Odysseus digs a trench above-ground on a rock at the confluence of two rivers, but the 'souls' or 'corpses' come up from underground. They are corporeal, but, by comparison with live people, they are feeble not only physically but mentally. Their only physical function that retains its full vigour is their voice, but the sounds they emit, though loud, are not articulate words; they are screeches. These shades are not altogether senseless, for Odysseus is able to fend them off by threatening them with his drawn sword. (It is strange that they should be intimidated by a physical weapon; since they are dead already, presumably they cannot now be killed.) They are thirsty for the blood of animals that Odysseus has sacrificed. The blood has been poured into the trench that Odysseus has dug; and, when the 'souls' or 'corpses' drink the blood, this temporarily revives their human faculties. They regain their power of speech, and they talk to Odysseus rationally.

Existence in the realm of Hades is hateful. The shade of Achilles tells Odysseus that he would rather be a live agricultural labourer, the bondsman of some indigent non-freeholder, than be king of 'all the dead corpses'.

The contrast between existence in the realm of Hades and life in Elysium is extreme. The shade of the murdered Agamemnon is in Hades's realm, but Agamemnon's brother Menelaus is to be exempted from having to die. Menelaus is privileged in virtue of his being the son-in-law of the supreme god, Zeus. Menelaus's unfaithful wife Helen is Zeus's daughter, so the gods have decided to transport Menelaus, alive, to Elysium. Presumably Menelaus will retain all his physical and psychic faculties intact.

The Israelites believed that at least two human beings, Enoch and Elijah, had been exempted from death and had been transported to Heaven bodily. Christians believe that Jesus, after having been put to death, came to life again and eventually ascended bodily into Heaven, after having appeared in bodily form to some of his disciples on a number of occasions between his resurrection and his ascension. Christians also believe that all the dead will be resurrected bodily on the Day of Judgment.

The scriptural accounts of Jesus's appearances after his resurrection are ambivalent. On the one hand, the physical reality of his reanimated body is emphasized. He eats food; he shows his wounds. On the other hand, he is elusive, like a ghost. He passes through doors that are closed and locked; he suddenly appears and suddenly vanishes. Though his reanimated body is corporeal, this body is not subject to those laws of physical nature that govern the movements of ordinary bodies in time-space.

Consignment to the realm of Hades or Sheol is automatic except for individuals – Menelaus, Enoch, Elijah – who have been exempted from it by the fiat of a god. By contrast, Nirvana can be attained only by unaided spiritual efforts that are so strenuous that some Buddhists have been daunted. As an alternative, they have been tempted to seek aid from a *bodhisattva* for admission into a paradise that is less difficult to reach, though at least in theory, a sojourn in this paradise cannot be permanent but can only be a prelude to an eventual rebirth that will either bring a person nearer to the attainment of Nirvana or will carry him farther away from this ultimate goal. A Pharaonic-Age Egyptian sought not Nirvana but personal immortality, but the effort required for this pursuit, too, was so strenuous that easier alternatives were devised. Like the Homeric notion of existence in the realm of Hades, and like the Christian tradition regarding Jesus's bodily condition during the days between his resurrection and his ascension, the Pharaonic-Age Egyptian concept of the sequel to death presents some unreconciled incompatible features.

The Egyptians built tombs for themselves, and they filled these tombs with grave-gifts. The tombs were as durable and the grave-gifts were as valuable as the future incumbent could afford to make them. The tombs of Pharaohs and of other grandees were endowed with property producing an income for the maintenance of priests who were to perform rites, in perpetuity, for the service of the dead. This practice reached its acme in the building and endowment of the huge pyramid-tombs of the Pharaohs of the Fourth Dynasty. Apparently the tomb was thought of as being a house that the dead person was to inhabit after his death. More care and more wealth was expended on it than on the house in which the tomb-builder lived during his lifetime, and this was logical; for life on earth is brief, whereas the sequel is permanent, according to the expectation of people who do not believe in periodic rebirths. Since Pharaonic-Age princely Egyptian tombs were massive, and the grave-gifts were lavish, the dead person must have been expected in some sense to live corporeally in his tomb after his death. The practice of mummification implies the same belief. Mummification preserves a corpse from disintegration, and the preservation of the corpse must have been thought to guarantee the perpetuation of the dead person's life in its original corporeal form.

But where does the dead person reside? In the mummy deposited in his tomb? Or in a portrait-statue of him that has been animated by the performance of magical rites? Or in an incorporeal and invisible soul that haunts the tomb and enjoys the grave-gifts and the permanently endowed rites and offerings? Or in a second incorporeal and invisible soul that goes either to the underworld of Osiris the god of the dead or to the abode of other gods in Heaven? A dead human being may also board the bark of the sun-god Re and may travel with him on his ceaseless journey westwards across the sky and night-time return journey eastwards underneath the earth.

Whatever may be a human being's destiny after death, the prospect will be less alarming if, in advance, he is furnished with authoritative instructions, prescribing the action that he is to take. Odysseus and his companions returned, safe and sound, from their hazardous visit to the realm of Hades thanks to detailed instructions that were given to Odysseus by the sorceress Circe and were then carefully obeyed by Odysseus himself. The esoteric instructions given to early Pharaohs were eventually incorporated in the Book of the Dead – a guidebook for the sequel to death that became accessible to all Pharaoh's subjects. In the Greek world the devotees of the demigod Orpheus were provided with similar instructions, and these were one of the attractions of this cult.

The Pharaonic-Age Egyptians went to greater lengths than any other people has gone, to date, in equipping themselves materially for a life after death, but the practice itself has been normal. It has been followed, for example, by the Mycenaean Greeks, the Etruscans, the Chinese from the Shang dynasty to the Ming, by the Japanese, and, in America, by the Maya. The grave-mounds of some of the prehistoric rulers of Japan are among the largest in the world. These surpass the Egyptian pyramids in their mass, though not in their structure. In the modern western world, Renaissance-Age Italian princes enlisted the genius of contemporary Italian architects and artists for building and adorning their tombs. The nineteenth-century English poet Robert Browning has recaptured this fifteenth-century Italian concern with the sequel to death in his poem *The Bishop orders his Tomb in Saint Praxed's Church.*

This concern has been usual. Human beings of the now extinct Neanderthal species already disposed of their dead ceremonially. They did not throw away human corpses as if they were rubbish. The material evidence for human culture from the Neolithic Age until a recent date consists mainly of graves, tombs, urns for preserving the ashes of incinerated corpses, mummies (Peruvian as well as Egyptian) and grave-gifts. If our archaeologists had had access only to the equipment provided for people's use during their lifetime, and if they had not recovered any of the equipment provided for the dead, our evidence for the history of human culture in the preliterate age would have been far scantier than it is. Man's concern with life after death has been posterity's stand-by for the satisfaction of its curiosity about the life before death of people in past ages. Most of the surviving products of past generations are parts of the equipment with which they furnished the dead.

In the past, people were not merely concerned with life after death; they also looked forward to this with either hope or fear, and both emotions led them to dwell upon the prospect. The archaeological evidence suggests that, among the Etruscans during the last three or four centuries BC, fear was the predominant emotion, whereas the Pharaonic-Age Egyptians seem to have been confident, for the most part, that, by taking sufficient pains, they could secure for themselves a blissful post-mortem future. Buddhists take pleasure in the contemplation of Nirvana, though they may quail at the spiritual efforts that are required of them if they pursue the quest of Nirvana in earnest, to the exclusion of more easily attainable objectives. A human being who is able to take pleasure in the prospect, as he sees this, of the sequel to his death will not shrink from contemplating death itself. For him, death will look, not like the end of existence, but like the opening of a door that offers the possibility of access to a mode of existence which will be durable and desirable by comparison with a human being's brief, precarious, and painful life on this side of the grave.

This was the attitude of the Pharaonic-Age Egyptians and of the imaginary Renaissance-Age Italian bishops in Browning's poem. In our own time it seems to have been the attitude of Winston Churchill. He is said to have spent time, and to have taken pleasure, in giving directions, in advance, for the conduct of his own funeral. The ironical point of Browning's poem is that his imaginary bishop is, with half his mind, a sceptic; his pleasurable concern over his tomb is aesthetic, not religious. Whether or not the bishop believed in the Christian doctrines of immortality and the resurrection of the body in his heart of hearts, he adhered to these doctrines nominally at least. In the modern age in the West, particularly since the recent spectacular advance of physical science, the belief that death spells the extinction of the personality has been gaining ground, and *pari passu*, a horror of death itself, and a reluctance to face the hard fact of death's inevitability, has been becoming the characteristic reaction of present-day Western Man, in contrast to the attitude of his Christian forefathers, who were concerned with death and with death's sequel, whether they looked forward to this sequel with confidence or with anxiety. This effect of the advance of science is illogical. The study of phenomena, including the study of psychic phenomena, does not yield verifiable information about the sequel to death. Yet the recent spread of the belief that death spells the extinction of the personality does appear to have been due, at least in part, to the modern increase in our scientific knowledge.

We have now surveyed a series of beliefs about the sequel to death. This series ranges from a belief that death entails an extinction of the personality, through a belief that it entails the reabsorption of the personality into a timeless supra-personal spiritual reality, to a belief in the survival of the personality; and this belief in survival takes a number of different forms. The personality may be believed to survive death, disembodied. It may be believed to survive automatically in an enfeebled physical form in the realm of Hades or in Sheol. Alternatively, it may be believed that the survival of the personality can be secured artificially by material means (tombs, mummification, statues, grave-gifts) or by non-material means (spells and rites), or by a combination of these two kinds of expedients. There has also been a belief in a full-blooded physical resurrection, or a series of physical resurrections, at a future date after a period of survival without embodiment.

Zoroastrians believe that the resurrection of the body is going to happen to all human beings simultaneously at an unknown date in the future, and this Zoroastrian belief has been adopted by Jews, Christians, and Muslims. Hindus and Buddhists believe that reincarnation has happened many times in the past and may happen for an infinite number of times in the future. Hindus believe, like the adherents of the four Western religions, in the reality of the soul, and at least one school of Hindus believes that the human soul is identical with a supra-personal spirit that is the ultimate spiritual reality in and behind the universe. Buddhists agree with Hindus in believing in the reality of successive incarnations, but, unlike both the Hindus and the adherents of the Western religions, Buddhists hold that the non-material element that links successive incarnate lives is not a soul; Buddhists conceive of this link as being an undissipated bundle of psychological states which is generated by greed and which creates an ethical credit-and-debit account that runs on from one incarnate life to the next, unless and until the account is cleared Buddhists also hold that this account can be cleared by the cumulative effect of good conduct, in a series of lives, and that, if and when the *karma*-account is cleared entirely, the way is open for an exit into Nirvana that will bring the series of reincarnations to an end.

Our survey has shown that the spectrum of concepts of the sequel to death is both broad and variegated. At one extreme we find a belief in a reincarnation or a series of reincarnations. At the opposite extreme we find a belief that death spells the extinction of a human being's personality.

In the present-day Western world, and among the contemporary intelligentsia in the rest of the world, there are adherents of each of these two extreme concepts. A majority of the living generation still adheres to one or other of the historic regional religions, and some representatives of this majority hold their ancestral faiths as unreservedly and as sincerely as their forefathers. The adherence of others is only nominal; in their heart of hearts they now believe that, at death, the personality is extinguished; and the number of the frank believers in extinction is growing. The loss of the traditional beliefs about the sequel to death is a recent event. Even in the Western world, disbelief continued to be exceptional until the second half of the nineteenth century of the Christian Era. Till that date, a majority of Western men and women continued to believe in 'the resurrection of the body and the life everlasting'.

Since 1914, the Western civilization has been in manifest disarray. The miscarriage of public affairs has been a consequence of a contemporary disorder in the hearts and minds of the participants in the Western society, and this disorder has surely been a consequence of the distracting spiritual revolution by which Western man had been overtaken in the course of the preceding half century. Throughout the previous fifteen centuries, most Westerners had believed in the truth of the statements about the sequel to death that are made in the creeds of the Christian Church. These statements give positive answers to the formidable questions about a human being's destiny that present themselves to human minds, and these answers are spiritually fortifying for people for whom the traditional dogmatic answers carry conviction.

Human beings have spiritual ideals that transcend the average level of their spiritual performance. They have concerns and objectives that transcend the most and the best that can be accomplished in one human lifetime. A human being seems to be a participant in a world that is greater, in every sense of that word, than the ephemeral flash of space-time in which he lives his short and troubled life on earth. Christian doctrine – and Jewish and Islamic doctrine likewise – assures a human being that the world in which he finds himself is not confined to the physical, mental, and temporal limits of a human lifetime, but is adequate spiritually to man's spiritual potentiality. This assurance eliminates the incompatibility between potentiality and actual capacity which is so harrowing for a human being who believes that a single lifetime on earth, under the manifestly unsatisfactory conditions of terrestrial human life, is the sum-total of a human being's existence.

A belief in the permanent survival of a human personality after death also reinforces a person's innate sense of responsibility for his conduct during his terrestrial lifetime, if the belief in survival is accompanied by a belief in a post-mortem judgment – and these two beliefs are associated with each other in the doctrines of Zoroastrianism, Pharisaic Judaism, Christianity, and Islam, as well as in the Osiris-doctrine of the more ancient religion of Pharaonic Egypt. An adherent of any one of these five religions believes that his conduct during a single lifetime on earth is going to decide his post-mortem destiny eternally. This belief arouses in him hopes and fears that may stimulate him to control the passions and to resist the temptations that assail every human being in the course of his terrestrial life.

In the third place the belief in the post-mortem immortality of a human personality gives consolation to someone who has been bereaved of the companionship on earth of a fellow human being whom he loves. The anguish of bereavement is mitigated by the assurance that the parting which is inflicted by death is only temporary. The survivor looks forward to rejoining his beloved comrade for ever in a mode of existence that is happier than the terrestrial life. The life after death will not, as life on earth does, first attach human beings to each other by a vulnerable link of love and then cruelly separate them by removing one of them and leaving the other still alive. According to Christian doctrine, the pain of separation is one of the temporary trials of a human being's life on earth.

These articles of Christian faith were the spiritual foundations of terrestrial life for the forebears of the generation of Westerners that is alive today. For many representatives of the present generation, this foundation is now lacking. They no longer believe in the life everlasting, and a fortiori they do not believe in the resurrection of the body. Belief and disbelief are not under a human mind's control. A fortifying and comforting belief cannot be maintained or be resumed deliberately if it has ceased to be compatible with the former believer's general Weltanschauung. Moreover, if a revolutionary change in the prevalent Weltanschauung has put a traditional belief out of court, there is no guarantee that the consequent spiritual vacuum is going to be filled by a new belief that will perform the spiritual service which was formerly performed by the traditional belief that has now ceased to be credible.

In the year AD 1975 an increasing number of Westerners are living in a spiritual vacuum. The discomfort and dismay of these present-day heirs of the Western civilization goes far towards accounting for the crisis by which the Western world is now being beset.

Expectations of Alternative Sequels to Death

For people who believe that death brings with it the extinction of the expiring human being's personality, the sequel to death does not present itself in the form of alternative possibilities. Nor are there alternatives for people who believe that death brings with it a reabsorption of a temporarily separate personality into a timeless spiritual reality which is a counterpart – though this in a different mode – of the physical reality that is one of the components of a human being while he is alive on earth. Nirvana is an enigmatic concept; for a non-Buddhist it is difficult to decry whether Nirvana implies the extinction of personal identity or the survival of it in a purified form in which it has rid itself of all kinds of desire. However, the concept of life after death which includes Nirvana does also include an alternative expectation; and alternative possibilities are likewise foreseen in all the concepts of the sequel to death in which the dead person's personality is believed to survive the person's death and the subsequent physical disintegration of his corpse.

The alternative to Nirvana, in Buddhist belief, is a potentially interminable recurrence of incarnations. This recurrence is believed to be automatic and inevitable unless and until, in some one of a series of psychosomatic lives on earth, a human being has cleared his karma-account by extinguishing completely the cupidity that, hitherto, has entailed rebirth. The Buddhist concept of karma is both more credible and more ethical than the Augustinian Christian belief in predestination. According to this bizarre and shocking variety of Christian belief, a human being is consigned, in advance, to an eternal post-mortem residence in either Hell or Heaven by the fiat of an omnipotent God whose awards of post-mortem anguish or bliss are arbitrary – or at any rate are inscrutable by human minds. By contrast, in the Buddhist concept, karma is not imposed on a human being by an irresistible external power, and its incidence is not arbitrary. Karma is generated by the person to whom it attaches. It is the residual debit in the ethical account that a human being creates for himself while he is alive; and, in the course of a lifetime, a person's karma-account can be, and will be, modified, for better or for worse, by the conduct of the accountable person himself. It is possible, though it is difficult, for him to clear his karma-account completely, and its complete clearance opens the door for a permanent exit from psychosomatic mundane life into Nirvana.

In the Buddhist concept of the sequel to death, the belief in karma is associated with a belief in rebirth, but these two beliefs are not necessarily inseparable. The belief in the operation of karma is also compatible with the belief that a human being lives a single psychosomatic life only. It is also compatible with the beliefs that a human being's personality survives his death and that, after his death, he will be judged by an authority other than himself and will be either rewarded or punished in accordance with his judge's verdict. If these non-Buddhist beliefs are held, the state of a person's karma-account at the close of a single non-recurrent lifetime will still be important. This will be the principal evidence on which the judge's verdict will be based. Karma is irrelevant only if it is believed that a human being is consigned in advance to Heaven or to Hell, without regard to the balance-sheet of his good and bad conduct during his lifetime or his series of lifetimes.

The belief in rebirth has been unusual. However, at about the year 500 BC, this belief was taken for granted, as if it were a recognition of a manifest truth, not only by the Buddha but also – and this perhaps more logically – by the Buddha's Hindu opponents who, in contrast to the Buddha, believed that a human soul is a reality and is not just an illusion produced by a misinterpretation of the true phenomenon of psychic life. In the same age, this same belief in rebirth was held in the Greek world by the Pythagorean school of philosophers and by the practitioners of Orphic rites. In the West, the belief in rebirth was never widespread, and it did not survive the conversion of the mass of the population to Christianity and Islam; in India and east Asia, this belief is still one of the explicit fundamental tenets of Hinduism and Buddhism.

The belief in rebirth has perhaps been implicit over a wider range of time and space. In many societies it has been customary to give a child the name of one of its grandparents, and this practice may be taken to imply a belief that the grandchild is a reincarnation of the grandparent after whom he has been named. However, the explicit belief in rebirth, and the incorporation of this belief in a body of systematic religious doctrine, is known to have been held in two places only: in the pre-Christian and pre-Muslim Greek world and in India and eventually also in eastern Asia. The resemblance between the Hindu-Buddhist and the Pythagorean-Orphic doctrine of rebirth is so close that it seems improbable that it is fortuitous.

The two locations of this belief are geographically remote from each other, and circa 500 BC the means of communication between them were poor. One possible conductive medium was the First Persian Empire; for, by this date, that empire included both the western fringe of the Indian subcontinent and the eastern fringe of the contemporary Greek world – including the island of Samos, the birthplace of Pythagoras and his home before his migration to the colonial Greek city-state Croton in the 'toe' of Italy. The Persian imperial government in its early days took some steps to improve its system of communications. It built trunk roads equipped at intervals with supplies of post-horses, and it opened up waterways that linked the Indus and its tributaries with the lower course of the Nile via the Indian Ocean and the Red Sea.

However, it is perhaps more likely that the belief in rebirth was conveyed to both south-east Europe and India by a *Völkerwanderung* of pastoral nomads who, in the eighth and seventh centuries BC, burst out of the Eurasian steppe into the Indus basin south-eastwards and into Thrace south-westwards. At the present day there is a widespread belief among the pre-Russian inhabitants of Siberia that the souls of their shamans (medicine-men) can, and do, leave their bodies and return to them in the course of a single lifetime. This belief is not identical with a belief in the reality of rebirth after death, but it might have generated this belief, and it seems probable that, in northern Asia, the beliefs and practices of present-day shamanism are age-old. The fifth-century BC Greek historian Herodotus reports that Aristeas – a citizen of the Greek colonial city-state Proconnesus, on the Asian shore of the Sea of Marmara, who had visited the Eurasian steppe and had written a poem about its nomadic inhabitants – vanished and reappeared twice, and that, long after his second disappearance, he reappeared – this time not in his native city, but in a far-away other colonial Greek city-state, Metapontum on the coast of south-eastern Italy. Herodotus also tells a story of Zalmoxis, a spirit honoured by the Getae, who were a Eurasian nomad people, encamped in present-day Wallachia. According to this story, Zalmoxis had originally been a human slave and disciple of Pythagoras at Samos, and he had then tricked his tribesmen, the Getae, into believing that he had died and had come to life again after the lapse of four years.

Rebirth is held by Buddhists to be an alternative to making a permanent exit into Nirvana. Another pair of hypothetical post-mortem alternatives, which has also been mentioned in the preceding chapter, is the normally automatic relegation of a dead person to the realm of Hades or to Sheol, and the exceptional translation of a human being, alive, to Elysium or to Olympus or to Heaven.

The feature of this second pair of alternatives that distinguishes it from Buddhism's pair is that, in this case, the persons who are consigned after death either to a pleasant or to an unpleasant destination have no power of even influencing, not to speak of deciding, their post-mortem destiny by their own conduct before death. The everlasting abode of all but a chosen few among the dead is dismal; the vestigial life that they lead there is miserable; they resent their fate; and, though it may be better than what the wicked deserve, it is certainly worse than what is worthy of the good. The shade of Achilles is evidently speaking for all its companions in the realm of Hades when it indignantly inveighs against its present condition in its colloquy with the not yet dead Odysseus. The scandal is the greater because the contrast between the misery of an after-life in the realm of Hades and the felicity of an after-life in Elysium is extreme, and the few who, without having died, are transported to Elysium have done nothing to deserve their good fortune. It has been mentioned already that Menelaus was destined for Elysium simply because he happened to be Zeus's son-in-law. As for Enoch, who 'walked with God, and he was not, for God took him', it can be read between the lines that Enoch owed his good fortune, as Menelaus owed his, to a 'special relation' rather than to any special merit of his own.

The predestination of human beings, before birth, to either Heaven or Hell, which is the distinctive tenet of Augustinian Christianity, is equally unethical. In order to conform to Christian orthodoxy, Augustinianism has to profess that the dead are judged before they are consigned to the destinations that have been fore-ordained for them; but manifestly the judgment is only a formality and the verdict is a farce; for, according to the Augustinian doctrine, a human being has not been a free agent in his life before death. Whether he has done evil or has done good, his actions have not been of his own doing; he has been an automaton, and the acts on account of which he is either saved or lost after death have not, in truth, been his own; they have been the acts of the divinity who has pulled the strings which have determined the movements of this God Almighty's human marionette.

In Pharaonic Egypt in the age of the Old Kingdom, it was believed, as has been mentioned, that a human being did have it in his power to secure post-mortem immortality for himself in a desirable mode of after-life, on condition that he commanded sufficient wealth to provide for the building of a tomb, for the mummification of his corpse, for the carving of his statue and for its animation by magical rites, and for the endowment of priests to perform liturgies on his behalf and to supply his entombed mummy with food and drink in perpetuity. A Pharaoh could also furnish the nearest and dearest members of his family, his household, and his court with the means of securing immortality in company with their sovereign. In this case, too, the privilege was inequitable and unethical, and eventually it evoked effective countermovements. The regime of the Old Kingdom was overthrown by a political and social revolution; the procedures for securing immortality, which originally had been monopolized by Pharaoh and his favourites, were gradually made accessible to all Pharaoh's subjects through being provided in less elaborate and less expensive forms; and the attainment of immortality in a blissful post-mortem abode was made dependent not on favouritism but on merit.

The earliest evidence that we have for a belief in a post-mortem judgment of the dead, and in the consignment of a dead person to either

Paradise or Hell according to the post-mortem verdict, is the Egyptian concept of judgment after death by the god of the dead, Osiris. If the verdict was favourable, the dead person was believed to go to Kentamentiu, a paradise on earth in the west or, according to another concept, to go to a paradise in Osiris's underworld where the righteous dead would live in the presence of Osiris himself. Osiris played the three roles of impartial judge, benevolent saviour, and divine patron of the host of righteous souls who were domiciled for ever in Osiris's paradise.

When the destiny and destination of the dead was deemed to be decided in accordance with the merits or demerits of a dead person's conduct during his lifetime, the living had to face the prospect of post-mortem punishment, as well as the prospect of post-mortem reward, and a fear of being consigned to Hell had to accompany the hope of being admitted into Paradise. By about the year 500 BC, when in both India and the Greek world a belief in rebirth had gained currency, the incompatible belief in a post-mortem judgment, resulting in consignment either to Paradise or to Hell, had become current simultaneously. The Greek picture of Elysium resembles the Egyptian picture of Kentamentiu. We may guess that the Greeks derived this picture from the Egyptians, and we may also guess that the Greeks were following the Egyptians when they took to believing that an admission to Elysium was a reward of merit, not an unearned privilege that was conferred arbitrarily by a divine fiat.

In the Egyptian picture of the alternative expectations, the righteous dead's attainment of Paradise looms larger than the sinners' consignment to Hell. In the Greek picture, on the other hand, the torments of Hell are illustrated graphically by descriptions of the fates of some particular mythical arch-sinners. This picture was taken over, and was painted in still more lurid colours by the Etruscans; and one of the attractions of the Epicurean belief that death brings with it the extinction of the dead person's personality was that this belief liberated the living from the fear that death might hold in store for them the legendary fates of Tityos, Ixion, Tantalus, Sisyphus, and the Danaids.

It is a known historical fact that communications between the Aegean basin and Egypt, which had been interrupted during the post-Mycenaean dark age in the Aegean, were reopened in the eighth century BC, and this makes it probable that the post-Homeric Greek pictures of Hell and of Paradise were derived from Egypt. Osiris, the post-mortem judge, had a Greek counterpart in Rhadamanthus. Meanwhile, about the year 600 BC, the Iranian prophet Zarathustra (Zoroaster), the founder of the religion that bears his name, had introduced the idea of a

'Last Judgment', in which all human beings, both those then alive and those already dead, were going to be judged simultaneously by a judge who would be the deputy of the good god Ahura Mazda. This event was to close the current period of the world's history, during which the world is the arena of a war between Ahura Mazda and his adversary the bad god Angra Mainyush. Ahura Mazda was held to be destined to be victorious eventually. It was held to be the duty of every human being to contend, in the meantime, on Ahura Mazda's side for the triumph of the good. When this predestined conclusion of the strife between good and evil had been reached, all human beings, alive or dead, were to be tested by the ordeal of trying to cross a narrow bridge. The righteous would be vindicated by crossing successfully; the wicked would fall, on the way, to perdition in a sea of molten metal.

The Zoroastrian concept of a universal judgment at the end of an epoch of the world's history is different from the Egyptian concept of the judgment of each individual immediately after his death; and, though the Zoroastrian concept is the younger of the two, there is no evidence, and no likelihood, that it was derived from the Egyptian concept. Zarathustra is believed to have lived and preached somewhere in what is now Soviet Central Asia at some date before this region and Egypt were both incorporated in the First Persian Empire. It seems improbable that there was any contact between Egypt and Central Asia before that. On the other hand, it is certain that the Zoroastrian concept of 'the Last Things' influenced, and eventually changed radically, the Jewish concept of the sequel to death.

Zoroastrianism may have begun to influence Judaism as early as 539 BC, the year in which the whole of the neo-Babylonian Empire was annexed to the First Persian Empire. Palestine was part of the neo-Babylonian Empire at that date, and therefore the Jewish exiles who returned to Palestine, as well as those who stayed on in Babylonia, were exposed to the influence of Zoroastrianism after the Persian conquest of Zarathustra's Central Asian mission-field. This Zoroastrian influence on Judaism did not cease when the First Persian Empire fell and was replaced in Palestine successively by two of the Persian Empire's Greek successor-states – the Ptolemaic monarchy after the death of Alexander the Great in 323 BC, and the Seleucid monarchy after its conquest of Palestine from the Ptolemaic monarchy in 198 BC. The Zoroastrian influence on the Jewish concept of the sequel to death came to the surface after 168 BC, the year in which the Seleucid King Antiochus IV Epiphanes began to persecute Judaism in Palestine.

Until that date, most Jews continued, apparently, to believe that the dead, righteous and unrighteous alike, were consigned at death to Sheol. They had not yet adopted the Zoroastrian belief in a full-blooded bodily resurrection of the dead *en masse* on a coming Day of Judgment. The Jews had, however, found psychological compensation for their temporary deportation to Babylonia and for their failure thereafter to regain their political independence. They had come to believe that their god, Yahweh, was going, not merely to restore to them their independence, but to make them the ruling people in a world-empire on the First Persian Empire's scale, through the agency of an anointed (i.e. a ritually legitimate) king. The anonymous sixth-century BC Jewish prophet whom modern scholars have labelled 'Deutero-Isaiah' cast for this role the Iranian founder of the First Persian Empire, Cyrus II. Later on, it came to be expected by the Jews that the anointed king (the messiah) who was to be Yahweh's agent for making the Jews into the world's imperial people would be a scion of the House of David.

The resistance movement against the Seleucid Greek regime which started in 166 BC gave immediacy to the messianic hope. The messiah was expected to make his appearance in Palestine and to establish a Jewish empire in this world which was to last for one thousand years. This millennium was expected to be a golden age, and therefore it seemed intolerable that the Jewish martyrs who had sacrificed their lives in order to help to establish it should be excluded from participation in it through the very fact that they had sacrificed their lives and were thus already dead. Consequently it came to be believed that the dead Jewish victims of Antiochus IV's persecution, and, by extension, all the righteous Jewish dead of past generations, would be resurrected in order to enable them to participate in the Jewish people's triumph. Since the messiah's empire was to be an earthly empire, the resuscitated righteous Jewish dead were expected to re-emerge from Sheol in full-blooded corporeal form.

This expectation of the bodily resurrection of a small band of righteous Jews did not carry with it any expectation of bodily immortality. The messiah himself was expected to die – according to some accounts in battle and not by a natural death. The resuscitated martyrs were expected to die in the regular course of nature after they had taken part in the inauguration of the millennial Jewish world-empire.

Immortality, as well as a bodily resurrection, a Last Judgment, and the despatch of the righteous to Heaven and of the wicked to Hell, eventually became part of the expectation of the Pharisees – a sect that transformed Judaism by supplementing the written Mosaic Law (the Torah) with an allegedly authentic unwritten Mosaic tradition, which was declared to have been transmitted orally. In this Pharisaic expansion of Jewish beliefs, the scenario of the Last Judgment and of the execution of this judgment's verdict is surely derived from Zoroastrianism. If the Last Judgment had not figured in the Zoroastrian picture, it seems unlikely that this scenario would have been composed by the Pharisees independently. The belief in the bodily resurrection of the second-century BC Jewish martyrs was a very special case, and there was nothing in the native Jewish tradition that would have suggested the extension of this special case to all Jews and to all Gentiles too.

The Sadducees, who were the ecclesiastical and political 'establishment' of the Jewish state that had been reconstituted in the course of the years 166–129 BC, denied the authenticity and therefore also the authoritativeness of the Pharisees' oral law. Like the Samaritans, the Sadducees recognized the written Torah alone as being Yahweh's genuine and binding word. Since the Torah did not contain any mention of the resurrection of the body, the Sadducees rejected this article of Pharisaic Jewish faith. It did not become an obligatory part of orthodox Jewish belief until after the Romano–Jewish war of AD 66–70. The Sadducees did not survive this disaster, the Pharisees did survive it, and therefore, since that date, Pharisaic Judaism has been undisputedly the orthodox form of Judaism. In consequence, the Zoroastrian picture of 'the Last Things' is incorporated today in the orthodox doctrine of Judaism and of Judaism's two daughter religions, Christianity and Islam.

The scenario of the Last Judgment and of the subsequent agony of the damned in Hell and bliss of the saved in Heaven is so dramatic and so momentous that its effect on human hearts and minds has been potent. Its potency is illustrated by the Book of Revelation, by the Koran, and by Dante's *Divina Commedia*. The Zoroastrians expect the present world-order to last for several thousand more years; the first generation of Christians supposed that the Last Judgment was imminent; and the disappointment of this Christian expectation for six centuries did not deter the Prophet Muhammad from producing, in his turn, the imminence of the Last Judgment's advent. This was, indeed, one of the chief weapons in his missionary campaign for the conversion to Islam of the pagan majority of his Arab fellow-countrymen.

By Muhammad's time, Zoroastrianism, Judaism, and Christianity had already won converts all round the fringes of Arabia, and thus the ground had been prepared for Muhammad's preaching. During Christianity's early formative centuries, Zoroastrianism was the principal religion of Iran, to the east of the Christian Church's mission-field, while, to the west of it, the Pharaonic Egyptian civilization and religion, including the doctrine of an immediate individual judgment after death for every human being, was still a going concern and was spreading, like Christianity, round the Mediterranean basin. Consequently the Egyptian concept of a post-mortem judgment, as well as the Zoroastrian concept of it, has become part and parcel of the corpus of Christian beliefs.

It has been noted, at a previous point, that the Egyptian and the Zoroastrian concepts of a post-mortem judgment are not compatible with each other; but the adoption of incompatible beliefs is possible in a field of inquiry in which hypotheses cannot be verified by observation or by experiment, and theology is a field of this kind, in contrast to natural science. If the Egyptian belief in an immediate individual judgment after death had not been incorporated in Christian doctrine, neither Hell nor Heaven would have been ready, in Dante's day, for the reception of saints and sinners, and Dante's vision would have been premature, pending the sounding of the Last Trump.

At the present day the belief in a re-embodiment of the dead is still officially obligatory for all Zoroastrians, Jews, Christians, Muslims, Hindus, and Buddhists; and these six religions, between them, still command the adherence of a great majority of mankind. The teaching of the first four of these religions is that a human being lives only a single life; that his soul survives his death, disembodied; and that, at some unpredictable future date, every soul will be re-embodied in order to undergo the Last Judgment and, according to the verdict, to enjoy physical bliss in Heaven or physical anguish in Hell. The teaching of Hinduism and Buddhism is that a soul (or, a Buddhist would say, a not yet cleared *karma*-account) is reborn in psychosomatic form not just once but a number of times. According to Buddhist teaching, the series of rebirths can be terminated if, in one of the recurrent bouts of psychosomatic life, the *karma*-account is cleared, for its clearance opens the way for an exit into Nirvana. Hindu teaching does not offer this way of escape. According to Hinduism, rebirth continues at least for the duration of the current epoch (Kalpa) – and the time-scale of Hindu cosmology is as vast as modern astronomy's.

To be afraid of death is natural for people who believe that a human being lives and dies once only. For them, death is a compulsory departure from a familiar world to an unknown destination, which may be either extinction or else a shadowy after-life which will be neither blissful nor painful, but will be dreary. Alternatively the sequel may be a judgment that will consign the surviving personality to either Paradise or

Hell. For believers in rebirth, death does not have the same finality. For them, on the far side of death there is a vista of repeated future rebirths in the familiar psychosomatic form. This vista makes death itself less terrifying, but the terror of death is replaced by a shrinking from the monotonous prospect of being reborn again and again to live a series of painful lives. The degree of this fear of rebirth may be gauged by the intensity and the austerity of the spiritual exertions that a believing and practising Buddhist is willing to make in order eventually to escape from the sorrowful round of rebirths into the timeless tranquillity of Nirvana.

It is difficult to believe in the reincarnation of a dead person, whether his reincarnation is deemed to happen only once or to happen repeatedly. An inquirer who has some acquaintance with modern organic chemistry and also with modern psychical research will find it easier to believe that, if the sequel to death is not the extinction of the personality, the personality survives unembodied.

The belief in the existence and the presence of unembodied spirits is ancient and widespread. It has been mentioned already that the classical Greek poet Hesiod, writing about the year 700 BC, represents his 'Race of Gold' as surviving, disembodied, after its extinction in its original psychosomatic form. This belief in the survival of souls, disembodied, became the normal belief in the pre-Christian Greek world. The concepts of both the realm of Hades and Elysium became obsolete, and the novel concept of the resurrection of the dead was a stumbling-block for Saint Paul's Athenian audience. 'When they heard of the resurrection of the dead, some mocked, and others said: "We will hear thee again of this matter."' This second rejoinder was evidently a polite device for bringing the meeting to an end. Paul's converts at Athens are reported to have been only a handful.

Degrees of Concern over the Sequel to Death

The degrees of concern are no less diverse than the concepts and the expectations. The conscious 'surface' of a human psyche is individual, and its individuality generates a concern over the individual's destiny after death and a desire for the post-mortem survival of the dead person's personality. The faculty of consciousness makes man the most individualistic of all known species of living beings. However, man is also a social animal. If he had been a 'loner', he could not have survived when he descended from the shelter of the trees and entered into competition with stronger, swifter, and better armed and armoured animals at ground-level. Man certainly would be unable to survive if he were to lose his capacity for social co-operation at the present stage of his history. Man's sociality is an inalienable feature of human nature, and this generates in man a concern for the survival of his family, his community, and his species.

This altruistic concern for a collectivity that transcends the individual human being reveals itself in the willingness of parents to sacrifice themselves in the interests of their children and in the willingness of soldiers to sacrifice themselves in the interests of their state. The boon that Abraham seeks from God is not personal immortality for himself; it is a progeny that will be numerous enough to ensure the survival of Abraham's race for ages after the date of Abraham's own death. This, too, is a form of immortality, but it is an immortality that, instead of being individual, is collective. Moreover, this is the form of immortality that is the objective of life in the biosphere. If it is legitimate to personify life metaphorically, we can say that life's dominant concern is to perpetuate a species, and, for this purpose, life will sacrifice prodigally any number of a species's specimens. The specimens are expendable; the species is precious.

When man feels, thinks, and acts as a social animal, the individual's concern over the sequel to his own death is minimal. The attitude that is attributed to Abraham in the Book of Genesis is an expression of Israel's concern for the people's future in this life – a continuous collective life that is handed on from one ephemeral generation to another. In the eighth century BC the prophets of Israel and Judah began to feel their way towards a direct personal relation between the prophet as an individual and his god; yet Deutero-Isaiah, writing in the sixth century BC, leaves it to his readers to guess whether the 'suffering servant' whom he portrays is an individual or is the Jewish community.

The Buddha, who was Deutero-Isaiah's younger contemporary, did break his way out of his ancestral community; he repudiated his heirship to his father's crown; he deserted his wife and child; he found for himself the way of release from the sorrowful round of recurrent rebirths; and he showed the way to other sentient beings. The Buddha's assertion of the individual's rights against the community's claims was radical and revolutionary. Yet, as has been noted already, it is not clear whether Buddhists believe that an individual's personality survives the extinction of all desires which opens the door for an exit into Nirvana. Moreover, the Buddha repudiated his ancestral community only to found a new community – the Buddhist monastic order (the Sangha) and this community of Buddhist monks is not socially autarkic. It is a minority which is dependent for its livelihood on the alms of a majority, and this lay majority of the Buddha's adherents is a community of the traditional kind. The experience of Buddhism illustrates the strength of the hold upon man of his concern for his collectivity; the revolt of the individual against the community did not begin in earnest till about 2,500 years ago; and, until it began, the individual's concern over the sequels to death was overwhelmed by an overriding concern for the preservation of the community and of the race.

This lack of concern over the sequels to death which is characteristic of collective-minded primitive man is also characteristic of man when he becomes so sophisticated that he believes that his death is going to bring with it the extinction of his personality. This prospect is outrageous for a human being who has diverted his concern from his community to himself. If a human being has put his treasure in his own career, and if he has then come to believe that his career is going to be terminated by his death, he is likely to avert his mind from this painful prospect and to surrender himself to a temptation against which mankind has been warned by the Buddha and by all later religious seers. A sophisticated sceptic will pursue the will-o'-the-wisp of power, wealth, and fame in this transitory life on earth; and the probability is that he will find himself frustrated before death has had time to deal him the *coup de grâce*.

The concern over the sequels to death is at its maximum in the heart and mind of a believer in Nirvana who strives to make his exit into it, and of a believer in post-mortem judgment and in Heaven and Hell who strives to make sure that his post-mortem destiny shall be Heaven. A person whose attention and effort is concentrated on his own personal release or personal salvation is likely to subject himself to self-inflicted torments if his fellow human beings do not oblige him by making him a martyr. In the history of the Christian Church the age of the ascetics was opened when the age of the Christian martyrs was ended by the Emperor Galerius's edict proclaiming the toleration of Christianity. There was a pause before the date at which Christians began to make martyrs of the adherents of non-Christian religions and of dissident Christian sects.

The martyrs and the ascetics have been the arch-exponents of individualism. The mundane individualists – the conquistadores and the captains of industry – have walked through the breach in man's traditional concern for his community that the religious individualists have opened. In the history of Buddhism, the concentration of the seeker after Nirvana on his self-set task of working for his own release has eventually been condemned by one school of Buddhists as being an unedifying indulgence in selfishness, and a less unsocial ideal has been found in the figure of the *bodhisattva* – a potential Buddha who, like the historical Buddha himself, has deliberately postponed his own exit into Nirvana in order to help his fellow sentient beings to attain the Nirvana from which the *bodhisattva* himself is holding back. Is the reaction of northern Buddhism against southern Buddhism 'the wave of the future'? Is mankind going to revert to the attitude that is attributed to Abraham? Is the concern over the sequels to death going to yield precedence, in the hearts and minds of future generations, to a concern for the welfare, not of the individual human being, but of the human race for whose survival each individual human being is nature's appointed trustee for the duration of the individual's brief life between his birth and his death?

This is perhaps the gravest question that confronts mankind in our time. On the whole, it seems likely that human beings will continue to feel concern about the sequel to the individual's death, concurrently with concern for the survival of the race. It seems improbable that either of these concerns will completely eclipse the other.

We may guess that there will be a reaction against the extreme economic individualism of modern captains of industry, financiers and industrial workers, as, in the past, there was a reaction against the religious individualism of Buddhist monks and Christian ascetics. The unprecedented increase in the potency of technology in the course of the past two centuries has now reached a degree at which it is threatening to lead the human race into destroying itself. Military technology has produced nuclear weapons; civil technology has depleted the biosphere's irreplaceable natural resources; medical technology has caused a population explosion by drastically reducing the rate of premature deaths before the majority of mankind has begun to depart from its age-old habit of breeding up to the limit. The biosphere is now in danger of being over-populated, polluted, and exhausted.

If Abraham were to be reborn in the novel environment that has been created by the Industrial Revolution, his concern for the survival of his race would lead him to ask Yahweh to give him, not a progeny as numerous as the sands of the sea, but only a progeny that would not exceed the numbers for which the biosphere is able to provide sustenance. The growth of the gross national product, and of the individual's share of it, which has been the paramount objective of Western man and his non-Western imitators since the later decades of the eighteenth century, seems likely to give place to the objective of stability which was the paramount aim in Pharaonic Egypt and in Imperial China. Our successors seem likely to be schooled, by painful experience, into acquiescing in the stabilization of economic life at a level of affluence far below that of four-fifths of the population of the United States during the first three-quarters of the twentieth century.

This re-awakening of an altruistic concern for posterity would in itself be one form of a revival of religion; but it seems unlikely that it would be the only form. In human nature, individualism, as well as sociality, is innate; and, if individualism has to be debarred from seeking an economic vent, it is perhaps likely to find a religious vent. Religious growth, unlike economic growth, is not condemned by nature to be confined within impassable material limits. There is no limit to the communion of a human being during his life before death with a supra-human spiritual presence behind and beyond the phenomena; and the re-awakening of this personal form of religion seems likely to be accompanied by an accentuation of concern about the sequel to the individual human being's death.

This concern seems all the more likely to revive and to persist because it seems improbable that the question of man's post-mortem destiny will ever be answered conclusively. At many times and places it has been believed that the survival, disembodied, of the personalities of the dead has been indicated by the experience of the living. It has been believed that the dead and the living are in communication with each other. It has not been denied that the kind of communication that is carried on between two live embodied persons ceases instantaneously when one of the two dies, and that it sometimes ceases before his death if, while he is still alive physically, he becomes mentally deranged or senile or if he falls into a coma. The dead person's disembodied spirit is believed to communicate with the living, and to be accessible to communications addressed to him by them, in ways that, as between living persons, are perhaps not unknown, though perhaps usually only vestigial. The supposed but unproven communication between the living and the dead may be conducted through a medium or else direct, through thought-transference without any verbal or visual physical intercourse. Some experiences of this kind are described, at first hand, by Mrs Heywood in the present book.

During the last hundred years these and other psychic phenomena have been studied in an objective spirit and with an intellectual rigour of the standard set by the contemporary scientific study of inanimate nature. The exploration of the subconscious levels of the human psyche has opened up, for study, a non-material realm of reality which, in its own mode of being, is vast (to borrow a word from the vocabulary that has been coined for describing the physical mode of being). In its immensity, the modern psychologists's and the antique shaman's psychic field of experience is on a par with the modern astronomer's physical field. This aspect of man's concern with life after death is dealt with in Part III of this book. When the reader considers Part III, he will be likely – so the writer of Part I expects – to conclude that the degree of concern over the sequels to death is probably going to persist and also to increase, *pari passu* with an increase in the concern to try to secure the survival of the human race on earth during the remaining aeons during which contemporary physical scientists estimate that the biosphere is going to continue to be habitable.

The Current Change of Mental Climate

While the present part of this book was being written, the mental climate of the Western and the Westernized portion of mankind was changing perceptibly in response to recent discoveries in the field of both physical and psychical research. The remarkable features of this current change of outlook were a decrease in mental assurance, a consequent relaxation of dogmatism, and an accompanying expansion of the mental spectrum. The mental assurance that was now diminishing had been founded in the past on one or other of two beliefs: a belief in the infallibility of utterances or scriptures that were held to be the word of God, and a belief in the infallibility of the logic of the human reason at the conscious level of the human psyche. In the West, confidence in reason had been gaining ground progressively at the expense of confidence in revelation from the closing decades of the seventeenth century of the Christian era till within the lifetime of the present writer, and this increase of confidence in reason had narrowed the range of the possibilities that could be envisaged by minds that had accepted logic as their sole and sovereign criterion of truth.

Logic cannot admit that two statements, two beliefs, or even two experiences can both be true if they are contradictory, incompatible, inconsistent, or incongruous with each other. The logical thinker, when faced with incompatible alternatives, has to make a choice between them. 'He will hold to the one and despise the other.' By the date at which the present book was being written, it was beginning to be suspected that the field of logic, as well as the field of Newtonian physics, is not co-extensive with the whole of the universe but is only a narrow zone of the total field of possible experience. Other zones were coming into view in which two experiences that were incompatible with each other might nevertheless both have to be recognized as being equally valid glimpses of the truth.

In this respect the post-rationalist mental vista resembled the pre-rationalist vista, which had been based on a belief in the infallibility of what had purported to be divine revelation. In both these non-rational vistas, two phenomena that were incompatible with each other could, and perhaps must, both be accepted as being authentic. On the other hand, the post-rationalist vista differed from the pre-rationalist and from the rationalist vista alike in being undogmatic. The post-rationalist inquirer faithfully follows experience, wherever this may lead, as his predecessors followed, respectively, revelation and reason. Psychic experience, as illustrated, for instance, by the cases described by Mrs Heywood, leads to glimpses of possible reality that logical reasoning might find itself constrained to reject as being illusions. Here we are being wafted into the 'higher spheres' of experience in which Goethe reaches the climax and conclusion of the second part of his tragedy *Faust*.

> 'All that is transitory
> Is only an image.
> Here [in a higher sphere of experience]
>   imperfection
> Becomes achievement.
> Here the ineffable
> Is accomplished.'

If experiences at this level are considered with an open mind, they throw flickers of light on the unverifiable possibility of life after death which has been man's concern ever since the unknown date at which our ancestors awoke to consciousness.

Part II

•

The idea of the hereafter:
past and present

2
Primitive Societies
Cottie A. Burland

•

The mystery of death has always been present for human beings. Of the most ancient and primitive people we know nothing. Their few scattered bones show they were physically akin to us, but beyond that we have only mystery. The first known burial was that of a Neanderthaler, curled up in a nest in the ground with a bison leg beside him. Presumably this was intended as meat for his travel to some other place. Later cave burials of Homo sapiens show that some twenty thousand years ago people of our physical type sometimes buried their dead in the dwelling cave. There was often provision of food and probably drink, but the evidence of death had been left until the decomposed flesh could be scraped from the bones, which were then painted with red ochre and carefully buried in order. At Monte Carlo the Grimaldi burials included beautiful bangles and a cap of tiny shells and bones. People were well dressed for their new life. Thus we have ancient evidence that our ancestors most certainly hoped for a life after death. Only the material evidence survives.

The last of the primitive hunters have been gathered together in camps and reservations. Some tribes have simply died away and left no descendants. But fortunately many of their myths have survived, and burial customs have been recorded so that we have some record of what was thought about the other life. They were simple folk who lived on the bounty of nature, hunting and gathering as they walked around their tribal territories. Such a life restricts the numbers in the social group. In most cases the hunting tribe has been restricted to family groups of some twenty or thirty individuals. If there were more the food supply would be insufficient. Where there was a large tribal territory hunters would split into conveniently small bands, each working over a defined area, and meeting only on one or two occasions in the year for a short period of celebration. In such a world death is always sad, but the body is invariably given some honour. It may be bundled up neatly and tucked out of the way in the bush, or placed in a special place to decompose so that a relic may be kept by closer relatives, in some cases the jaw bone, in others the skull. In the Andaman Islands widows wore the skull of their deceased husbands, and among the most primitive people known, the Tasmanian aboriginals, the dead were cremated and relatives carried a bundle of the ashes neatly tied up in skin or kelp on all their wanderings.

The Australian aboriginals were the last surviving human beings to live entirely in a late Palaeolithic phase of culture. They developed varying attitudes to the matter of death. The best known is the belief in continuous reincarnation which was characteristic of the tribes of the Australian desert, in particular the Aranda, who placed the souls in stone plaques called *churinga*. The ancestors became alive, they had the forms of animals and men. They became very large, and travelled around the tribal territory leaving special marks. Then they disappeared, but each left souls behind. The souls emerged from the stone *churingas*, they became people. Then they passed through the various initiation rituals through which their spirit power and inner knowledge increased. Eventually one by one they died again, each going in invisible form into his *churinga*. The elders who had learned the holy secrets hid the *churingas* away in clefts of the rock where no person, certainly no woman, would go near. The men acted the myths of the ancestors, they entered the Alcheringa, the dreamtime. They were painted and decked with white down and became the ancestors, at once men and totem animals. They danced and initiated the younger men, step by step, into the sacred knowledge. When all the rituals were complete, a man, now elderly, would be fully aware of the myths and their meanings. When a young woman wandered near the sacred grounds it might be that a spirit would escape from its *churinga* and enter her belly. When the baby was born an elder would be called on to look at it to consider its movements and appearance, so that he would recognize which soul had returned to live among the tribe. Then the child was given a name. Secretly the *churinga* was removed from those others where souls still rested.

There is no evidence to lead us to believe that the soul in the *churinga* was thought to be conscious, though some accounts suggest that it was expected to choose its mother. It is clear that the sojourn in the *churinga* was not thought to be long, because the new child was expected to be recognized by the elderly man who guarded the stones. In other areas of Australia the souls temporarily inhabited a sacred tree or a cleft in the rocks, but no women were initiated in the cult and every effort was made to keep them away from the holy places. They were not supposed to acquire the knowledge of the myths even though they bore new bodies for the souls to inhabit. This may be something to do with the antithesis between feminine nature and the life of the hunter, who must work his magic secretly. But in many parts of Australia feminine spirits play an important part in myth, and in Arnhem-land the cult of a Great Mother is important.

This may be due to cultural ideas drifting in from the agriculturists in New Guinea. Here, too, there is another concept about death: there is an island of the dead from which the ancestors came in the form of twin sisters. The sisters were in effect the Morning Star and Evening Star. They were culture-bringers who established the way of life for the future aboriginal tribes of Arnhem-land. It is said that they were giant-esses, but their descendants were normal people, who when they died went back to the island homeland. This may well have reflected some cultural contact with the peoples of the Torres Straits.

In south-eastern Australia, there are early records of a gradual disposal of the body as it loses contact with the spirit. At first the body was strapped to a frame to decompose and dry. At this stage the ghost was very close, and people were careful never to mention the name of the deceased for fear that it might lead to their being taken with the ghost as companions. The body was temporarily buried, until the bones were clean. Then the elders dug them up and scraped them. The spirit was close at hand. Sometimes a child was then named for the dead man. They were regarded as one when a remembrance feast was held, and the gifts to the dead man were given to his new representative while their souls went to him in a more magical form. But after the bones had been cleaned there was a general leavetaking. The jawbone was removed, and painted to remain as a memorial. The rest of the skeleton was packed away and neglected. People performed a long ceremony to drive away the ghost, and it was thought to have lost power. Only the widow and a few close relatives would wish to visit the dead person in dreams. It appears that the spirit was thought to lose power and finally to have no further existence. But the tribes which performed such ceremonies have long passed away and the original legends are lost, so that there is no modern confirmation of the early reports. In any attempts to reach the true beliefs of primitive peoples, the white man often imposed his own ideas, though usually unaware of his influence, and the native folk tended to hide their sacred mysteries and to say only what they thought would please the powerful stranger.

The other surviving group of late Palaeolithic hunters in our world were the Bushmen. In the old time their land was so prolific in animal life that they ran no risk of starvation, and lived in hordes of up to a hundred individuals. They were afraid of the ghosts of the dead, and yet hoped that deceased relatives would help them in the hunt by giving advice. The dead were buried in shallow pits, covered by a heap of stones with a particularly large one at the top as if to keep the body down. There was no particular effort to keep away from the dead, and when the painters were alive a century and a half ago burials might take place in a corner of the rock shelter. The modern Bushmen of the Kalahari have stories about a powerful creator loosely described as The Captain, who lives in a fine grass-covered house in the sky. This house has upper rooms in which the spirits of dead Bushmen live happily. They need neither food nor drink. However, this sounds very much as if it had been elaborated from some missionary teaching. Some of the earlier legends suggest that Bushmen might become stars.

Of the sea hunters and gatherers of Tierra del Fuego so little remains that all one can say is that they too believed in the persistence of ghosts.

It is evident that in the hunting and gathering Stone Age cultures beliefs in the continuation of life after death are universal, but they differ greatly one from another. The beliefs are strong although in this primitive state of culture the sight of the decay and destruction of the material body was quite common. So far as we have records, the concepts of reward and punishment in the after-life are absent. But then the idea of theoretical systems of right- and wrong-doing was not part of everyday culture. Life and death were facts, and it seemed to be generally believed, largely on the strength of ghost stories, that the deceased have not ceased to live.

The Eskimos until recently lived a highly specialized hunting life. Their culture was surprisingly rich when we consider the terrible conditions of life in the Arctic lands. The majority of Eskimo bands were of only one or two extended families, because larger bands would soon exhaust the food potential of their area. They lived a life rich in ceremonial, magic, and social dances, especially in the winter when people could not stray far from the settlement. Many of their myths concern the adventures of ancestors and the world of spirits. Tales tell of ancestors who became stars in the skies; others of heroes who dance eternally in the aurora borealis. The general belief was that most spirits went to a great underworld where life continued at a rather lower and less happy level than life on earth, but there are many tales of the return of ghosts to visit their families.

Most Eskimo communities believed that the other world was the domain of a superhuman being, Sedna, who was the originator of life in the seas. Sedna had once been human, though presumably of giant stature. She was linked with her cruel father, who determined to kill the girl and on a canoe voyage cut off her fingers and limbs and sank the corpse into the sea. However, he too was drowned. The limbs of Sedna became whales, walruses, and seals, her fingers and toes became the fishes. She continued life as a Great Mother, who was the centre of most religious belief. There were many other spirit beings in Eskimo mythology, and all were accessible through the trance mediumship of a *shaman*, who might be either male or female.

There were many dangerous spirits frequenting the ice. These were Tupilak, curious creatures, half human – half animal, always thin and hungry, and seeking to trap hunters and lonely people. They devoured their victims and sent their souls below to the lands where Sedna or her father ruled. There was little fear of death as such. But death robbed the community of a handy hunter or skilled seamstress. There was a fear of ill-intentioned magic causing death. Yet in the case of elderly people who could no longer help in daily life, death was quite acceptable. One quiet night some member of the family would remove the top ice block in an igloo and the old person would simply die of exposure. Their last service to the family had been to go away.

The personality would then go to the underwater world of Sedna. But for a few weeks after the death no member of the family, nor anyone close to the place of death, would use a knife or any cutting implement. Ghosts, who would remain near by for a while, could be cut or hurt by knives. But the taboo would be removed after a few weeks.

The other-world was not a very happy place, but apparently some Eskimos hoped that some aspect of the soul would be reincarnated some day. It was a confused belief and early records tell of a double ghost and further spirit qualities which all separated at death. It was also possible to have news of the dead as if they were real people living elsewhere. Sometimes people dreamed of the dead and a few saw their ghosts. The *shaman* might become entranced and his spirit go on a journey to the other-world, whence he would return with advice and kind messages from the dead relatives. Some of the lonely communities isolated in their world of ice would fear that the powerful Sedna or her evil father might cause misfortune and even break into the upper world to seize victims. This was countered by the *shaman*, who would find a quiet corner in the igloo where a coil of hide ropes would be made, standing high with a narrow opening at the top. With two or three people as assistants and the whole family gathered around chanting and drumming would commence. At length the floor would be felt to heave and sway and sounds of splintering ice would be heard. The *shaman* would leap out of his trance and drive his harpoon into the hole left in the coils of rope, thus spearing the spirit. Sometimes his success was proved by strands of long hair sticking to the blade of the harpoon. Thus as the magic session came gently to a quiet ending the family felt they had been saved from disaster for months to come.

The Eskimo view was that the souls mainly but not permanently lived in a lower region. There was contact through ghosts and *shamans*, and real danger to the living through the efforts of the controlling powers of this other-world to entrap the living. Yet dream visits to the land of the dead were neither uncommon nor particularly dreaded.

Farther south, the hunters of the Great Plains of America had advanced to simple agricultural life, before the introduction of the horse changed the orientation of their culture by making buffalo-hunting easy. They had always believed in the continuation of life after death, and they exhibited little fear of earthly dissolution. They were well acquainted with the dissolution of the body, since the dead were wrapped up in bison skins and left on raised platforms on the western side of the village. People remembered whose body was wrapped up in which bundle. After a time the bundle fell to pieces, the bones were collected and the skulls were cleaned. Then often the skulls were painted and arranged in a circle where relatives would go and communicate with the power above through the spirits. Somehow the bones and the spirit were thought to have some remaining connection.

The general belief was that the spirits went to a paradise, described as the 'Happy Hunting Grounds', where life was like that of the living, but more pleasant and glorious. This happy land was sometimes thought to be below the ground, or to the west. A few accounts say that it was above the sky dome, but this upper world of great beauty was believed to be the abode of the gods and of a few heroes rather than the generality of humankind. Of course there were many variations of this belief, and it altered through time, though the change from the tribulations of this life to the land where the ancestors lived in happy adventures of war and hunting was a constant factor.

Changing circumstances developed these beliefs into the Ghost Dance religion. When people were driven into reservations by the white men, they were forbidden to go on raiding parties, forced to give up their way of life, and to subsist on the food and clothing supplied through white agents. Despised by a more powerful race which was ignorant of the spirit world they now took refuge in consulting the ancestors. The state of mind in which prophets arose and contacted the ancestors to plead for help against the evils inflicted by the white man was not new. It had been repeating itself in a small way for some two centuries. But the movement really took shape when the great medicine-man Wovoka was stricken by the spirits. The sun was eclipsed in 1886 and Wovoka fell into trance. The sun had died and Wovoka went up and saw all the people who had died. Then he was granted a vision of God, who told him he must not remain above but was to return to earth with a message to the people. He was to teach them a new dance and to tell them they must not fight, nor steal, nor speak untruths. They must love one another.

When Wovoka returned into his body he told the people of his wonderful vision, and gave the full message of hope. The white men would come to ruin and disappear in a terrible period of disaster from which the Indians would emerge after three days. Then on the cleansed earth the buffalo would return, the dead of the Indian tribes would come back rejoicing, and there would be Indian life again without the horror of white destruction. To bring this desired new heaven men must give up the white man's habits: there must be no alcohol, and no farming, and also no Indian mourning for those who died, for soon they would be all saved and return to life on the newly purified earth, in 1891.

Wovoka was a Paiute Indian, and as soon as he had organized his people to perform the circular ghost dance strangers from other tribes became interested. They were filled with hope, and returned to preach the new religion to their own people. By 1890 the movement spread and reached the twenty-six thousand-strong Dakota people. Heaven was at hand, a new heaven and a new earth; the evil men would be destroyed and the Indians find peace. Alas the stronger tribes became aggressive and the white agents told the soldiers of the new Indian revival. A body of miserably poor people, strong only in their new hope, were caught up by soldiers. The white man's guns killed three hundred of them at Wounded Knee. That tragedy seems to have broken the hearts of the Indians. The ancestors did not return, the cruel whites remained in power. The Ghost Dance faded from view and the Indians remained hoping that their peyote-induced dreams would come true. Even this did not destroy the American Indian belief in the survival of the personality after death: one must wait a little longer for deliverance. The belief in the heavenly land had been translated by a visionary, and hopes fostered only to be frustrated. But the Ghost Dance tragedy could never have happened if the beliefs of the Indian nations were not strong and full of hope. There was little mysticism in their belief. Reincarnation was a possibility, but no multiple soul. The whole person was in the other world and the whole person was expected to return when the day of liberation dawned.

Phenomena somewhat similar to the Ghost Dance occur in many other regions, particularly in Melanesia and Africa. A prophet arose in Melanesia who exhorted the tribespeople to destroy their past, to stop all contacts with the Europeans and to await the coming of cargoes sent by the ancestors from their heavenly abode. The ancestors are always alive in the other world and ready to protect and help their descendants. In some parts of Melanesia, quite apart from the Cargo Cults, fishermen believe that souls of grandparents and perhaps even earlier generations remember their descendants and come back in the form of birds to lead them to shoals of fine fish. They are near, and only gradually fade from memory, a process which seems to have been thought of as mutual.

As for the more advanced Polynesians, their ancestors left south-east Asia during the Bronze Age, but in the islands to which they were borne they found no easily accessible metals. Their culture was based on the descent of their chiefs from the gods. When discovered in the eighteenth century they were enjoying an advanced Neolithic type of civilization, based on fishing and cultivation of garden plots. Warfare was endemic in each group of islands, and strongly organized clans strove for supremacy. Beliefs in the survival of the personality after death were strong and clear. Naturally these reflected social conditions on this earth. Social distinctions were retained because they were based on the number of generations dividing the individual from the divine ancestors. At death the soul remained three or four days near the body and then took the road towards the sunset, which usually included a trail to a sacred western headland whence the soul either plunged into the sea or embarked on a soul boat towards the land of the setting sun. A tremulous red trail over the waters was often seen.

The other world was thought to be in the west, but at the same time most people thought of it also as somewhere below, with a layered structure which also included realms above. To the Maori in New Zealand these layers of the other world were each sacred and only to be reached in a journey by means of a series of ceremonies undergone to banish the sacredness (*tapu*), which would be strengthened as one ascended, or reduced as one returned to lower levels. The exact place of these worlds of the spirits was never clear. It was as vague as the Celtic Avalon, which was somewhere across the sea, always to the west. The Polynesian could reach the other world by canoe, and in sailing to the west the boat went up or down to other levels.

From the Marquesas comes the story of how Kena sought the soul of his dead lover, Tefiotinaku. He went by canoe and came to an island in the land of the dead, but he had to travel beneath the sea to another deeper island, and then twice again he had to move on, finding at every stage beauties who detained him for loving. But in the fourth under-world he came to the house of the goddess who ruled over the world of souls. He was given permission to take the soul of Tefiotinaku wrapped in barkcloth in a basket. When he returned to his village he released the soul, but although the girl appeared real, when he clasped her in his arms she proved an insubstantial wraith. The whole terrible journey to the underworld had to be repeated, and the goddess once again sent Tefiotinaku back to earth in a basket, but this time Kena was warned that he must make sure the purification ceremonies were held before he released the soul, which struggled to escape all through the journey. However, all was done properly and this time Tefiotinaku was returned as a beautiful young woman to her lover. They afterwards had some fine children.

The story depicts the soul as a dream-like creature which was aware that its place after death was in the underworld where noble souls went, close to the household of the goddess. Hence the struggles to escape until the rituals had returned her to earth. The soul meanwhile had not lost its earthly semblance, and retained its physical beauty. There was no division in the process except that the body had been discarded for a while.

The Maori of New Zealand saw the lands of the dead as a series of layers, below and above this world. The status of the souls depended on their close relationship to the gods who were their ancestors. Constant rivalry with the gods came from the great power of cheating and destruction, Whiro, who sought to ruin all good things. The fate of mankind was to enter another world rather like this, but a little sadder. There was no choice of the final abode by reason of good or evil done during life.

These Polynesian ideas about the way of death are part of a complex theological construction. It probably originated in south-east Asia in the first millennium BC and spread throughout the islands as the canoe men advanced over the ocean. The world of the spirit was aristocratic in nature, and socially stratified. But this reflected earthly life with its chiefly families towering above the commonalty. Everywhere it was possible for human beings to find the spirit world in dreams, and the spirit world sometimes came into contact with people through ghosts of relatives and visions of their abode. Dead relations took an interest in the welfare of their descendants.

The unity of culture and the high state of chiefly organization of the Polynesians is more characteristic of Bronze Age cultures of other areas. It is possible that their concept of a layered other world with its strongly hierarchical organization was a natural reflection of their ordinary way of life. Their neighbours in the Pacific, the Melanesians, were probably more characteristic of the farming and fishing cultures of Neolithic life. Tribal groups were quite large, often of several thousand people living in a group of villages united for defence. Chiefs were necessary, but not always hereditary. There was little social cohesion outside the tribal group, and a state of warfare was common in all extra-tribal relations. Hence a certain narrowness of outlook, in which the people along the coast would be enemies by definition. Such a state of affairs was reflected by a wide variation in the arts in any area larger than just a single village.

The Melanesian attitude towards the dead was one of ceremonial respect. The funerary rituals must be observed and offerings made for the departed. In most cases ghosts were expected to appear. People remembered any little faults which might have antagonized the dead. However, the ancestral ghosts were generally helpful. They watched over the fortunes of their family, inspired the fishermen, and gave strength to the warriors. There appears to have been little thought of an earthly resurrection. In New Britain ceremonial Malanggan boards were carved with elaborate patterns, mostly of birds and serpents as well as formalized heads. Often a figure in the round representing the deceased was included in the general design, painted red and white. Eventually the carvings fell to pieces, but they would probably last about three generations. During this time the spirit was available to help. He was remembered as a living person. Later he was forgotten and the monument was no more either. So the soul had flown away. However, for a long time he had been an inspiration to his immediate descendants, guiding them to good fishing grounds and defeating the forces of evil which threatened their welfare

In the Solomon Islands there was a similar social separation. A group of two or three villages was a big social unit. Though the basic culture of the people was closely similar, there were variations in art styles and local customs. In Roviana dead chiefs had power from beyond the grave. This was not simply ghostly but was associated with physical relics. The skull of the deceased was temporarily buried, then exhumed and cleaned until the bones were smooth and white. The head was then placed in a sacred house, a kind of house-shaped cage from which it peered through the gable end, with white shell circlets round its eyes. Normally this skull-house was kept inside a cairn of stones in the sacred burial ground. But when danger threatened, the skull was taken out of its resting place, and together with magical shell ornaments it was installed in a leading war canoe. The spirit of the chief was somehow within it and above it all at once. The boat was guided to an enemy village, and it was given power by the skull. The warriors fought more fiercely because they were defending their palladium in the form of the skull. They hoped they would return home with enemy heads as a glorious token of their victory.

The difference between Polynesian and Melanesian attitudes towards the dead reflects the living social arrangements. The Melanesians conceived of local gods, and had few ideas of an overall hierarchy, whereas the Polynesians had a strong ancestor-cult based on relationships with a divine hierarchy, which has an Asian aspect. The Melanesians thought of the dead as closely linked with their descendants, at least as far as they were remembered. But the Polynesian was in no danger of forgetting the names of the dead because of the presence of 'remembrancers' attached to the retinue of chiefs.

We find even among the more advanced Polynesian societies a linkage between the spirit and some preserved bodily relic. It was applied in Hawaii to the physical remains of Captain James Cook, some of whose bones had been wrapped in bundles of tapa through reverence for his powerful spirit, which was somehow associated with Lono (Rongo), the creative power among the gods. In New Zealand we find that the Maori also believed that the soul went to another world and tried to take the heads of enemy tribesmen in order to use them to weaken the spirits of the other tribe. The ceremony involved the head, carefully dried, being laid on the floor of the house while the elderly women danced round it, cursing it and exposing their naked bodies in order to weaken the will of the opposition and bring bad luck on them. The dried head was clearly thought to have some contact with its one-time companions. Of course many other human communities went in for head-hunting. In most cases the head was a mere trophy, though in many ways it seems to have retained some kind of life. For instance the heads worn by the Jivaro Indians of Ecuador were shrunken and worn as symbols of bravery by the warriors; but the mouth was stitched up for fear that it should speak and curse the wearer. Even among the Iron Age Celts the trophy heads were thought capable of speaking and of chanting songs.

There was a quality of thought which almost suggests a belief in a duality of soul, one part going to the other world, the other remaining near the physical relics.

The concept of a multiple soul is rather characteristic of African belief. It may well be that the idea drifted southwards from Pharaonic Egypt. Certainly in ancient times there were trade routes through the grasslands between Nile and Niger, and across the deserts from the Mediterranean. But the beliefs are not universal and even the affectionate desire to be in contact with dead relatives is not uniform and is sometimes absent. The Nuer of the upper Nile at the turn of the century did their best to dissuade their dead from returning. The body was taken out through a hole cut in the wall of the hut, then buried with some sacrifices and a farewell ceremony. It was carefully placed in a remote spot and buried facing away from the village. The dead were to go to their own place and stay away.

In other parts of Africa, however, the dead were remembered with affection. In many places images were made so that they could return and inhabit them for a while to commune with their descendants. In this case we are dealing with a type of multiple soul. The person is somehow within the image, yet the local people expect that a ghost may be at large, and at the same time the real soul is in a happy world above. Such beliefs are most marked in the West African coastal regions and the Sudan, south of the Sahara, and also in the Congo. All these people had migrated from the north. In some cases the idea of some spiritual linkage with the relics of the dead was closely linked with kingship. We must think of the preserved umbilical cords of the BaGanda kings of Uganda. They were a kind of palladia, linking the life-spirit of the rulers through time, each with its personal history. They were a means of contacting the spirits, not available to anyone except members of the royal clan. Among the mass of the BaGanda people, children were usually named after an ancestor who had entered the spirit world. It was hoped that some part of the ancestral personality would enter the child and remain to give help and good thoughts during life. The kings were also available as advisers, living mysteriously in the hut where the sacred jawbones of dead kings were kept. Each king had his house and servants. His priest, consecrated by drinking from the ancient skull, might enter the hut and emerge in a state of ecstatic trance. He would bring advice from the spirit, and before the living king he would be inspired by the spirit so that the past and present kings could talk to one another. Spirits were thought to have the same form as they had in the prime of life, but any mutilation of the body during earthly life would persist in the ghost form. It does not seem clear whether the spirits were alive in the sky or beneath the earth. They were certainly around their descendants on earth, and were regarded with equanimity when one happened to appear.

In south and south-east Africa, living people were believed to be able to keep their soul in some place safe from bewitchment. It could live in an amulet, or could be protected in a rock or tree. This kind of detached personality was also the secret life force of the individual. In the higher African civilizations a personality might also be enshrined away from the living body. A well-documented example is the personal stool made in Ashanti. The central column of the stool is in some sense a shrine for the life-force of the owner. The stool is preserved and cared for, and at death it is laid on the grave and offerings poured over it. Eventually it must rot away, but then it is no longer needed. The life-force has moved on as the soul of the owner has entered the world of spirits. There is no specific place, for the souls are mobile, shape-changing and free. They are not gods, but they have powers far in advance of their earthly attributes, and can be approached through diviners or through some offerings with prayers. They care for their descendants, and not surprisingly they are occasionally manifest as ghosts. They are living beings able to dispense life-force to give strength to members of the family. It appears as if the human has more than one spiritual portion in life and a greater unity in death.

In Africa there is no unity of belief, and the home of the dead seems to be mainly in the sky, but a great number of people felt that their dead relatives were around them on earth, though usually invisible. The greatest area of unity of thought is around the stories of the origin of death. Everywhere we hear that the creator from his home above the sky sent a messenger with the message that men were to live for ever, but that some enemy, usually a powerful evil spirit, induced the messenger to rest while he sent a false message. In some cases humans were given sexual powers to make their permanent earthly life inconvenient. But God had always intended man to live and his intentions were thwarted.

Another area inhabited for a long time by peoples of advanced Iron Age culture is Indonesia. Among those more remote people who have not been converted either to Hinduism or Islam, there remains belief in a universe of spirit beings where human souls are remembered and remember life. Among the Batak of Sumatra souls are plural, though traditions vary as to the number of spiritual qualities included in the category. The external soul dies when the person dies, but the soul may remain in the world of spirits and inspire *shamans*. It has the quality of life to be found in the seed of rice, which lies dried in a basket until brought out for planting. The soul may also reincarnate, often in some animal form such as the feared and honoured tiger. Meanwhile the skulls of important people were kept in great stone sarcophagi like boats with spirit images carved at the prow. In Borneo some tribes buried their dead and opened a gate into the other world by taking a thin pole and splitting it. On returning from the funeral the mourners, one by one, stepped through the cleft rod. When all were through the village priest closed up the rod and tied it. The mourners went away and scrubbed themselves thoroughly so as to remove the contagion of death, while the spirit was supposed to awake next day, see the grave offerings and realize that he was dead. He would therefore go away to the land of the dead, and not remain to frighten the living.

It would take too long to record the many variations of human belief about the fate of the soul contained in the preliterate phases of society, but it is possible to say that there is not a great deal of unity. The evidence does not suggest that anything beyond the simple belief in survival is archetypal and built into the human personality. One may link the various stories of the journey of the soul to the other world with dreams of the passage through life, which often assume a numinous quality. But the basic belief is simply that the personality persists and may be awoken from its sleep, or else it may continue without break. This is reinforced, no doubt, by experience. The most universal of all phenomena experienced in connection with death is the reality of ghosts. No culture appears in which specially gifted individuals are not able to fall into trance and converse with disembodied souls. Many of the behaviour patterns characteristic of the primitive *shaman* can be scientifically investigated in the modern seance room. The descriptions are the same while the details reflect the cultural norms of the audience.

One cannot extrapolate recent recorded belief back in time through preliterate societies, but as far as we have evidence from archaeology of deliberate burial we find care for the body, either dressed in ornaments or reduced to a skeleton which has been painted with red ochre and usually placed in the normal posture of sleep. Even the Neanderthal burials of some eighty thousand years ago had joints of meat buried with the dead. That implies a sacrifice of food and labour of no little value.

A belief in an after-life seems to be endemic among the human race.

3
The Religions of Africa
Adrian Boshier

•

Among the Black nations of southern Africa, the Bantu-speaking Negroes, it is believed that all persons possess a spirit with which they are born. Moreover, during life they may, from time to time, inherit the spirit of members of their family that have passed away. The influence of these spirits can be most powerful and might change utterly the behaviour of the recipient. Thus when an African man or woman acts in a strange manner the tribesfolk, in their usual philosophical way, attribute such behaviour to the nature of that person's spirit or *moya*.

One of the most powerful of these spirit manifestations is one which demands that the possessed individual be trained and initiated as a *sangoma*, witch-doctor. (In this context the author employs the term 'witch' conscious that it stems from the earlier word 'whit' or 'wit' meaning knowledgeable.) An ordinary person may be described as having the spirit of a hunter due to his love of and success in the chase. The same can apply to any other trade or profession, but when a person is reputed simply to have 'the spirit' then it is understood to mean the religious characteristics that pertain to witch-doctorhood.

Moya (which also means breath and wind) can manifest in any adult and its presence in men and women of any colour, creed or race is openly conceded to by African folk. This originates from their belief in one supreme God under whom all people fall. It is, however, considered presumptious and indeed virtually impossible to approach God directly. Instead there exist intermediaries upon whom mortals can prevail to have their thoughts conveyed to God. These are the spirits of departed ancestors. This belief has erroneously earned the

Africans the title of 'ancestor worshippers'. The African is, in fact, worshipping God, but this communion is relayed through the ancestral spirits.

On earth, race, language, class, indeed a multitude of factors divide mankind, whereas African belief states that in the spirit world these barriers disappear. Accordingly it is possible for an individual of any ethnic group to be accepted into tribal African society, depending upon the harmony between his spirits and those of the tribe.

Such traditional beliefs were quite unknown to me when I entered the African wilds twenty years ago. In an effort to discover the kind of Africa reported upon by bygone explorers I sought those regions that appeared as blank areas on maps. Having no financial resources whatsoever I travelled on foot and lived off the land. It was not long before I came into contact with tribal belief and was informed that I had 'the spirit'.

Not long after committing myself to desert, mountain, and African bush I found it essential to return periodically to civilization and the company of my own kind. Such visits rarely lasted for long and soon I was off again, seeking those elements of the wilderness which spelt such excitement for me. The occasional journey to town and friends demanded that I maintain some standard of civilized appearance. Consequently, it became necessary to organize some form of income. Snakes had always held a fascination for me and whenever I had encountered them on my wanderings I had always felt compelled to catch them. Now this sport became my livelihood and I purposefully sought and milked them for their venom as there existed a ready market for this substance in the medical world. By becoming a professional snake-catcher I quite unwittingly associated myself with the creature most inextricably bound up with traditional native belief.

After wandering through much of southern, east and central Africa, my extreme interest in tribal peoples led me to a rugged range of mountains in the north-western Transvaal, not very far from the Limpopo River. These mountains, the Makgabeng, had received very little attention from outsiders and when I first entered them in 1959 it was like discovering an ancient ghost-city. Everywhere I looked remains of bygone peoples were abundant, stone ruins, fortified caves, terraced hillsides and, most exciting of all, a veritable gallery of cave paintings. Cave after cave contained scenes with human, animal, and symbolic figures executed in a variety of colours which, despite the years, still retained their radiance.

In spite of their reputation for disliking outsiders the Makgabeng tribesfolk tolerated my presence, whereupon I set about recording this amazing wealth of rock-art. Although this self-appointed task took almost all of my time I still felt compelled to make occasional trips to civilization for my periodic dose of 'balance'. Alternating between city and wilderness I found myself equally thrilled and involved in the reports of space shots as I was with the sacrifice of a beast in a tribal rain ceremony.

While on such a visit in 1962 I married, and my artist wife returned with me to the mountains to make copies of the cave paintings. During the same year my activities came to the notice of two anthropologists and so for the first time I received both financial assistance and professional guidance. Walter Battis and Raymond Dart insisted that I continue studying the people first-hand as I had always done, but very gradually they began slipping in projects aimed at certain aspects of tribal life. Two years later an extraordinary set of circumstances interrupted my work in the Makgabeng and led me to investigate a mountain in the kingdom of Swaziland which was about to be exploited for its vast reserves of rich iron-ore.

My initial work on the mountain, known as Bomvu (red) Ridge, revealed that the ore deposits were riddled with some very ancient man-made excavations which had subsequently been refilled. From the local Swazi tribesmen I learned that the site about to be exploited by a large mining company had been mined by their own people since very early times. In fact, as far back as their oral tradition stretched man had always worked the red ores of Bomvu Ridge both as an iron ore and as a source of their much valued red pigment. Testimony to the Swazis' claim lay in the vast ancient workings that I had found all over the mountain. Later when my colleague Peter Beaumont submitted the various workings and layers to radio-carbon dating it transpired that red haematite and its sparkling black form, specularite, had been mined from this mountain for many millenniums. Actual dates embraced the third, fourth, sixth, tenth, twenty-third and twenty-ninth millenniums before the present. The earliest date obtained was 43,200 years ago. Therefore, Bomvu Ridge qualifies as the oldest-known mine-working in the world. In addition it transpired that approximately one hundred thousand tons of haematite had been extracted and that most of this remarkable enterprise had been achieved through the employment of stone tools! During my preliminary investigations the Swazis became extremely agitated as it was prophesied that the spirits would not tolerate the presence of modern miners with machinery and dynamite. The fears of the tribesfolk regarding that wrath of the great snake

Inyoka Makhanda Khanda and the ancestral spirits towards the proposed exploitation of the ore deposits became so strong that the company involved was induced to present a section of the mountain to the Swazi nation.

By no means is haematite or red ochre an unusual element in the archaeological record. It first appeared in Europe in Mousterian times when Neanderthal man employed it in his funerary practices. Simultaneously or somewhat earlier it was being mined in Sub-Saharan Africa by the first modern men, Homo sapiens sapiens, and from there it spread to almost every corner of the world. Throughout Europe, Asia, Africa, Australia, and the Americas it has been used in the burial rituals of man, with particular emphasis upon his concern with life after death. Beginning far back in pre-historic times and persisting amongst some peoples to the present day, the belief has existed that the earth is a living body. Analogous to this claim deposits of red ochre are described as being the blood of this mother earth. No better example is found than the present name by which it is known, *Haematite*. Thus it was bloodstone to the early Greeks just as it is to the Australian aborigines, some of the African tribes and as it presumably was to Cro-Magnon and Neanderthal man.

Contemporary with the Mesolithic ascendancy of reason there arose the concept that blood was the source of life. Whether man slew his human foe or animal prey the most tangible evidence of that being's death was its loss of blood. Excessive loss of blood resulted in death with the exception of women who shed blood as regularly as the moon completed its mystic cycle. There was, however, an interruption to this female phenomenon and that was when the blood was withheld for nine moons while it was engaged in creating a new life. Moreover the entrance of that new life into the world was accompanied by a flow of blood which again was not fatal to the mother.

The associations between blood and life-and-death are manifold, especially to primitive man. Reflecting upon the years that I lived as a hunter I vividly recall the endless days of tracking and following wounded game. Either alone or in the company of Bushman or Bantu hunters nothing conveyed more the vision of success than the sight of a blood spoor impelling us on over incredible distances.

Accepting that our ancient forebears, those who first began pondering causes and reasons, saw the role of blood as the anthropological record suggests, one wonders how they acted to increase, promote, guarantee, and even induce life. Undoubtedly many rituals arose to these ends and even today the world is by no means short of fertility ceremonies. What concerns us in this study, however, are those rites aimed at ensuring man's life after death.

The act of burial is, by itself, an attempt to help convey the departed into the hereafter. As an added measure guaranteeing this passage, additional methods were adopted such as positioning of the body and the inclusion with the body of items deemed important in the other world. Among these grave-goods none is more commonly encountered than haematite. The quantity may vary from a few lumps such as were found with the Neanderthal burial at Chapelle-aux-Saints (35,000–45,000 years old) to cases such as the Red Lady of Paviland whose fossilized remains were encrusted with an abundance of powdered ochre included at the time of burial.

Ochre burials are universal and have continued in some areas up to the present century. Thus we see the world-wide belief in the life-giving powers of the mother earth whose sacred blood can restore life. As surely as excessive loss of blood determined death so the inclusion of the blood of the earth could bring it back again. So powerful was the life-force attributed to this substance that, as we have already seen, it was responsible for man's earliest mining venture; moreover, its continual demand in that region of Swaziland alone accounted for the extraction of thousands of tons of haematite using nothing but crude stone tools. Hence the universal employment of ochre as a means of ensuring a form of re-incarnation and the ancient mining of haematite (the world's greatest source of iron) indicate that man's concern with life after death was the prime motivation of industry.

Having completed the preliminary research of Bomvu Ridge and after indulging in a little study on the aforementioned symbolism of red ochre, I set off once more for the remote Makgabeng. Thus began my fifth year in these mountains and for the first time my wife and I were returning with a Land-Rover. Shortly after our arrival I was asked to attend a meeting of the local African chief and senior tribesmen. This gathering, it transpired, had been called to discuss the severe drought that had been raging for years and had earned the region the title of 'belt of sorrows'.

Beside the last of the producing waterholes on the edge of the mountains, I listened as elder after white-headed elder stood and expressed his views on the dreadful workings of nature. Uppermost among all the fears voiced that day was the almost unanimous apprehension that the ancestral spirits had been offended. 'Did not many of the young folk go off and find work in the cities and on the mines, thereby neglecting the ways of their fathers?' 'What of the white man's God? Did not the missionaries tell our fathers that he would dry the breasts of our women and stop the rains from falling unless we adopted their belief?' At one stage a particularly ancient man suggested that as I dwelt in the caves deep in the mountains surely I was closest to the ancestors, as the forebears of this tribe had also been cliff-dwellers. What, therefore, were my opinions on the matter? As the old man was speaking my mind flashed to a beautiful set of sacred, wooden drums that I had discovered concealed in a cave some years before. In replying to the tribal elder I indicated the distant outcrop below which these holy relics lay hidden and asked why the sacred *komana* drums of the tribe had been relegated to such a place to rot? Their reaction was one of surprise and alarm, for how had the spell been broken that rendered the drums and their hiding place invisible to all but the keepers of the *komana*? Waving aside their concern I demanded an explanation for this strange behaviour because these drums, wherein dwelt the spirit of the tribe, had not even been maintained in good order. Assuming that only the spirits could have revealed the whereabouts of the cave to me, they explained that the position and condition of the drums exemplified the dilemma of the tribe. It had been impossible for their parents to accede to the demands of the missionaries, so instead of destroying their sacred objects they had hidden them away. The unknown power of the white man's spirit had prohibited proper use of the drums as effectively as their traditional belief had refused the Holy Bible. The Makgabeng people were therefore in spiritual deadlock and now asked me what course they should take to appease God and the ancestors.

I must confess that in spite of my own Christian upbringing my concern lay with the happiness of the tribe rather than the missionaries who had visited the area so briefly at the close of the last century. Accordingly I encouraged the chief to order the drums to be restored to a place of honour. In reply to their fears I assured the tribesmen that the white man would in no way avenge such actions, nor would his 'ancestors'. During the ensuing debate regarding various technicalities over the restoration of the drums and the rituals involved, I was alarmed when they questioned from where could they obtain the necessary blood. Human sacrifice is by no means unknown in some parts of Africa where ceremonies are held in an effort to break serious droughts. Seeing myself involved in a ritual murder I begged the council to consider no such action, but was quickly assured that the blood they required was not human blood. Then to my astonishment they told me that the sacred blood of *Mamagolo*, the Great Mother, was not obtainable in the region. Hardly daring to believe that the tribesmen were referring to haematite

I pressed for further details of this 'blood'. Their description left no doubt whatsoever that the Great Mother's blood was indeed red ochre, whereupon I immediately promised to obtain some for them. Graciously they declined my offer explaining that the tribal potters had already incurred the wrath of the spirits by employing the red powder obtainable at the European trading stores as a substitute for the genuine mineral. The material they required came from below the earth in those places where the great snake dwelt. Long ago, they explained, it had been mined by individuals who then travelled across the country trading it for a livelihood.

Suppressing my excitement I described in detail the Bomvu Ridge ancient mines from where I again offered to get them a load of ochre. Still somewhat dubious because of the powder-paint glazes which the potters had bought from white traders, the Makgabeng elders said they would first have to see the Bomvu ochre before accepting it. Nevertheless they conceded it was worth the effort involved, for without the sacred blood it was impossible to give life to the drums; and in turn unless the drums were fed with this lifeblood they could not fulfil their function of communicating with the departed ancestors.

Marvelling at the sequence of events that had led to my acquaintance with red ochre, its whereabouts, and above all the survival of the ancient symbolism of its life-giving powers, I departed for Swaziland.

Within a month I was back in the Makgabeng with some two hundred pounds of haematite in rock form. As soon as they saw it the elders excitedly declared it to be the one used by their forefathers, whereupon they handed it over to a group of old women to be ground to powder. As it was forbidden for men and menstruating women to grind the ochre only those women past menopause were allowed to prepare it.

Some weeks later I noticed that the drums had been removed from their hiding place, but no mention was made of them nor of any of the matters discussed that day beside the water-hole. To my great joy, however, the following season was accompanied by the finest rains for decades, the drought was broken, and the land displayed its remarkable powers of recovery. Eighteen months after the red ochre incident I was living alone in a cave in the Makgabeng still engaged in recording the cultures of the people both past and present. One day at sunrise a man approached my cave-home and invited me to a meeting to be held at a certain village two days hence. Rather surprisingly, the man denied any knowledge of the nature of the gathering, knowing only that I was expected there before sunrise. Somewhat suspicious, I nevertheless assured him that I would attend at dawn as requested.

Two days later I found the appointed village, the home of the most senior of the local witchdoctors, alive with activity as large numbers of tribesfolk moved through the courtyards or sat about in groups talking. After the customary exchange of greeting I was astounded by the announcement that the impending ritual had been organized to ascertain whether the ancestral spirits would accept me as a tribal initiate. An old male witch-doctor explained that the menfolk had decided some time previously to grant me full membership of the tribe, but as this was the first time a white person had been considered it was necessary to obtain the consent of the spirits. Overcome with shock and emotion, I was led to the central courtyard where an old woman sat partially covered by an embroidered cloth. This was Maledi, highest of all the Makgabeng *sangomas* and a woman from whom I had tried for years to elicit information. At this moment she was awaiting the return of the spirit of her grandfather, who acted as her principal guide. Apparently he had come a little earlier but informed his granddaughter that he was on his way to the top of a neighbouring mountain to collect some wild tea. Upon his return he would 'talk'. My inquiry as to why he desired tea was answered matter-of-factly, 'because he likes it', and when I asked how he would travel they replied, 'with the wind, spirits always fly with the wind'.

Eventually the spirit returned, whereupon Maledi and her assistant began speaking in an archaic tongue that only the spirits and their servants, the witchdoctors, understand. Consequently an old diviner who was not participating in the ceremony had to translate everything for me. For hours the two possessed *sangomas* danced and sang to the accompaniment of some wonderful drumming, stopping occasionally to deliver a message from the world of the departed. I was amazed at the stamina of old Maledi, whom I knew to be a grandparent herself, but when I mentioned this to her husband he told me that it was not she but the spirit that danced.

The whole question of becoming an initiate had arisen so suddenly that only later did I realize how much hinged upon the decision of the tribal ancestors. Most fortunately, however, they approved my entrance into the school for young men, whereupon I was officially given my new tribal names.

As soon as the *sangomas*' spirits departed, Maledi, her assistant, and two of the male doctors led me off into the mountains to a cave, some two miles away, that I had found on my second trip to the Makgabeng. Some of the symbols painted on the ceiling of this small cavern resembled a few of the figures that adorned Maledi's village walls, and intrigued by the similarity I had frequently asked the old woman about their significance. For almost seven years she had denied all knowledge of the cave and had always assured me that the paintings on her village walls were merely decorative. Now as we stopped before the stone wall that fortified the cave mouth she officially welcomed me to her spiritual home, where she came to commune with her ancestors and where she initiated the young girls of the tribe. Inside the cave Maledi then set about interpreting the geometric symbols and admitted that those on her hut walls had identical meanings. When reminded of her professed ignorance of these matters in the past she replied quite unconcernedly that only now that I was an initiate could she disclose these secrets to me. Prior to my acceptance the ancestors would have punished her severely for such revelations.

The next seven days were the most exciting of my life as the Makgabeng witch-doctors began the task of instructing me in the lore of their people, knowledge which all male initiates must possess. During the course of our discussions the witch-doctors referred to the excellent rains that had fallen and declared that this was evidence of the successful rituals involving the sacred drums and the red ochre. Indeed they repeated several times the immense relief experienced by the tribe since God and the ancestors had shown approval of their return to the ancient blood offerings of their forefathers.

Following this first initiation I was accepted as a witch-doctor among several tribes, then, seven years later, back in the Makgabeng, I went through the next stage in tribal education, the school for old men. The first school is a period of instruction preparing the young for adult life and teaching them tribal history, belief, and custom. The second school embraces higher learning and places more emphasis on religious belief and ritual. Being trained as a witch-doctor takes the religious side further still, for tribal doctors are the priests and priestesses of their belief.

From both the tribal and witch-doctor schools my tutors' instructions continually emphasized the remarkably close ties the living have with their departed relatives. Virtually all their waking life they contend with the whims and fancies of these very real entities. More likely than not their sleep will also be influenced by them for dreams are considered direct communications from the spirits. Their discussions about these ever-present beings are absolutely matter-of-fact and completely free of embarrassment, much like any European relating the behaviour of a living member of the family. The witch-doctors, being most closely in touch with the ancestors, are the greatest source of information on the behaviour of the spirits and, when in the right mood, can talk for hours about their characteristics. On very rare occasions they even indulge in humorous songs like bemoaning the vain nature of a long deceased great-aunt whose continual demands for ornate bangles and colourful beadwork leaves no money for food.

Very often one reads of the stern, forbidding nature of the African witch-doctor. Although this can be the case with some individuals, most of those with whom I work have all the humour so characteristic of the African folk as a whole. The ability to maintain this humour even about themselves and their profession makes them pleasant and enjoyable companions. Typical of this is an exchange I overheard between an elderly female witch-doctor and her rather cheeky niece, also a *sangoma*. Admonishing the younger woman for her disrespect the old aunt threatened to return after she died and give her niece a headache. Although in this case the remarks were playful I suspect a somewhat ulterior motive behind the incredible care and respect with which the aged are treated, for just as the lifelong characteristics of a living person will be maintained by the returning spirit, so the manner in which a person is treated on earth can greatly affect the way in which they pass on. A well-cared-for soul who has received respect and affection to the end is likely to produce a contented spirit. This is most important, as it is held that the closest ancestral spirit usually has the greatest influence over a person. No matter what the motive, however, their traditional belief certainly guards against neglect of the old and infirm.

The power of spirit 'personality' is best seen among the *sangoma*s when in trance state. As most of these doctors are females one frequently witnesses the most feminine woman suddenly transformed into a figure of undoubtedly masculine nature as a male ancestor possesses her. Her facial expression becomes harder and sterner and a definite male stance transforms her body as she speaks with a deep masculine voice. Upon the departure of that ancestor the *sangoma* may be taken over immediately by yet another male spirit whose voice, manner and possibly even language is quite different. Then, before regaining her normal state of consciousness, it is possible that one of her female ancestors might visit her whereupon her behaviour will change completely, once more. Ndlaleni Cindi, the *sangoma* we have studied most thoroughly, has both male and female spirits. Over the years we have seen her in trance state so often and the pattern of behaviour for each ancestor is so characteristic that we now know which spirit is in attendance before she has spoken a word.

Contrary to some reports, neither the witch-doctors nor the average tribesfolk appear greatly concerned with death and I believe this has much to do with their familiarity with those who have already died. The spirit world is so real and such a part of everyday life that there can be no doubt whatsoever of survival after death. Exactly where the spirit resides after death is a matter of debate, although not a very heated one, as few Africans seem at all concerned about the actual locality. Suggested places are above the clouds, below the earth, under the water, the various cardinal points of the compass, and right here on earth, amongst we mortals who, with few exceptions, lack the ability to see them.

Although the ancestors can travel at will, the strongest spot for making contact with them is on the site where their bodies are buried. Thus, individuals are continually making pilgrimages all over the subcontinent to family graves for the purpose of delivering prayers or making offerings. Likewise, parties of tribesmen frequently travel to the site of a past chief's grave as the chief's spirit is the most powerful in the tribe and certain requests must be channelled his way.

The horror of death seen among some peoples does not occur to the same degree with the Bantu; however, the grief expressed by friends and relatives upon the physical departure of a person is very real indeed. The people will mourn the individual, although he lives on, having merely shed the anchor which made him visible and kept him confined to earth. Now, as he inherits new abilities and enters another realm those left behind perform certain rituals to ensure his well-being. For the spirit must still eat, drink, and partake of various luxuries like snuff, beer, and tobacco. In the tribal areas embracing the Makgabeng, the fields are divided into sections, each portion bearing the name of a member of the family. When a person dies the land bearing that person's name is not ploughed for one year so that the spirit may grow his or her own crops to be harvested and consumed in the spirit world. In the case of the head of the family no planting is done at all on the family fields and with the death of a chief no one in the tribe may plant anything that year. So it would appear that the more senior members of the tribe benefit from more attention in the hereafter.

Whereas a Christian must lead a righteous life to guarantee his personal salvation, the traditional African seeks no such end. If one must seek a cause as to why we lead a moral life on earth then with the African such conduct rests upon the integrity of his ancestral spirits. Upon bodily death all traditional Bantu will enter the spirit world; the question of entry is not dependent on final judgment. While one lives on this mortal plane, however, one's behaviour is under continual judgment by a set of very critical spirits. The ancestors demand constant attention and the slightest negligence concerning their welfare immediately reveals their despotic and temperamental natures.

A drawback to ancestor-belief when viewed by an outsider is the extreme intolerance on the part of these ancestors to the introduction of anything new. This state of affairs, however, seems to exist throughout the world amongst older and younger generations of the living, so in Africa as elsewhere it acts as a kind of braking system, perhaps maintaining an equilibrium between progress and stagnation.

In spite of the gradual relaxation that is evident among the newer generation of spirits they still demand absolute obedience from their descendants. Consequently, even in the huge urbanized complex of Soweto, outside Johannesburg, the *sangomas*, and there are at least a thousand living there, are still completely subservient to their ancestors. Occasional accounts are circulated of offended spirits taking the lives of wayward mortals, and within the confines of concrete and steel sacrifices to the dead are still regularly made. Only after initiation did I encounter sophisticated and highly educated Africans who openly admitted their continued belief in the ancestors. In the cities such views are normally concealed for fear of ridicule, whereas in tribal areas there is no one except the missionaries from whom the traditional belief in life after death need be hidden.

As the ancestors are the servants of God so the witch-doctors are the servants of the ancestors. When a person dies the body is placed in a grave and the appropriate rites are held. One, ten or even fifty years later any African will admit that if one should open that grave the remains of the dead individual will still be found. The spirit or *moya* of that person, however, survives and from the moment that it departed from its body it began seeking another body through which to express itself. There is no belief in equality amongst tribesfolk, thus there are people with great spirit and others who make up the humble nonentities of society. The latter have spirit, as do all beings, but theirs is less demanding, requiring no more than the very minimum of attention. The former, on the other hand, tend to be sought by more powerful spirits to the degree where, with the right blend of characteristics, the individual is completely possessed and compelled to devote his or her life to the ancestors.

A person so selected by one or more spirits is led, usually through their dreams, to the home of a qualified doctor, where training commences. The apprentice is taught how to bring out the spirit, to understand it, and to induce it to perform such tasks as divining illness and locating lost objects. The initiate discovers that these ancestors can be outrageous exhibitionists, extremely wilful, and unashamedly vain. This vanity is reflected in their mortal menials, who are continually urged, through dreams and inner compulsions, to obtain beads, bangles, feathers, and all manner of beautiful attire.

The spirits are as individual in their mysterious realm as we mortals are on earth. Accordingly, their whims and desires result in no two apprentices or doctors appearing the same. Style of dress, manner of eating, drinking, dancing, and general behaviour are all dictated by one's ancestors. In fact, it seems that the individual personality of a *sangoma* is almost completely overshadowed by his or her ancestral spirits.

The witch-doctors under whom I studied passed on what they had learned from their own teachers and ancestors. Yet I was repeatedly urged that above all I must follow the instructions of my own spirits for absolute success.

In spite of all the individual temperaments encountered in the African spirit world, there are certain rites that are favoured by the majority of guiding spirits, such as drumming, dancing, and singing. Another demand which is almost universal among the tribal doctors is the insistence that their services to the people be well rewarded. Failure to charge a patient or client is a most dreadful insult to the spirit, the one who is, of course, responsible for all cures and successes. Finally there is one observance that every novice and qualified doctor must heed and that is the offering of blood, the most essential of all elements, to the spirits.

Periodic sacrifice to the ancestors is crucial, for without this life-giving blood they are unable to assume their full power and who, whilst dependant upon his departed ancestors for survival, would starve the source that fed him? Occasional offerings to the dead of goats and cows illustrates the witch-doctors' continued belief in a practice once observed in ancient Greece and recorded in Homer's *Odyssey*: 'The spirits of the dead could be summoned up; they gathered around in droves when an animal's throat was cut so as to drink its blood and become alive for a time, however brief.' The Eucharist illustrates the best-known example of blood and life, or rather a symbol of blood, where the red wine is taken to represent the blood of the son of God. So far as we know at present, however, that remarkable genesis of industry in Swaziland, the ancient mines of Bomvu Ridge, heralded the earliest-known example of man's concern with life after death.

4
The civilizations of pre-Columbian America
Crispin Tickell

•

Ancient American civilization came to a violent end about four hundred and fifty years ago. We can only see it through a dusty telescope in time. Like most other peoples, the Aztecs, Maya, Incas and their predecessors over thousands of years believed that life continued in some fashion after death. But our knowledge of their beliefs is pitifully small and fragmentary. It is anyway distorted by the shock which destroyed their society, and the medium through which it reached us.

The story of that shock – how small groups of Spanish adventurers, greedy for God and gold, overthrew a whole civilization – is at once intensely romantic and profoundly disagreeable: on the one hand a late Iron Age society with the advantages of gunpowder, horses, the crusading spirit, and individual initiative; on the other a late Stone Age society, rich, collectivist, self-contained, and well adjusted to its environment. Unhappily the riches made the Spaniards behave, as one observer said, like wild beasts; the intricate mechanisms could not survive the malfunctioning of the mainspring; and change in the environment – from the introduction of smallpox in Mexico to the silting up of the irrigation systems in Peru – brought about social disintegration which is still evident.

Today we are perhaps more tolerant of otherness, or at least better aware of the relativity of all human ideas and organization. But it is worth asking ourselves how the modern explorers of the moon would have behaved if strange but none the less wealthy lunar inhabitants had tried – somewhat ineffectually – to shoot down visiting spacemen, rejected all terrestrial pretensions, and asked simply to be left in peace. Those leading the next expedition would surely be fired by self-righteous zeal to put the lunatics in their place, look after their wealth for them, and teach them – if they turned out to be teachable – the virtues of whatever system of ideas was then fashionable.

So it was with the Spaniards in Mexico and Peru. Far from recognizing the values of the civilization they had discovered, they systematically set about their elimination. The only God was their God, the only beliefs were their beliefs. Indeed it was a nice question, argued out subsequently at great theological length, whether the Indians could properly be regarded as having souls, let alone the right to an after-life. In the meantime none doubted that Aztec religion was the work of the devil himself. The cult of human sacrifice, served by priests with long hair matted in dried blood and bodies punctured by maguey spines, seemed the final proof. There is no horror like that perpetrated by others.

The result was the destruction of a whole society in its spiritual as well as material aspects. The glue which had stuck it together was dissolved, and with no more than a few of the pieces we cannot understand what it really looked like from outside, let alone felt like to be within. There is a further problem. The Aztecs and Incas, the dominant powers in the early sixteenth century, were no more than late arrivals on the scene of civilization. They dealt roughly with their predecessors, and what they did not reject they absorbed and made their own. As was recorded of the Mexican leaders at the time of the emperor Itzcoátl more than a century before Cortés:

'It is not fitting that all the people should know the paintings. The common serfs will be led astray, and the earth will be made crooked, because in the documents are many lies . . .'[1]

The Spaniards themselves could not have put it better. To examine now how Aztecs, Maya, Incas and their predecessors judged life and death – and life after death – is an enterprise in conjecture which it is as well to recognize as such.

The evidence can be briefly described. In Mexico there are about a dozen painted paper books or codices – Maya, Mixtec and Aztec – surviving from before the conquest, and a greater number composed afterwards. No more is left of the thousands which once existed in the libraries of the main towns. A remark made by Bishop Landa of Yucatán is worth repeating: 'We found a large number of books of these characters, and as they contained nothing but superstition and lies of the devil we burned them all, which the Indians regretted to an amazing degree and which caused them great anguish.' In Peru there were no written documents. Painted boards in the main Inca temple at Cuzco illustrated certain myths and theological propositions. For the rest the Incas transmitted administrative information by the distribution of knots on different coloured cords, the quipu. They can now tell us little. Even less comes from the ideographic painted beans of the Mochica people long before the Incas.

Perhaps most illuminating for our purposes are first the writings of the Aztecs, Incas and others in the convenient new European alphabet, expressed sometimes in local languages, sometimes in Spanish; and secondly the writings of the Spaniards themselves, soldiers, priests, lawyers and administrators, who wanted for a variety of reasons ranging from missionary propaganda to doubts over land-ownership to determine the practices of a rapidly vanishing past. The work of the Spaniards, although invaluable, has to be read with some scepticism. Inevitably they fitted what they were told into their own scheme of things, thereby distorting its character; and their informants, mulling matters over in their fashion, almost certainly gave them an improved or selective account including a high element of what they thought the Spaniards wanted to hear.

Next is the evidence of archaeology, rich but inevitably unspecific. It is our only source about the remoter past. While the temples of Tenochtitlán were razed to make the foundations of the city of Mexico, the great Maya sites abandoned five hundred years or more earlier have survived almost intact in the jungle. In Peru virtually all our knowledge of pre-Inca civilization comes from the contents of tombs: mummies, jewellery, food, and some of the most eloquent pottery ever made.

Finally there are the living traditions. The passage of four hundred years and the inlay of an alien civilization have not eliminated the specific character of the substance beneath. It may now be a distortion of the past, and point towards the bedrock rather than the superstructure of ancient civilization. But the Mexican way of death and view of life thereafter still stand out. By squinting up these curious perspectives we can at least guess at the thinking of ordinary people down many generations.

In any case the bedrock is the right place to start. All ancient American societies, from the most primitive to the most elaborate, had a common origin. Beginning some forty thousand years ago, the hunting peoples of Asia moved across the low-lying land of what is now the Bering Straits into Alaska and spread southwards, adapting themselves as they did so to new and immensely varied conditions. The rise in sea level following the end of the last ice age raised the drawbridge, and subsequent communication with the outside world (a subject of much controversy) was at best intermittent. The invaders were far from uniform from the beginning, and over the millennia widely diverged. But whether through interchange among themselves or by virtue of their heritage, they continued to hold certain ideas and practices in common.

Their religious beliefs are of course unknown, but from the traces that have survived they must have resembled those of hunting peoples everywhere. With the introduction of agriculture and settled communities, an elaborate system of beliefs, managed by gifted individuals or a class of priests, was constructed on the basis of the natural yearly cycle. From the time of the first farmers specific concern with the after-life is evident. In Mexico the corpse was often buried with small clay female figurines, apparently symbolizing fertility and the continuity of life. They were perhaps designed to accompany their owner into the unknown. In Peru the food and artifacts placed in the tomb also indicate the desire to meet the soul's future needs.

As society became more complicated, traditions from the hunting past and agrarian present were brought together into the religious system. In the case of both the Aztecs and the Incas the element represented by hunters, soldiers, and people from the mountains found expression in the worship of sky gods, in particular the sun, with corresponding mythology; and the element represented by peasants and those living in tropical and coastal regions had rain, moon, and sea gods, also with corresponding mythology. Here the dichotomy of male and female also found expression. As in so many other religions the combination of these two sets of beliefs was matched by another arrangement. At the bottom was a religion of the simple and uninitiated: polytheistic, animistic, magical, and local. Next came the religion of the educated and the aristocracy: still polytheistic but of wider scope and with some measure of intellectual organization. At the top was the esoteric religion of the priesthood: unitary, somewhat abstract, concerned with mathematics, astronomy, and chronology, and expressed in terms of symbols.

In the fragmentary state of our knowledge we have to be careful not to wish consistency on to a religion which absorbed rather than rejected, or to think that the beliefs of any one of the tendencies described above were necessarily shared by the others at any one time. A visitor from space who had only the Athanasian creed, Dante's *Inferno*, the *Phenomenon of Man*, *Old Moore's Almanack* and the oral evidence of an Irish or Sicilian peasant would be hard put to it to work out a coherent statement of modern Christian belief in the after-life.

Thinking about the after-life was in fact very different in the two areas of high civilization in ancient America: on the one hand the region now covered by Mexico and its southern neighbours (meso-America); and on the other Peru and its neighbours to north, south, and east.

It may seem misleading to generalize even about meso-America and to draw conclusions from where our knowledge is greatest. But certain attitudes and elements seem to have been common in varying degrees to all the higher cultures. First and perhaps most significant is the belief that death is no more than a turning point in life: indeed death and life are two aspects of the same thing. This is well brought out by the early potters of Tlatilco in the Valley of Mexico who made double-headed images, one a living face, the other a grinning skull. The life and death of an individual were predestined from the moment of his birth. There are moments in all our lives which by accident or design determine what follows. For the ancient Americans one of those moments was death. If a person died in one way, he had one sort of after-life; if he died in another, he had another. At no time in his life did he have a power of individual choice as we fancy it for ourselves. He was never more than an infinitesimal part in a cosmic process of life, death, and regeneration.

It follows that the morality of his life was relevant chiefly as it concerned the manner of his dying. The meso-American peoples had a rigid moral code, but they were not anxious about the problems of individual sin. It is here that we are furthest away from Christian tradition: the notions of personal struggle, personal conscience, and personal redemption were quite foreign. So was our familiar dualism between God and devil, good and evil, right and wrong. Their dualism was in the supreme God Ometéotl – the Dual Lord and the Dual Lady – at once the father and mother, and creator of all gods and men, and a mystery not unlike that of the Trinity. The other gods, like men, had good and bad aspects, and characteristics which changed according to time and circumstance. There was no certainty that what men might regard as good would triumph in the end. Quetzalcóatl – the Feathered Serpent – who stole the first maize for men and was in some respects the protector of mankind, fell from grace, came to grief at the hands of Tezcatlipoca – the Smoking Mirror – and rose through sacrifice to be the evening star.

But if personal morality had little place in the process of life and death, the collective acts of mankind were vital to life itself. The present world was the fifth since creation. Its four predecessors had ended in catastrophe, and there was no doubt this one would too. In the meantime men had the responsibility to see that the cycle of life continued.

Sacrifice of many kinds was practised. Quetzalcóatl had tried snakes, birds, and butterflies. But Tezcatlipoca had defeated him, and only human sacrifice would do thereafter. Thus the drowning of children was necessary for Tlaloc the rain god; before the crops would come up Xipe Totec the corn god demanded the dripping blood of a victim whose skin was stripped from his body, flayed, dyed yellow, and worn by the priest; most important Huitzilopochtli – Humming Bird on the Left – the tribal god of the Aztecs, representing the sun at its zenith, needed human blood – precious water – to fuel his daily journey across the sky. For the Aztec there was honour rather than cruelty in human sacrifice. Before the obsidian knife cut out his heart, the victim would salute the priest: 'O beloved father'; and the priest would reply: 'O beloved son'. Sacrifice simply represented the means for maintaining life in a hard and above all fragile world.

The Aztec view of the after-life illustrates both the priorities and origins of Aztec religion. There were three paradises (not to be confused with the thirteen layers of heaven reserved for the hierarchy of gods, stars, planets, and the moon). First was the East Paradise of the Sun where went soldiers killed in battle and those sacrificed on temple altars. At dawn each day their souls would gather and joyfully accompany the sun to its zenith. After four years they might return to earth as humming birds or butterflies. Second was the West Paradise of the Sun for the souls of women who had died in childbirth. As the sun passed its zenith they would take over from the warriors and escort it down to the western horizon. They might also return to the earth in the guise of moths. More sinisterly, they could take up position by crossroads on the night of the full moon and eat children. The third paradise or South Heaven was for souls chosen by Tlaloc the rain god. Here went those who had been drowned or struck by lightning or had committed suicide or died of diseases associated with water – leprosy, dropsy, and rheumatism. It was a green abundant garden of flowers where people sang, played, and chased butterflies. The fresco of it at Teotihuacán (the city in the Valley of Mexico ruined in the ninth century) demonstrates its antiquity.

For those who failed to qualify for the three paradises the prospects were bleak. The soul went to the North Heaven or Place of the Dead on a journey which took four years through eight underworlds to reach its final destination in the ninth. Before cremation or burial the priest warned the corpse of the hazards ahead, and equipped him as best he could with food, water, paper flags, and a dog (the hairless xoloitz-cuintli). A bead of jade was placed in his mouth as a substitute heart, and presents were left for him to take to the Lord and Lady of the Underworld. In some ways the journey itself represented a return to the origins of the American people in the far north. Details vary. According to one account the soul had first to cross a wide river, holding on to the tail of his pet dog; next to pass through high mountains which periodically banged their sides against each other; next to traverse a pass where the wind was as cold and sharp as blades of obsidian; next to make way through flags; next to avoid showers of arrows; next to fend off jaguars and other ferocious beasts who tried to eat his heart; next to creep through defiles of brittle rock; and finally to arrive in the place of darkness and merciful oblivion. According to some the soul could return once a year for food on earth before returning to the shades.

This thinking is simple and obviously suspect. Much is unaccounted for. Whatever the pessimism of the Aztecs, it is hard to believe that their leaders – from priests to soldiers who died in their beds to merchants to the emperor himself – accepted it literally or did not have other solace, perhaps under the patronage of the gods peculiar to their calling. Durán, writing in the 1580s, records a speech made by the king of Texcoco on the death of the Aztec emperor Axayacatl in 1481:

'. . . You have now gone to the place where you will meet your fathers, Relatives and noble ancestors. Like the bird that flies You have gone there to rejoice in the Lord of All Created Things, Of the Day and Night, of the Wind and Fire . . .'

Then the king of Tacuba spoke:

'. . . You have reached the land of your lordly kinsmen and ancestors, There you lie, there you rest in the shades of the sombre fields Of the nine mouths of death with your ancestors; There you lie in the glittering house of fire of the Sun . . .'[2]

This does not sound like the terrifying place just described. But even emperors could have illusions. There is a strange story that the emperor Moctezuma, in despair at the approach of the Spaniards, decided to abandon his throne and take shelter in the underworld. Unhappily the envoys he sent came back with the following message from the god:

'. . . The inhabitants are no longer as they were in the world but different in form and manner; previously they had enjoyment, rest, and contentment; now all is torment; this place is no delectable paradise, as the old refrain pretends, but a continual agony; go tell Moctezuma that if he saw this place he would freeze from sheer terror, and would even turn to stone . . .'[3]

We must also reckon with the pervading scepticism in surviving Aztec poetry. It is full of nostalgia for the delicate but transitory things of life and the uncertainty of the future. The beauty of the world is all the greater for being only on loan. Men are like flowers which quickly wither or songs which die on the air.

'. . . In a day we are gone, in a night we are unfleshed . . .' The shining mirror as the perfect world can be contrasted with the smoking mirror – Tezcatlipoca – as the real world.

'. . . Are flowers carried with us to the kingdom of the dead?
It is true, it is really true we must depart.
But where, O where do we go?
Are we dead there, or do we live still?
Does existence exist once again in that place?'⁴

The answer was that no one knew. Orthodox beliefs might give comfort or dismay. But death retained its mystery.

The myths in other parts of meso-America seem to have been variations on the same theme. It is true that according to Mendieta the people of Tlaxcala (the independent principality over the mountain from Mexico) believed that after death lords and princes turned into clouds, gaudily feathered birds or precious stones; while the common people became weasels or foul-smelling beasts. But this seems an isolated story of class distinction. Even as far away as Yucatán the Maya had a cosmology similar to that of the Aztecs, albeit under different nomenclature. By the time of the Spanish conquest their civilization was in decay, and like the Aztecs they had been subject to Toltec influence. The result is that it is almost impossible for us to disentangle specifically Maya from general Mexican characteristics. They also believed in a thirteen-layered heaven and a nine-layered underworld, but their view of the destination of the soul was different. So far as we know there was only one Maya paradise, a place of abundance where soldiers killed in battle, sacrificial victims, women who died in childbirth and suicides enjoyed themselves for ever. The underworld where all others went was a cold, hungry, miserable place ruled by torturing demons.

Again all this seems too simple. It obviously goes back a long way, perhaps to a time before the Aztecs had added the East and West Paradises of their tribal god the Sun. But it hardly seems to fit the great intellectual traditions of the Maya priesthood, and could well represent a story told to foreigners or the simple-minded.

In modern Mexico death still occupies a special place. People like to be a little casual on the subject, to show an indifference which scarcely matches the national fascination with it. The readiness with which it is dealt out to others may not be so much lack of empathy as ingrained habit over generations, and even, deep down, the feeling that it is the collectivity of life which counts and that death is anyway part of the process of making new. Among those of Indian origin the souls return for their nourishment on the day of the dead. A special bread is baked, and in some villages the graves are laden with food and marigolds. All night long a vigil is maintained by candlelight, and in the morning the food has mysteriously lost its savour. For those in towns the festival is more the excuse for a party; but the skulls in sugar and chocolate, the special bread, the skeletons with fireworks in their fingers, or aloft as kites in paper helicopters, make sure that death gets the last laugh. One other link with the past should be mentioned. For the ancient Mexicans hallucinogens possessed a divine substance. Hence the Aztec name for the sacred mushrooms: teonanácatl, the food of the gods. Hallucinogens were everyman's way into a sense of the divine. For some they still are.

We are in another world when we turn to the beliefs of the civilizations which once clustered over the central Andes, touching the tropical forests on one side and reaching to the western shores of South America on the other. There is an extraordinary contrast between the abundance of archaeological evidence from the earliest times onwards for belief in an after-life and the sparse and vague references to the subject in writings after the Spanish conquest. This may follow from the character of religion itself under the Incas. It consisted of a range of popular beliefs of an essentially regional kind, including a remarkable cult of the dead, but focused on holy places, local gods, and familiar spirits; and secondly of the apparatus of a state religion which brought together the beliefs of ruling and subject peoples, and constituted indispensable means of political management. The second naturally rested on the first and drew its strength from it. Not surprisingly the first long outlived the second. Indeed in some respects it is still alive.

But what ordinary people actually believed about the after-life remains obscure. We look helplessly at their remains but cannot lodge ourselves in their minds. Among both the mountain and coastal peoples corpses were carefully preserved after evisceration by methods still unknown to us, and in the peculiar conditions of cold mountain or dry desert air nature completed the process of mummification. Practices naturally differed according to time and place. In the case of some coastal tribes, for example, the corpse was wrapped in a cocoon of woven cloths, animal skins or garments, surmounted by a false head constituting a wooden mask with jutting nose and round staring eyes, and equipped with the objects which had meant most to the person in life. These could include pottery of all kinds, weapons, tools, jewellery, and jewel boxes, three-note flutes of bone, work baskets containing bobbins, needles, spindles, and thread, children's toys, cases of make-up with tiny tweezers, embroidered belts, and of course food and drink – gourds holding maize, snails and other molluscs, and bowls which must once have contained chicha beer. Among the Mochica and others, small oval or circular sheets of gold, silver or copper were placed in the mouth of the corpse, and sometimes a hollow cane led from the mouth to the air above ground. Mochica pottery, sometimes zoomorphic, sometimes representing scenes from daily life, shows a joy in living and the visible world which shines out even now. To judge from these and other artifacts a feline god was of particular significance. Skeletons of little dogs have also been found (as in Mexico), and according to the literature wives, companions, and selected servants were sometimes killed and buried with great men. The Jesuit Blas Valera maintained that there was an element of choice. Candidates for sacrifice might offer presents such as llamas in their place. On such occasions funerals were followed by the celebrations of those who had met the requirements of the dead while saving their own lives.

So far as we know the mummies of the coast, once interred in and around their pyramids, were left in peace. But some of those in the mountains, buried in caves, quadrangular towers or even earthenware jars, were paraded from time to time through the villages or round the fields as part of religious festivals. The mummies of the royal line of Incas since Manco Capac were brought out in chronological order under parasols of multicoloured feathers into the main square at Cuzco on the main agricultural feast day of the year. At other times they were looked after by a staff of servants, dancers, clowns, musicians, and others who brought them food, kept their clothes in good order, and tried to see they were amused. One of the Incas even had servants standing by him day and night to shoo away flies. For lesser men customs varied. For example along the coast the nearest relation of a newly mummified corpse was ducked three times into the river when the dead man's clothes were washed clean. After a ritual feast chicha beer was sprinkled over the ground to quench the dead man's thirst, and sometimes one of his widows – drugged with coca – would be buried alive with him to provide company. Some mountain peoples took out their mummies for three days and nights once a year to reclothe them and supply them with food and drink. Tombs are still favoured spots for banquets.

A variety of explanations has been suggested, from reincarnation to resurrection to ancestor worship. Neither reincarnation nor resurrection seems likely. Concern was centred on the present body rather than any future one. When condemned to death by the Spaniards the Inca Atahualpa preferred to be baptized and strangled rather than burnt and thus go up in smoke. There can have been no sharp distinction between body and soul. Nor is there any notion of a soul returning to inhabit the body. As for ancestor worship we know nothing to suggest that the mummies were regarded as divine in themselves. Blas Valera wrote that the Indians prayed to the gods

'. . . to look after the dead man, not to let his body be spoiled and lost in the earth, not to allow his soul to wander, but to gather it in and keep it in some region of happiness.'[5]

The answer is perhaps simpler than it looks. The Indians saw life and death as parts of a single process. They did not know what would befall the dead. They may even have thought that the place of their burial was literally the scene of their after-life. At least they felt a responsibility to perpetuate as long as possible their visible conditions of life so as to make tolerable their existence in these or other perhaps more hazardous circumstances. In return they expected the dead to protect their descendants and the community in which they had lived. Although the Indians may not have worshipped mummies, they certainly venerated them in the same way as other *huaca* or sacred things. Huaca could be almost anything impressive, alarming or curious, from the Andes themselves to a juxtaposition of trees to six-toed human beings. They were in a sense vehicles through which the supernatural essence, good or bad, passed and made itself known in the world. The dead were part of their mystery.

The concept of huaca is elusive and must anyway have changed over the generations. Moreover it was applied quite differently in different places. The same must be so of thinking about the after-life. There is a rich variety of oral traditions, some probably of great antiquity, some equally old but later given a Christian tincture, some more recent. According to one a curiously shaped rock high in the Andes is at the top of a trail which led the souls of the dead to the sky. Male souls were bent with one kind of burden, female souls with another. They underwent tests to show their moral character. If they passed they could enter into joyful immortality through gaps – large or small according to sex – in the rock. If they failed they remained eternally but invisibly before it. Among the Chibcha the soul had to cross a wide river in a boat made from spiders' webs before travelling to the centre of the earth through gorges of black and yellow rock. In one part of the coast souls had to reach what was called the Dumb Land on a suspension bridge made of human hair and could count only on the help of black dogs.

It was on this sort of substructure that the Incas must have put together their complicated religion as part of the organization of state. For them there was a supreme creator god known – at least by the later chroniclers – as Viracocha in the mountains and Pachacamac along the coast. For the Incas his most important servant was the sun-god, from whom the ruling family was supposed to be descended. While the Inca himself took his sister as first wife, the marriages of his rapidly expanding family were an agency of genealogical imperialism by which newly subject rulers were brought into it. The other main gods and goddesses – some indigenous and some adopted – were of the earth, the moon, the stars, thunder and rain, and the sea. Elaborate rituals, geared to the yearly cycle, were performed by a powerful priesthood, and included collective and individual purification, divination of the future, healing of the sick, and regular sacrifice (including human sacrifice of the unblemished on special occasions and in special places). From the little we know from the Spanish chroniclers (writing for a Christian public), there was a heaven for good souls, plus the ruling class, and a hell for bad souls. Heaven – the Upper World – was in the sky with the sun. Food and drink were plentiful and life was much as on earth. Hell – the Lower World – was in the interior of the earth. It was a cold and disagreeable place and the only food was stones.

In describing this simple arrangement of the after-life Cieza de León remarked on the success of the devil in persuading the Indians to 'give more attention to beautifying their tombs and sepulchres than anything else': in short they seemed more interested in learning to die than to live. This is an impression he could easily have got. But he would surely have been mistaken. For the Indians the turning points in living were followed by the turning point of death. The dead should be given all the help they needed for what awaited them unseen round the corner. But in a single process each part was as important as the other, and the line, however crooked, was continuous. The fact of sacrifice, human and otherwise, shows that the death of individuals could contribute to the health of this very collectivist society as a whole.

For none of the ancient Americans was death the hushed-up disaster it has become for us. If it was not the passport to privilege thereafter, as in the anguished religion of the Aztecs, it was an integral part of the mystery of existence, and events before and after it were not dissociable. As in other religions, people did their best to legislate for the after-life by projecting the categories of the known to the unknown. Their efforts may seem to us cruel, pathetic or absurd. But there was no more certainty for them than for anyone else. The Aztec poets held to their scepticism, and Inca families were glad to sacrifice llamas rather than themselves. Life itself was good; and from the mist procession of living things came a glow which was also surely an after-glow. Who anywhere can say more than that?

Notes

(1) Irene Nicholson, *Firefly in the Night* (1959), 25.
(2) Diego Durán, *The Aztecs*, trans. Heyden and Horcasitas (1964), 174-5.
(3) Nigel Davis, *The Aztecs*, 236.
(4) Irene Nicholson, op. cit., 186, 190.
(5) Roger and Simone Waisbard, *Masks, Mummies and Magicians*, trans. Patricia Russell (1965), 55.

5

Religions of the East

Geoffrey Parrinder

●

India has been one of the greatest sources of religious and philosophical development for at least the last four millennia, and its contribution to interest in life after death has been outstanding. What has broadly been called Hinduism has affected all other Indian creeds and still fashions the dominant outlook. Buddhism and Jainism, now small in numbers in India, profess ancient and in some ways divergent beliefs, and they are regarded as non-Hindu or heterodox because they have their own scriptures, but some of their basic doctrines concerning life after death parallel or supplement Hindu teachings. The Sikhs arose much later, but in this special field they share much with their Hindu neighbours, and of minor religious groups very few have or had nihilistic attitudes towards life after death.

Certain teachings, if not peculiar to India, have developed there, notably the idea of the transmigration of the soul, or its reincarnation, and the associated ethical belief in *karma*, the effect and entail of actions performed in this life. Not only Hindus, but theistic Sikhs and apparently agnostic Buddhists and Jains share these fundamental Indian interests, and through missionary Buddhism they were taken right across Asia to flourish in the formerly difficult soils of China and Japan. Yet these beliefs are not found in the most ancient Indian texts now extant and it may be that they were present at lower levels of prehistoric society, the influence of whose ideas remained when the texts or physical monuments disappeared.

Survival after death is taken for granted in the Vedas, the sacred texts of which the oldest were perhaps composed in the second millennium BC.

As in many other cultures, a simple form of life beyond death was indicated in pictures which suggested that it would be in heaven but as a glorified form of life on earth. The chief of the world of the dead was Yama, the father of mankind and the first of those who had died. He lived in a heavenly paradise where he drank with the gods under leafy trees, accompanied by constant singing and flute-playing. The dead were also said to dwell in the third heaven, the highest step of the god Vishnu, who had made three strides across earth, air and sky, similar to the daily journey of the sun. Funeral hymns claimed that the spirit of a dead man would go into the world of light and there with the ancestors, Yama, and the gods, he would 'unite with the fathers, unite with Yama, unite with a vigorous body'. In a new body without the weaknesses and imperfections of earth, the spirit entered into a life of bliss where all desires would be fulfilled.[1]

A picturesque but more sophisticated sketch of progress into the life beyond is given in one of the classical Upanishads, philosophical discourses which are dated before and after 500 BC. Here the departed soul is said to rise up to the moon which is the door of the heavenly world and if he passes it successfully he proceeds to the worlds of fire, wind, sky, and the gods. There he is received by hundreds of nymphs, who adorn him with robes, garlands, and ointments, and knowledge of the divine being. He proceeds to a lake and an ageless river, which he crosses with his mind and shakes off good and evil deeds. These return to his loved and unloved relatives respectively. He arrives at a celestial city, a palace, an extensive hall and a shining throne on which the creator God is sitting. There he is interrogated, 'Who are you?' and he replies, 'I am what you are, the Real.'[2]

When Indian thinkers of various schools began to develop the simple notions of survival, diverse opinions were expressed and there was no imposed orthodoxy. Sometimes doubts were expressed about the possibility or nature of survival. The famous philosopher Yājña-valkya, having discomfited his rivals in discussions on the nature of the soul, asked them to put questions to him. When they were silent he propounded his own question in the form of a poem about a tree. This poem has a strong resemblance to the verses about a tree in the Book of Job (14, 7–14), where the Hebrew writer says that a tree will sprout again but man dies and wastes away. Similarly Yājña-valkya compares a man to a mighty forest tree, his hairs are like leaves and his blood like the sap within the trunk. When a tree is felled it shoots up, but how can man rise up when he is cut down? And if a tree is uprooted it cannot grow again and man has no root to emerge from death. A final verse sings the praise of the divine Brahman, the goal of wisdom and bliss, but this might be a later addition, though Job also at the end took refuge in God.[3]

In another dialogue Yājña-valkya is asked what becomes of a person when his voice, breath, eye, and soul have left him. He leads his questioner aside, saying that this should not be discussed in public. Then he speaks about action (karma), one becomes good by good action and evil by evil action. This is almost an agnostic Buddhist answer which, as we shall see later, held that there was no apprehensible soul, and therefore the link between one life and another was simply karma, the actions and entail which affect each psycho-physical organism.

But that Yājña-valkya was not satisfied with these negative conclusions appears in the many dialogues in which he considers the nature of the soul, both waking and asleep. Sleep is analysed in a subtle fashion by showing that the dreaming soul takes with it materials from conscious life, to create the roads and streams and chariots of the dream world, for the soul is a creator. Then the condition of the soul at death is described as like a heavily laden cart, which is the body mounted by the soul. When a man is dying he frees himself from the body, as fruit drops off a tree. Then sight, smell, taste, speech, hearing, thought, touch, and knowledge all fade away, to be unified in the soul which leaves the body by one of its apertures and returns to life.[4]

Yājña-valkya further compared the soul to a caterpillar which draws itself up on a blade of grass before passing on to the next blade, or to a piece of gold which a goldsmith fashions into another form. So the soul passes to another life, 'making for itself a new and more beautiful form'. Such ideas led easily to the doctrine of transmigration, passing from one life to another – metempsychosis – probably involving rebirth on earth or reincarnation.

It seems that the idea of rebirth was not known to the Aryan invaders who came to dominate India and their Brahmin priests who composed the Vedas, and it may have formed part of an ancient and powerful substratum of belief among the indigenous population of India. In a dialogue which appears in two of the oldest Upanishads a young Brahmin is asked by some leaders of the princely caste if he knows where the dead go to, how they return again, what are the different paths for the dead, and why heaven is not full up. He has to confess his ignorance and returns to reproach his father for not instructing him properly. The father is another eminent philosopher, Uddālaka, and he goes to the rulers, who confirm that this knowledge had not come to the priests before but was only known to the ruling class. Then they describe to him the lot of the dead.

Those who are enlightened ascetics rise up after death in the cremation fire and the light of the waxing moon and the northern course of the sun, and eventually arrive at the world of the gods from which there is no return. But those who cling to rituals and works pass up in the cremation smoke, the dark half of the moon and the southern course of the sun, into the ancestral worlds. There they work out the consequence of their actions and then return through space. They come down in cloud and rain and are born on earth as plants, and if they are eaten as food and emitted in semen they can find continued life in a new womb. This rather crude progress is then given a moral note, in addition to the rewards of deeds in heaven. Those whose conduct has been good will be born through a pleasant womb, to women of priestly, princely or merchant classes. But those whose conduct has been evil will be born through unpleasant wombs, to bitches or sows or outcaste women. Because of this transmigration heaven is not full up, and the variations in population in different ages can be explained by birth into animals as well as human beings.[5]

From these beginnings the doctrine of rebirth entered Indian literature and has been a basic assumption ever since. It is taken for granted, not argued, as a fact of life. Whatever view may be held of the soul, the effect of *karma* on the next life is assumed as evident. Once accepted, it provides a watertight explanation of the joys or ills of life, for misfortune and disease now must be the product of evil in the past, and each man is responsible for his own destiny. However, it is not an unchangeable fate, for the nature of the next life can at least be improved by good actions here.

Transmigration (*sam-sára*, 'going through') is fundamental to the Indian world view, and it may well be a belief of very great antiquity, since it is as basic to Jain and Buddhist cosmologies as to Hindu. The Buddhists call it 'circling on', or 'the round of existence'. In this round every being is born here and dies here, dies here and is born elsewhere, is born there and dies there, dies there and is born elsewhere.[6]

Transmigration of the soul is but part of the great transmigration of the universe, the microcosm of the macrocosm. The world also revolves in great cycles of birth and death, or evolution and devolution. There was not a creation out of nothing but a constant appearance and dissolution, with no final end since the whole process took shape and developed again after dissolution. The years of the gods, which were thousands of times those of men, were divided into four ages (*yugas*) of different lengths. The first was the Krita age, going on to the Tretā and Dvāpara, and ending with the Kali age. The first age was the best and the last, in which we now live, the worst. In this last and nastiest period religion declines, morality is abandoned, permissiveness reigns, women forget modesty, and the lower classes lord it over the priests. Then nature flares up and there is a flood under which the earth sinks into the boundless ocean. Such eschatology is common to all Indian religions, but it is not final. For as dissolution had followed creation, so a new creation or appearance must inevitably come next. A new world is born, like a new body for the transmigrating soul. Moreover, all Indian religions taught the possibility of release or salvation of the individual from the round of transmigration.

One objection raised by Western critics of theories of reincarnation is that we have no memory of past lives, and therefore we cannot profit from their mistakes or achievements and the purpose of spiritual progress appears to be defeated. To this at least two answers may be given. The first is that many people in Asia claim to remember their past lives and though the scriptures rarely refer to such stories there is no doubt that they are universally believed at the popular level. Western thinkers, such as Jung, who have given some consideration to the notion of reincarnation seem not to have ruled out the possibility of memories of past lives at conscious or unconscious levels. The other Indian answer, however, would be that belief in transmigration does not depend upon memories of past lives. Indeed it is a striking fact that the classical Hindu texts never cite memory as a proof of past existence on earth. The proof is rather in the very nature of the soul, its indestructible essence, which neither death nor life, nor things past nor things to come, can destroy.

In one of the most influential Upanishads there is the story of a young man, Nachiketas, who was apparently sacrificed by his father. He went to the house of Death (Yama), but finding him absent had to wait three days without receiving the hospitality due to a Brahmin. In recompense Death on arrival offered three boons. The first two were formal but for the third Nachiketas demanded the secret of survival. There are doubts about a dead man, some say that he exists and others that he does not. 'What is there in the great passing-on?'

This was strange to ask of Death himself and the deity tried to wriggle out of an answer, offering long life, wealth, lovely maidens, and many children to put off the questioner. But Nachiketas persevered, since ephemeral things wear out and only truth endures, and finally Death declared the indestructibility of the soul. It does not die, because it has not been born. It has not come from anywhere or become anyone. The soul is never killed with the body, because it is birthless, endless, primeval, constant, and eternal.[7]

The two verses which state this conviction are quoted almost verbatim by the famous Bhagavad Gītā. Here the setting is different, for the warrior Arjuna is smitten with qualms of conscience before a great battle. If the fight proceeds both friends and enemies will be killed, the order of right will be overthrown and society destroyed. Arjuna refuses to fight and appeals for help to his charioteer who is the god Krishna. The latter proceeds at once to assure Arjuna of the eternity of the soul, citing the Katha Upanishad, and affirming that everyone has always existed and will never cease to exist. This doctrine is rammed home by repetition in the Gītā, and it is linked with cosmic transmigration in a stupendous vision where all creatures are absorbed into the body of God at world-dissolution.[8]

The soul has a natural immortality and its post-existence is as sure as its pre-existence. Both men and gods share in this eternity and although Krishna increasingly plays the role of the Supreme Being, yet when he expounds the succession of births he asserts that both he and his human hearer have passed through many lives. The difference between them is that God knows about his previous births but man does not. Somewhat similar claims were made for the Buddha by his followers.

If the soul has a natural immortality then its escape from the bonds of the body and the chain of existence should depend upon its own efforts, and not upon any deity who is likely to be as much caught up in transmigration as man himself. So there is stress upon knowledge and works, for true enlightenment will bring release from the delusions of life, and at a more pedestrian level perfect fulfilment of all duties will destroy all evil *karma*. But this release may take many lives and the way is by no means certain, so that theistic works, like the Gītā, come to insist more and more that the best way to salvation is through the grace of God and loving devotion to him.

The Upanishads speak of the undying soul or self (*ātman*) and also of Brahman, the world-ground, the Absolute or the All. It is possible to distinguish in the texts the individual soul from the world-soul, but often that cosmic ātman is spoken about in identical terms with Brahman. The lot of the individual soul, past and future, is inextricably bound up with the universal being, and whether that is an aggregation of souls or a transcendent deity may be deduced variously from different texts.

There appears early in the Upanishads the doctrine of monism, that all is one, or non-duality (a-dvaita) as Indians call it. In the West this is often termed pantheism, that all is God. Clearly this monism is very important for belief in survival of death, for if man is one with the universal being which proceeds unchanged through all ages, then he is naturally immortal. Yet if monism simply consists in saying that whatever is exists, that there is no duality or difference of beings, no subject and object, no real past or future, the apparent variations and individualities being 'illusion' (maya), then to say that 'I am the All' may be the baldest tautology and indicate simply that 'I am I'.

A collection of nine examples given by the sage Uddālaka in the Upanishads contains reflections on the theme of the individual and the world-soul. The first state that when a man is dying his voice and mind and breath and heat merge into the highest power, but the subtle essence of all is the Soul of the universe. 'That is reality, that is the soul (ātman), and you are that soul' (tat tvam asi, 'that thou art', the favourite text of the non-dualists or monists).[9]

Rivers flow into the sea and lose their individuality, as bees collect honey from different trees and the various types of honey can then be no more distinguished in the honeycomb; that subtle essence is the soul of the whole universe, and you are that soul. Similarly salt placed in water disappears from view while its taste is dispersed throughout, like the soul of the universe.

This apparently straightforward monism yet received divergent interpretations. The Upanishads themselves are often not monistic, and while monism may suit certain philosophers its identification of deity and humanity might seem to spell the death of religion, and of personal immortality. In the ninth century AD the great philosopher Śankara propounded the most elaborate system of non-dualism, which has attracted many followers among intellectuals and is probably dominant in those circles today. As against the Sānkhya philosophers, who taught that there are countless individual souls, Śankara regarded the individual as a mere appearance of the highest Self, Brahman.

Śankara said that the apparent differences of soul are like the differences between reflections, for when the sun seems to shake in one pool it does not do so in another. If there were many souls and they were all-pervading everywhere that would create confusion, so there is only one true self which appears as many. Śankara allowed for apparent differences which are due to illusion, but this is a mere effect of Brahman, impermanent and unreal. Similarly he gave concessions to religious worship, even composing hymns to various gods, but this was an admission of a temporary condition of which the last reality was the eternal and undifferentiated Brahman.[10]

A modified non-dualism was taught in the eleventh century by the philosopher Rāmānuja, and this was much more congenial to the popular movements of devotion to a personal God. Rāmānuja said that in the text 'you are That', the word 'That' refers to Brahman but it is co-ordinate to 'you', since souls are the body of God but not his entirety. The soul is not a mere effect of Brahman, with an illusory temporal existence, but souls are modes which constitute the body of God. Moreover, souls have their own consciousness which persists into eternity and they are not completely absorbed or annihilated in the life after death.

'This "inward" Self shines forth in the state of final release also as an "I"; for it appears to itself . . . On the contrary, whatever does not appear as an "I", does not appear to itself; as jars and the like. Now the emancipated Self does thus appear to itself, and therefore it appears as an "I". Nor does this appearance as an "I" imply in any way that the released Self is subject to ignorance and implicated in transmigration; for this would contradict the nature of final release.'[11]

The ancient and widespread theistic movements in India demanded some distinction between God and man, and also implied the survival of death by the grace of God. This doctrine goes back at least to the Gītā where the loving devotees, in contrast to the abstract philosophers, come to God with all their hearts. It is accepted that men may seek the vague unmanifested Absolute, by knowledge and austerity, but the way is hard and few there be that find it. The few may perhaps revere the indefinable and unthinkable, yet the many cannot do this and the way of love is higher and better. The Gītā proceeds to assure its readers that God becomes the Saviour who by his grace, quite independently of *karma*, lifts his devotees speedily out of the ocean of transmigration and into a timeless state of blissful communion with himself.[12]

Theory and practice both reveal beliefs in life after death. Some of the most important and regular religious duties of Indian householders have been those given to the care of the dead, the fathers and ancestors of the family. Every day food and water should be offered to the fathers and every month rice-balls (*pinda*) are given on the day of the new moon in a ceremony called Śrāddha ('faithful'), and on other occasions of rejoicing as well as mourning. These are not funeral rites but acts of homage to the senior members of the family now deceased, and their aim is to supply continued strength to the departed souls.

As in other cultures, ambivalent feelings were held towards the dead, both affection and fear. Because the dead person might injure the living, attempts were made to separate him off formally from them. In funerals he was provided with food and materials for the journey to the other world, and also asked to depart in peace. If the proper ceremonies were not performed, it was thought that the dead person would become a wandering ghost without a proper body, and only after the first Śrāddha would he take his place in the world of the fathers.

In ancient times some of the common people, at least, buried their dead and verses exist in which the earth is besought to protect a dead person as a mother covers her child with a robe. But cremation, perhaps introduced into India by the invading Aryan nomads in the second millennium BC, became the rule for Hindu funerals, and it is practised to this day except for very small children or saintly persons whose bodies are supposed not to decompose. The 'burning ghats' where cremations take place are notable in many parts and especially by the sacred river Ganges at the holy city of Benares. Cremation was regarded as an offering to the Sacred Fire, the God who was both priest and deity and who would scatter the body but lead the spirit to the ancestors.

Traditionally verses were recited beside a dying man and after his last breath the corpse was washed. It was taken on a bullock cart to the cremation ground and there dressed before being placed on the funeral pyre. In ancient times the widow lay down beside her dead husband and was then taken away by a younger brother, who welcomed her back to the world of the living and to his house if he was willing to marry her. The Vedas speak of an ancient custom in which the wife herself was burnt, along with her husband and gifts of food and clothes. But this Sati ('faithful wife', Suttee) has long been abrogated, and sometimes the widow was not even obliged to attend the cremation. Sati was revived by certain families and was notorious in places in the nineteenth century until it was finally abolished.

The practice of cremation implied recognition of the destruction of the physical body and there could be no doctrine of the 'resurrection of the flesh'. The spirit was believed to ascend to heaven in the cremation smoke or fire. But the performance of both funeral and memorial rituals depended upon the continuance of the family, who were both blessed and needed in these reciprocal ceremonies. The coherence of the family, guaranteed by the caste system, was vital for performance of ancestral rites. Classical texts indicate the disasters that could come from mingling of castes, women marrying outside their class, and offerings for the dead being neglected so that they slip further down the scale in the world beyond.[13] The importance of having sons, to perform ancestral rituals properly, is constantly emphasized.

Traditionally the monthly or annual Śrāddha rites were directed by learned Brahmins, priests who sat in an open place while the householder made burnt offerings in the Sacred Fire to the gods, and placed three rice-balls on bunches of sacred grass for his father, grandfather, and great-grandfather. Further offerings were for more distant male ancestors and water was poured on the ground in libation. The rice-balls were later divided among the priestly guests and a feast was given for other attendants.

In modern times the full Śrāddha ceremonies are rare and many people have neither time nor money for more than simple offerings. But men continue to die and proper funerals are regarded as essential for the welfare of both dead and living, so that ritual actions are enacted both to ensure the heavenly destination of the departed and their continued benevolence towards their families. Although the theory of reincarnation is firmly held the return to this life may not occur for a long time, and meanwhile the departed need both to receive and give help and attention.

The heterodox schools of Indian philosophy and religion are those which reject the authority of the Vedic scriptures, including the Upanishads, and establish their own sacred texts. Each has characteristic differences from Hindu doctrines, but there are also many similarities, especially regarding life after death.

There have been atheistical teachers, though little is known about them except through the writings of their opponents. The Lokāyatas were said to hold that only this world (loka) exists and that there is nothing beyond it. They denied heaven and hell, and asserted that the soul is only the body with its attributes and there is no future life. People like this were ridiculed in the Bhagavad Gītā, by the example of the rich fool who is sensual, successful, and proud, but ensnared by desires and delusions he will fall into that hell which he has denied.[14]

The Jains are a very ancient Indian religion, though with a following of only about a million and a half today. It has been suggested that the Jains and Buddhists preserved ideas current in the pre-Aryan ancient Indus Valley civilization, and they flourished in the ruler rather than the priestly castes. Both religions reject the gods of the Hindus, or rather they may include them as secondary figures but they repudiate creator gods since the world goes round in endless cycles. Both believe in some kind of future life and in its culmination in Nirvana. The Jains believe in countless souls (*jivas*), in human beings, animals, and plants. These souls are entangled in matter by good and evil *karma*, and salvation is the liberation of the soul from matter into the bliss of eternal isolation at the ceiling of the universe. The Jains rejected the monistic theory of one soul (*ātman*) pervading all things, because of the manifest differences between bodies and therefore souls. They were criticized in turn by Śankara and others, for supposedly teaching that the soul is of the same size as the body and therefore, he said, the soul of a man might go in his next birth into the body of an elephant and not be big enough to fill it, or into an ant and be too big. The Jain and Buddhist fondness for negative or alternative arguments about God, the soul or the future was also criticized by Hindu philosophers. Their doctrines were those of 'maybe' or 'many-sidedness': 'maybe it is', 'maybe it is not', 'maybe it is and is not', 'maybe it neither is nor is not'. By such expedients the Jains were said to avoid or ignore the existence of the Lord who alone is the source of souls.[15]

The Buddhists appeared not only to deny or ignore God but to go farther than the Jains in denying the existence of souls. In one of the first sermons attributed to the Buddha, on 'the Marks of Non-soul' or No-self, the five constituent elements of the psycho-physical organism are considered in an attempt to discover whether any of them can be regarded as the soul. 'The body is not the soul, for if it were the soul it would not be subject to sickness.' Then the feelings, perception, impulses, and consciousness are examined and each of them cannot be the soul because of its suffering.[16]

Later Buddhist dialogues discuss whether a man is the same now as when he was a baby, and whether the different parts of the body taken together can give an apprehension of the person. With its negations and ambiguities the Buddhist position still continues to avoid both speculation and dogmatism. An eminent scholar has said recently that 'the Buddha never taught that the self "is not", but only that "it cannot be apprehended".' He also asserts that the popular Western view that Buddhism is a do-it-yourself ethic without anything supernatural is quite alien to true and historical Buddhism, which 'is based on the revelation of the Truth by an omniscient being, known as "the Buddha".'[17]

Whatever its views on the soul, Buddhism has always firmly taught rebirth, the round of transmigration, and the hope of Nirvana. The Buddha himself, who is one of a succession of Buddhas but the only one for this present long world-age, has passed through hundreds of births. One of the most popular books is the Jātakas ('birth-stories'), which contains some five hundred and fifty accounts of previous births of the Buddha in various human and animal forms, in each of which he performed his lot perfectly. His last birth, which he chose from heaven, brought full and final enlightenment and led to complete Nirvana. At his enlightenment the Buddha looked back and saw all his previous births, all beings present, and all the future. This virtually divine omniscience is part of the attributes of the Buddha and ensures his central place in devotion for which he is 'the God above the gods.' Like Krishna, the Buddha knows all his births, whereas men do not.

The nature of the Buddha in Nirvana was debated with negative skill. Does the Buddha exist? Yes, but since he has completely passed away in Nirvana, in any sense that could lead to the formation of another being, it is not possible to point him out here or there. Nevertheless the Buddha can be pointed out in his doctrine and his followers invoke him every day: 'I go to the Buddha for refuge, I go to the Doctrine for refuge, I go to the monastic Order for refuge.'

Mahāyāna ('great vehicle') or northern Buddhism taught doctrines of three Buddha-bodies, divine saviours in *bodhisattvas* who gave themselves for all beings, and personified perfect wisdom. Some philosophers taught a doctrine of the ultimate Void or Emptiness, with no difference between transmigration and Nirvana, so that bliss consisted in the cessation of all thought. This again was attacked by the Hindu philosophers, holding that if you declare that 'everything is nothing' this is equivalent to saying 'everything is being'.[18]

The Sikhs were founded by Guru Nānak in the fifteenth century AD. They are monotheists, but although perhaps in some ways they were influenced by Muslim monotheism and mysticism, the Sikhs are firmly within the Indian tradition. The late Middle Ages saw the flowering of many devotional movements, some of them enthusiastic to the point of eroticism, with devotions to incarnate deities. Others, like the followers of Nānak and Kabīr, taught faith in a supreme but non-incarnated God.

Yet traditional Indian beliefs in life after death continued in these new contexts. Nānak sang of being born many times as tree, bird, and animal, and in many lives he had performed good and evil deeds. But he believed that nothing could be hidden from God and only the divine grace could save man from sin and transmigration. In Sikhism, as almost everywhere else in indigenous Indian thought, the theory of *karma* explains the present sad or happy lot of man, though it can be changed by good deeds now and by the grace of God. Modern Sikh writers emphasize the truths revealed by Guru Nānak and his successors, since 'countless sins are washed away by the illumination of the Word.' Transmigration rules until the soul rises up to Nirvana, and then 'rebirth is eliminated through the word of the Guru.'[19]

'There are seven hells', say both the philosophers Śankara and Rāmānuja, summarizing descriptions of places of torment in the hereafter that abound in Hindu works, such as the Purānas, as well as in Jain and Buddhist texts. There is a close similarity to Dante's Inferno, if indeed the Indian ideas did not influence medieval Christianity indirectly through missionary Buddhism and Islam.

It is often mistakenly thought that Indian and Asian religions generally do not believe in damnation, but the countless hells of Hindu, Buddhist, and other religions, which give lurid details of devils and tortures, are nothing but damnable. The Bhagavad Gītā itself, continuing descriptions of the fate of the rich fool, gives classical support to the notion of the eternal loss of the wicked. They revolve around in birth after birth, being born into more and more demonic wombs, and 'never attain to God'.[20]

No doubt 'never' must be understood in the context of the cosmic cycle, which after dissolution will turn again to creation. It is not strictly 'everlasting punishment', but then in the Bible too the eternal 'eon' for the wicked is not unlike the cyclic period of Indian thought. It is impossible to say how literally the descriptions of heavens and hells were taken in the past. No doubt their intention was to attract men to goodness by glowing accounts of rewards, despite more subtle warnings against doing any action for reward, and to frighten men away from evil. Nowadays these pictorial accounts are spiritualized and a Sikh writer states that 'heaven and hell are states of mind and not geographical localities in time and space. They are symbolically represented by joy and sorrow, bliss and agony, light and fire.'[21]

The inconsistencies that may appear to exist between concepts of hell or heaven, and transmigration and final Nirvana, were not found to be insuperable. The oldest texts refer to the dead rising up to heaven and there receiving the reward of good and evil deeds, then after the entail of *karma* is exhausted some return to earth. There is a double moral judgment, both in the state of life after death and in the high or low condition of rebirth.

Heaven must not be confused with Nirvana. There are many heavens, in the distant mountains or skies, and while for Hindus they are the abode of the gods and blessed fathers for Buddhism the Buddhas-to-be live there awaiting the next revelations of truth. Popular religious works contain innumerable glowing accounts of the heavenly mansions, which may be temporary abodes yet lasting countless years. The guide in the famous Temple of the Buddha's Tooth in Kandy today takes parties through rooms where the walls glow with coloured paintings of trees and streams, birds and blissful immortals, and he blandly indicates 'Nirvana'. The educated know that Nirvana cannot be described or painted, yet an anthropologist reports that most Buddhas, monks and laity, prefer heaven or even rebirth to the distant and inconceivable Nirvana, and for them rebirth is better than 'the cessation of rebirth'.[22]

Nirvana was taught first by the Jains and Buddhists and apparently came into Hinduism through the Bhagavad Gītā which, with characteristic theism, comes to see Nirvana in communion with God, 'the peace which culminates in Nirvana and rests in Me'.[23] Nirvana means 'blown out' (vāna being related to wind), and it is the achievement of blowing out desires and karma, so that there is no more cause for rebirth, and the chain of transmigration comes to an end.

In English usage, and some commentaries, Nirvana has been loosely called 'extinction' in the sense of the annihilation of the soul or spiritual principle, but it is clearly not that in Indian contexts. Even suppression of individuality does not necessarily imply complete identification with the Absolute in Hinduism, for Śankara and Rāmānuja differed on this, and many religious texts can be interpreted as teaching unity but not identity with the divine. In Jainism the souls continue in liberated bliss for all eternity, while in Buddhism the extinction of desire, which is the cause of suffering and transmigration, is achieved.

Buddhist teachings about Nirvana are marked both by negations and by attempts to indicate its quality. The popular Questions of King Milinda emphasize that one cannot point to the shape or size or duration of Nirvana, nevertheless Nirvana is absolute bliss. It is the extinction of craving for sensuous enjoyments or for further rebirth, and so it brings all sufferings to an end. It is like a mountain peak, inaccessible to the passions, but unshakeable, lofty and calm. It is the bliss of the eternal and indescribable goal of the fully enlightened.

Indian religion has often been described as world-denying, an ascetic and selfish retreat from the problems of life, and there have undoubtedly been many ascetics or spiritual athletes who have endured untold privations in the search for a spiritual goal. Yet the energy and dedication that have been directed to the ascetic life have served as examples to most people. They have not set the pattern for an entirely world-denying religion. It is not just the world beyond, but life on earth that has concerned Indian religion.

Indian culture has produced countless works of art all down the ages, many of them with an exuberant sensuality that is perhaps complementary to extreme asceticism. Indian literature, moral and social treatises, technical and political achievements, over many centuries, testify to the value placed upon worldly life. Even for priests asceticism was the last of four stages of life through which men were normally supposed to pass: the stages of student, householder, recluse, and ascetic. Only when a householder had seen his children's children, and ensured the performance of ancestral rituals, should he retire from active life and meditate on the eternal.

Indian moral and social duties were grouped under four headings, of which salvation or liberation (*moksha*) was the last. The others were virtue or morality, gain in wealth and influence, and pleasure in love and the arts. These four ends of man were held to be right and proper for the classes of society and the sexes with their various duties and opportunities. That high ideals are not always followed is a general human failing.

Liberation or salvation was primarily considered to be from the round of transmigration though, as with ordinary Buddhists, hopes might be placed on a more pleasant life on earth next time rather than on a translation into Nirvana. It has been stated already that liberation could be thought to be achieved either by perfect knowledge, or by long and perfect actions, or most popularly by the grace of a loving God.

The all-pervading belief in transmigration gave a vista of a potentially endless series of rebirths, within this present world-cycle. But the religions of grace, and these are by far the most popular, offer ways out of the chain of rebirth. The Gītā says that God saves men 'immediately from the mortal sea of transmigration'. Such salvation is not merely for an aristocratic minority but for all who take refuge in God, 'women, artisans, and even serfs will attain the highest goal'. And this salvation lifts the saints out of transmigration and the world-cycles, for having become like God they are not born at world-creation or disturbed by its dissolution.[24]

For the monists or non-dualists, notably Śankara, liberation brings the knowledge of one's identity with the absolute Brahman. The Absolute is the Self of everyone and by meditation men come to reject the erroneous opinion that the Self is liable to transmigration. The Self is eternally free in its nature but blinded by ignorance in a human body, and liberation is simply recognition that one is the Absolute, being Brahman. The apparently separate personality of man is illusory or transient, whereas the Absolute is the timeless non-personal reality. However, the extinction of separateness is not extinction of reality but of ignorance. The ultimate reality is Being-Consciousness-Bliss (*sat-chit-ānanda*). Therefore, while the soul loses its individuality in the eternal, it does not lose consciousness. Rather, it enters into the highest and perfect consciousness, which is the bliss of true being.

This absolutist monism is popular among intellectuals, and it has been compared with the Void of some Buddhists, though the latter does not appear to emphasize the supreme consciousness of Hindu teaching. But for other Hindu thinkers, and closer to the ideals of the masses, there is the more personal theism of Rāmānuja. He emphasizes union with God, yet this is not identity but a communion of I and Thou, and a life after death that is neither solipsism nor extinction. Rāmānuja declares bluntly:

'to maintain that the consciousness of the "I" does not persist in the state of final release is altogether inappropriate. It in fact amounts to the doctrine – only expressed in somewhat different words – that final release is the annihilation of the Self. The "I" is not a mere attribute of the Self so that even after its destruction the essential nature of the Self might persist – as it persists on the cessation of ignorance; but it constitutes the very nature of the Self.'[25]

Rāmānuja declares again and again that souls constitute the body of God and that the absolute Brahman, the highest Spirit, must be different from individual souls, otherwise they could not commune with him. 'The Brahman to be reached by the meditating devotee must be something different from him.' Rāmānuja closes one of his most famous commentaries by declaring:

'there is a Supreme Spirit whose nature is absolute bliss and goodness; who is fundamentally antagonistic to all evil; who is the cause of the origin, sustaining and dissolution of the world; who differs in nature from all other beings . . . Who is an ocean of kindness for all who depend on him . . . And frees them from the influence of ignorance which consists of *karma* . . . And allows them to attain to that supreme bliss which consists in the direct intuition of his own true nature; and after that does not turn them back into the miseries of transmigration . . . When once he has taken to himself the devotee whom he greatly loves.'[26]

Notes

(1) Rig Veda 10, 14; 10, 15; 10, 135.
(2) Kaushītaki Upanishad 1, 1–6.
(3) Brihad-āranyaka Upanishad 3, 9, 28.
(4) ibid. 3, 2, 13; 4, 3, 9f.; 4, 3, 35–4, 42; 4, 4, 3f.
(5) ibid. 6, 2; Chāndogya Upanishad 5, 3–10.
(6) Milinda's Questions 77.
(7) Katha Unpanishad, 2, 18–19; and see my *The Indestructible Soul.*
(8) Bhagavad Gītā 2, 19–20; 11, 26ff.
(9) Chāndogya Upanishad 6, 8–13.
(10) Vedānta Sūtras with Śankara's Commentary 2, 3, 50.
(11) Vedānta Sūtras with Rāmānuja's Commentary 1,1, 1; Thibaut's translation p. 70f.
(12) Bhagavad Gītā 12, 1–7.
(13) ibid. 1, 41ff.
(14) ibid. 16, 8–16.
(15) Rāmānuja's Commentary 2, 2, 31; Śankara's Commentary 2, 2, 34.
(16) Samyutta Nikāya 3, 66.
(17) E. Conze, *Buddhist Thought in India*, pp. 30, 39.
(18) Rāmānuja's Commentary 2, 2, 30.
(19) T. Singh in *Sikhism* (Patiala 1969), 69f.
(20) Bhagavad Gītā 16, 19f.
(21) T. Singh, loc. cit.
(22) M. E. Spiro, *Buddhism and Society*, 76f.
(23) Bhagavad Gītā 6, 15.
(24) ibid. 12, 7; 9, 32; 14, 2.
(25) Rāmānuja's Commentary, Thibaut's translation, p. 69f.
(26) ibid. 4, 4, 22.

6

Near Eastern societies
Father Joseph Crehan

•

Ancient Greece

Not long before or after 600 BC the Homeric hymn to Demeter presented to the Greeks ideas about death and the passage to another world which were to have a lasting influence. The myth of the rape of Persephone was probably very much older, and may have been Minoan originally. The hymn showed to the Greeks how the Mysteries performed at Eleusis could be regarded as memorials to Demeter's arrival at the house of Celeus and Metaneira while she was sorrowing for the loss of Persephone, and to the promise of immortality to the child Demophon (whom she nursed for Metaneira). This promise was frustrated by the ill-timed curiosity of the mother about what the nurse was doing to the child to make him grow so wonderfully. The moral from such a story must surely have been the characteristically Greek notion that it was not good to try to know too much about the next world and that even the initiate at the Mysteries could expect only a symbolic presentation of the facts.

Earth, Zeus, and Hades are all said by the hymn to have collaborated in the rape of Persephone, and the undertaking apparently given to Demeter (lines 399–403) that Persephone will dwell in Hades for one-third of the year and will return to live with the immortal gods make it likely that the cycle of decay and growth in nature was understood to be in some way symbolized in the Mysteries. It will not do to distinguish two stages in the Greek religion of the dead, the first being a peasant mythology of the corn-maiden who dies and is reborn and the second a sophisticated myth of eschatological import which puts man in his place in the universe. The Minoan origin of the myth suggests that it may have developed much farther east in the form of a sacred marriage ritual between an earthly maiden and the king of the underworld. The alternative form of the myth (in which Persephone stays in Hades and does not return to earth) was followed by Virgil. In Lokri there was a similar version current; and there are Greek paintings where the charioteer of Hades carries off a maiden to his realms.

That a sacred marriage was required to renew the vegetation year by year was a belief that can be found from Mesopotamia to the Pillars of Hercules. An inscription in Hebrew and Etruscan from Caere on the Italian coast records this as having happened in the fifth century BC. The high point of the Eleusinian Mysteries was the showing of the travail of Demeter, along with a marriage-song for her maiden, 'while Zeus placed in her lap the testicles of a goat, as if they were his own'. Defenders of the sanctity of Eleusis say that Psellos has combined in his account what was done at Eleusis and what took place in Alexandria, but we cannot be sure. Asterius (*Homily* 10; P.G. 40:324) hints at some kind of sacred marriage at Eleusis. Inscriptions in gold-leaf *lamellae* that were buried with corpses at Thurii in Magna Graecia and in Crete (c. 350 BC) contain invocations of Persephone as Queen of the Dead. Persephone is there clearly supposed to be dwelling always among the dead, and not migrating season by season between this world and the next. The idea of bliss among the dead for the 'pure' was familiar from Homeric times, for Menelaus was told that after death he would go to the plains of Elysium where life is pleasant (*Odyssey* IV:573). It is claimed that this promise goes against the general theology of Homer, where the dead are considered to dwell in a realm like the Hebrew Sheol. Yet other heroes such as Harmodios and Aristogeiton (who in 514 BC slew the tyrant Hipparchos) were celebrated in popular song as being in the Isles of the Blessed.

Pythagoras, late in the sixth century BC, is reported to have reminded many of those he met about their former life, in which their souls had lived long ago before becoming joined to their present bodies. For himself he made the claim that he had been Euphorbos, son of Panthoos, a Homeric hero. Such theories suppose a separation of soul and body at death, a separation to which the famous monument to the Athenians who fell at Potidaea in 432 BC bears witness: 'The aether received their souls, the ground the bodies of those who fell about the gates of Potidaea.'[1] The phrase 'the body is the cloak of the soul' was apparently a catchword of the Pythagorean school, and for this reason Persephone was depicted as weaving at the loom new bodies for old souls. Gold-leaf *lamellae* (from Petelia, Pharsalos, and from Crete) give directions for the soul when it leaves the body: 'You will find a spring on the left-hand in the realm of Hades, and by it a white cypress . . .' The soul was directed to ask for the water of remembrance from the spring, which would presumably guarantee that next time round it would be able to recall what happened to it in the life it had just left.

Plato makes Kr the Armenian recount his vision (*Republic* 614b) of what he saw while temporarily dead; there were judges seated at the parting of the ways and the souls arriving from earth, when judged, went either to the right and upwards to the flowery meadows of joy, or downwards and to the left, for suffering. This sophisticated belief cannot have harmonized with the popular cult of the dead as it was practised at the Anthesteria festival at Athens. Here on the evening of the flower-festival pots of cooked fruit were put out for the dead of the family. Those taking part in the ritual cannot have had any idea that their departed relatives were now living in *other* bodies.

In the *Phaedrus* (246c–248c) Plato tried to reduce the theory of transmigration to some order. The soul at the start of its existence seeks to rise through the spheres until it can see heavenly truths plain. But if it loses its wings, it is borne along until it lights upon a solid body and settles down there.

'It is the law of Destiny that the soul which sees some of these truths should be free from harm till next time round [as the spheres revolve], and if it manage to do this each time, it is free for ever. But if, through inability to follow up, it remain without sight of them and grow heavy through some chance forgetfulness and loss, and then losing its wings it fall to the earth, it does not go into an animal body on the first occasion, but the soul which came nearest to seeing goes into the body of a man who will become a philosopher or lover of beauty . . .'

Eight other categories are provided for the less successful: kings, politicians, gymnasts, and so on.

The team of judges of the dead as given by Plato (*Apology* 41a) consists of Minos, Rhadamanthys, Aeacus and Triptolemos. The first two are personal names from the Minoan empire of Crete, while the second pair are connected with Eleusis. Homer (*Odyssey* XI:568) already knew of Minos as a judge of the dead, and he records some of the legendary penalties (such as carrying water in a wicker basket) which were imposed on notorious sinners. Yet Homer represents the dead Achilles as saying to Odysseus, when the latter has come on a privileged visit to Hades, that he would sooner be a poor labourer on earth than lord of the dead in Hades. How this was meant to combine with the status of Minos and the other judges is not clear. Hermes is often styled the *Psychopompos* or escort of souls. In *Odyssey* 24:9–14 he is depicted as taking off to Hades the souls of the suitors of Penelope slain by Odysseus. The weighing of souls is also his work; he holds the scales in a famous vase-painting, while Achilles and Memnon are weighed in the presence of Zeus, with their mothers Thetis and Eos pleading for their lives. This was the myth that formed the subject of a lost tragedy of Aeschylus, but Homer (*Iliad* 22:209) makes Zeus himself weigh Achilles against Hector.

From the fourth century BC onwards there were, as Plato tells us (*Republic*, 365a) many Greek manuals claiming to be by Orpheus, Musaeus or some other sage, which were full of mythology and formulae for initiations. Socrates could ask his judges how much they would pay to be in the company of Orpheus and Musaeus (as he would be after his death), and the taunt is heavy with Socratic irony. These popular manuals did not lack instructions about the calling-up of the dead for consultation. Hermes was again the intermediary, but what success attended upon the efforts of amateur practitioners cannot be known. The magical papyri are full of formulae and suggestions, but not of chronicled successes. Cumont (*Lux perpetua*, p. 206) noted the amazing fact that in spite of philosophical discussion of transmigration, there was absolutely no trace of it in the sepulchral inscriptions of Greece or Rome. If it had been firmly held as a belief, one would have expected to find that here and there a prayer for a better deal next time round, or for a safe return to old haunts, would appear on the tombs. Orphism and Pythagorean speculations must have rested at the level of intellectual discussion, with no roots in the life of the people.

The old view of Greek religion of the dead drew upon the animism of E. B. Tylor and was fostered by Jane Ellen Harrison and Gilbert Murray. Now that animism is abandoned by the anthropologist, one can make a more realistic picture of Greek belief. It took the Homeric poems almost as scripture; they might be commented upon, but they were not to be gainsaid. Whatever Socrates might say or Plato, the Greek from the Kerameikos would keep his Anthesteria and shout happily at the end of it: 'Begone, spirits of the dead; Anthesteria is over', bidding his dear departed to wait for yet another year in Hades. The triumph of philosophy in the matter of the cult of the dead did not come until Greece had been dragged into the Roman orbit.

Roman Beliefs in Survival

The Romans were practical men rather than speculative, and it is important to survey their beliefs in survival through the medium of what they did with their dead. Burial customs are not easy to assess, for the placing in a grave of treasured objects may mean many different things: the knife or the jewel may be set beside the corpse because he is thought to need it in the next life, or because after his death no one else ought to have it, or perhaps as a present to the gods below, or simply because it was his and he always wore it. Cicero gives ancient Roman belief in these terms: 'It was a fundamental belief of the men of old that after death there was some consciousness and that by leaving this life a man was not so undone as entirely to perish' (*Tusc. Disp.* I:12:27). Tacitus, in his life of Agricola (ch. 46), his father-in-law, agreed: 'If there is any mansion for the souls of the just; if, as philosophers hold, great spirits do not perish with the body, may you rest in peace.' The dead body would be arrayed and placed on a couch in the tomb, as if at a banquet. This was the practice of the Etruscans, which Rome seems to have followed.

Propertius, who wrote his poems under the stress of a haunting pre-occupation with death, has described (*Elegies*, 11:13) what he thought his own funeral might be like. He would have no long procession (*pompa*) no trumpets of woe, no ivory bier, and no couch fit for Attalus. Instead, he would take his three books of poems as a present for Persephone, and his girl could walk after his corpse, tearing at her bared breast in mourning. In his case, a funeral pyre would be lit under the couch and the ashes then collected in a simple urn. Cremation was beginning to be practised in Rome during the last two centuries of the republic, though Pliny assures us that it was not primitive practice (*Hist. nat.* VII:187).

After death the soul joined the Manes (deified souls of departed ancestors), according to Roman belief, and these received some reverence from the extended family or *gens*. In Propertius (*Elegy* IV:7) there is an outright declaration that the Manes exist and that death does not finish everything. He describes the return of his dead girl, Cynthia, in a vision: she had the same look and the same hair style as when she was alive, but her dress bore the marks of the fire. She was able to speak and to breathe, but her lips showed a trace of the water of Lethe that she had drunk and her fingers rattled.

Whether this vision was real or imaginary, it does at least convey what a Roman poet of the Augustan age thought acceptable to the public. Burials in collective graves (or of jars of ashes on their separate shelves in large *columbaria*) kept up the idea of the Manes as somehow grouped together for a family. The monument (in Greek) of a Roman soldier who died on service at Dura-Europos in Mesopotamia (*Excavation Report*, 9:177) was erected by his widow, and it gives as a rendering of the habitual *Dis Manibus* the words ψυχαὶ θεαί ('the divinized souls').

Cicero in his *Philippics* (I:6:13) made a sharp distinction between the honour paid to the Manes of the dead and worship of the immortal gods: 'I could never bring myself to link any dead man with the worship of the Immortals, or to address supplications to one whose tomb was anywhere to be found that received the honours of family devotion.' The word *parentatio*, or family devotion, needs a word of explanation.

The Parentalia was a feast of the dead celebrated at Rome from February the thirteenth to the twenty-first each year, and on February the twenty-second the *cara cognatio* was a day of family gathering when the dead were believed to come to join with the living. Ovid in his *Fasti* (II:535–39) says that small offerings to the dead are all that is required at the Parentalia; a tile wreathed in a garland of flowers (for tiles were used to cover early graves), some grains of corn, a sprinkling of salt, bread soaked in wine and a handful of violets. These were to be left on the path by the tomb. Ovid subscribed to the tradition that Aeneas brought this ritual to Rome from Troy. Laws restricting the extravagance of Roman funerals were incorporated into the Twelve Tables from the Athenian code of Solon. Cicero vouches for the fact and tells us that he and many others had to learn the laws by heart in childhood (*de legibus* II:23:58). At the *cara cognatio* (or Caristia) incense was burnt and food put out in the home for the Lares of the family to partake. These Lares are said by Festus, the Roman etymologist, to have been 'the souls of men admitted to the company of the gods'. Wealthy Romans kept small busts of their ancestors in the *atrium* of their houses, and this habit led to the great proficiency of Roman sculptors in portraiture. Characteristically, one of the laws of Solon had forbidden any carving to commemorate the dead which needed more than three days' work by ten men.

The dead had to be buried outside the *pomoerium* or city area of Rome. This was laid down by the Twelve Tables. Cicero (loc. cit.), who reports the fact, guessed that the purpose was the prevention of fire in a built-up area, but he adds a significant fact: the college of *Pontifices* (the guardians of Roman religion) held that a public area (of the city) could not be considered to incur a private hallowing, such as would have come about from a burial in it. What Cicero called *privata religio* (private hallowing) was only set up, he says (*de legibus* II:22:57), when the ritual had been carried out and the corpse interred, or when clay had been cast upon the bones that were cremated. This casting of the clay (*gleba*) with the prayer *Sit tibi terra levis* ('May earth light upon thee') was the most solemn act of burial. Festus reports that those who had taken part in a funeral procession had on their return to step over a fire and to be sprinkled with water, and that this was a form of purgation called *suffitio*. One cannot infer from this and from the fact that the dead were taken out of the city for burial the idea that the dead were somehow unclean. The law of the *pomoerium* was responsible for much ribbon-development by the building of tombs along the roads out of Rome, as may still be seen on the Appian Way, but the reason for the law seems to have been the conflict of private and public *religio*, as Cicero hinted. The practice of *suffitio* may yet be illustrated from Ovid (*Fast.* 4:787–790), where he says that fire and water are the principals of life; the exile was denied fire and water and the bride was given them as she entered her new home. It may be that the ritual for those returning from a suburban funeral was to indicate that they had now left the dead for the living.

In the *Aeneid* (6:735–751) Virgil took a Pythagorean view of the state of the dead. The soul at death was considered to pass upwards through the air, then to traverse the waters that are above the air, and finally to go through the atmosphere that is exposed directly to the rays of the sun. This journey involved a purification of the soul by air, water and solar radiation, so that when it reached Elysium it was thoroughly cleansed. Here it might stay, or else be escorted back across the river of Lethe to a new existence on earth. The Stoic philosophy had brought in this notion of a cyclic rhythm in the life of the world; some of the very wicked dropped out of the cycle to undergo perpetual punishment, others were retained in eternal bliss, but the great majority of men went round a process of life, death, purgation, and new life, while the material world was renewed every thousand years. The Epicureans, by contrast, denied all immortality. The hand that wrote a couplet on a wall in Pompeii summed up their philosophy:

Balnea vina Venus conumpunt corpora nostra:
Sed vitam faciunt balnea vina Venus.

which means: 'The baths, wine, and women are the ruin of our bodies, yet these three make up our life, the baths, wine, and women.' A simple pagan would hardly be comforted by the inscription (C.I.L. VI:4: 29609) on a tomb which proclaimed: 'I am ashes; ashes are earth; earth is a goddess: therefore I am not dead.'

When the emperor died, there was a public apotheosis. Coins had shown the murdered Julius standing on a triumphal car on his way to the heavens. For Augustus there was the release of an eagle from the funeral pyre, to show the people that his soul had gone up. Cameos were made showing Pegasus coming to bear him aloft. Lucan (1:45) promised Nero such an apotheosis, and Statius (*Theb.* 1:27) promised the same to Domitian. Seneca mocked at the business with his *Apocolocyntosis*, a skit which might be translated: 'The Pumpkinification of Claudius'. A papyrus from Egypt tells how Phoebus was believed to have announced the arrival of Trajan among the gods (*Papyrus Giessen* 20: Klio 7:278). Poppaea was embalmed at Nero's order (Tacitus, *Annals* 16:6) 'in the manner of foreign rulers', and this change from the Roman practice of cremation may have started a new fashion of burial. It is clear that by the time of Hadrian inhumation was becoming the established practice.

In the sixth book of his *De Republica* Cicero defended against the Epicureans the immortality of the soul, using Pythagorean and Platonic arguments. As a counterpart to the Vision of Er in Plato's *Republic* he ended his work with the *Dream of Scipio*, in which it is plainly taught that: 'The mind of each man, that is himself . . . It is not you that is mortal, but your body' (6:24). Colotes the Epicurean had argued that it was unworthy for a philosopher to use a myth to convey his teaching. Cicero was not deterred by this attack on Plato, but employed the same tactic. Plutarch attacked Colotes, and in the later days of the empire Macrobius wrote a commentary on Cicero's *Dream*. A fourth-century copy of the *Dream* was carried about Europe by the monks of Columbanus and ended its days at Bobbio.

The Pythagorean brotherhood at Croton carried on a cult of Herakles, who was known as the escort of the dead. This cult was introduced into Rome by Appius Claudius Pulcer in 312 BC, and under the name of Hercules the hero was soon regarded as authentically Roman. Some private groups may have kept up Pythagorean traditions in the Rome of the late republic and early empire; the underground rooms at Porta Maggiore were explained by Carcopino as the meeting-place of such a sect, and so far no rival theory has provided as good an explanation of the evidence. Apollonius of Tyana, in the age of Domitian, was a product of Neo-Pythagorean teaching, and in the second century Albinus and Apuleius carried on the Platonic tradition. Before the end of Roman paganism Sallistius (circa 370 BC) composed a treatise *Concerning the Gods*, in which he defended transmigration of souls. 'If transmigration takes place into a rational being, the soul becomes that body's soul; if into an irrational creature, the soul accompanies it from the outside, just as our guardian spirits do ourselves. A rational soul could never inhabit an irrational creature.' As proof of the fact, he instances the birth of babies with congenital disease. Also, if the number of souls was not limited, then God must continually be making new ones, or there must be from the outset an unlimited number, which to him was absurd. His supporting argument was that God, being perfect, must have made the world perfect and could not be thought of as continually adding to it, but this is to prejudge the question of God's power. That there should be an unlimited number of souls in a limited world is not a contradiction if by 'unlimited' one merely means a number that men cannot estimate. Libanius, a contemporary, made a pungent comment on the idea of a perfect world when he asked why there was so much talk among men of the Isles of the Blessed.

The Hereafter in Israelite Thought

The gift of breathing which God gave to man was understood by the Jews to constitute life. This was what Adam received (*Genesis* 2:7), while Job (34:14-15) declared: 'If God should take back his [man's] spirit to himself and gather to himself his breath, all flesh would perish together, and man would return to dust.' The return to dust was not felt to preclude the survival of the spirit or breath in an attenuated form. The abode of the dead was named Sheol from early times. Thus Korah, Dathan and Abiram (*Numbers* 16:30) are said to be swallowed up by the earth and to go down alive into Sheol. Abraham (*Genesis* 25:8) was 'gathered to his people on his death, even though he died and was buried far from their abode in Chaldea'. Jacob said (*Genesis* 37:35): 'I shall go down to my son, mourning to Sheol', when he thought that Joseph was already dead. With this belief there sometimes went, as in the episode of Saul 'calling forth Samuel' (1 *Samuel* 28), the desire to consult the dead. This was generally reprobated, as in Isaiah (8:19), where spirits and soothsayers are said to speak like little birds and murmur like doves. The fallen state of Jerusalem is described by the same prophet (ibid. 29:4) as being like that of someone dead: 'Like a spirit's shall thy voice come from the earth and thy speech shall squeak from the dust.'

The dead are called *Rephaim* some ten times in the Old Testament, and this name is also used for the dead in two Phoenician inscriptions. It is not certain how its derivation ought to be explained. In *Deuteronomy* (2:11) the same name is used for a race of giants. It may be that since giants were thought to be extinct, the name was used generally for all those 'men of old' who were now dead. The king of Babylon is told

(*Isaiah* 14:9): 'Sheol is astir for thee . . . it makes to rise up for thee all the kings of the nations. They shall say unto thee: "Thou too hast been stricken like us; thou art become like unto us".' This certainly does not suggest that the dead were considered to be powerful and strong. 'There is no work or thought or knowledge or wisdom in Sheol,' said Ecclesiastes (9:10), but he later declares that the dust returns to the earth as it was, and the spirit returns to God who gave it (12:7). As Job says (26:6): 'Sheol is naked before God.'

The condition of existence in Sheol was viewed as a diminished kind of life: 'Sheol gives no thanks to thee, nor does Death praise thee, nor do the departed hope in thy truth', said Hezekiah in his hymn of thanksgiving for recovery from illness (*Isaiah* 38:18). 'Who will sing the praises to the Most High in Sheol, as do those who are alive give thanks?' asked the son of Sirach (*Ecclus* 17:27), and this time the comparative term ('not so much as those who are alive') should be stressed. With the idea of a judgment after death there came in a separation of good from bad. The tyrant of Babylon was told by Isaiah (14:15): 'Thou shalt be brought down to Sheol, to the recesses of the pit.' The uncircumcised are said to be in the uttermost parts of the pit, for Ezekiel (32:19–30) compiles a long litany of those enemies of Israel who will thus be punished: 'Assyria is there . . . all of them slain, whose graves are in the uttermost parts of the pit'; Elam is there, Edom is there, and the princes of the North. *Job* (3:17–19) might seem to be in disagreement with this picture, for he affirms that in Sheol, 'the wicked cease from troubling . . ., the small and the great are there, and the slave is free from his master.'

The rewards of the just are proclaimed in no uncertain terms in the *Wisdom of Solomon* (3:1–4 and 4:7–18): 'The righteous man, though he die will be at rest . . . God's grace and mercy are with His elect, and He watches over His holy ones.' 'The wicked' (ibid. 4:20) 'will come with dread when their sins are reckoned up'; the good are not really dead (ibid 3:2), but they live for ever (ibid 5:15). Thus towards the end of Old Testament times there had come a conviction of complete discrimination among the dead. On this foundation there was built the idea of the resurrection of the just. Hints such as those in *Proverbs* 11:7 and 12:28 had been given earlier that whereas at the death of the wicked hope perishes, when the just man dies, his hope does not perish. The Greek version of the passage (made circa 200 BC) said this outright, whatever the words of the Hebrew original then current.

Jewish tradition (in the Talmud, *Pesachim*, 118a) held that the purpose of including Psalm 116 (114) in the *Hallel*, or groups of psalms to be recited at Passover, was that it spoke prophetically of the resurrection of the body in its eighth and ninth verses: 'Thou hast delivered my soul from death; I walk before the Lord in the land of the living.' It may be that in its original context this verse was a thanksgiving for an escape from a premature death by accident or violence, but the words must have appealed to the Pharisee tradition when once belief in resurrection was established. This is most clearly taught by the prophet Daniel (12:2) 'Many of those who sleep in the dust of the earth will awake, some to everlasting life, and some to shame and everlasting contempt.' It could be argued that the word 'many' is selective and stands for the faithful in Israel only, but by a common idiom the prophet was probably speaking of two multitudes which together make up humankind. In *Ezekiel* (37:1–14) the vision of the valley of dry bones uses the idea of bodily resurrection from the grave as a picture of triumphant return from exile. Unless he was wont to express *obscurum per obscurius*, it must be that he considered that the idea of bodily resurrection was familiar to his hearers. What Elijah had done once and by miracle (*Ecclus* 48:5) for a dead man, God could be thought to do for all the just.

Since the Canaanites (at Ras Shamra) propitiated a god of death whom they named Reshef the Destroyer, lord of the arrows, it was perhaps inevitable that Israelites should from time to time personify Sheol. 'Shall I ransom thee from the power of Sheol?' asked the prophet Hosea (13:14), but he did not expect an affirmative answer. *Jeremiah* (9:21) with his image of death 'coming in by our windows' may have been thinking of the arrows of destruction. *Isaiah* (5:14) has the same personification of death, while later in his prophecy (25:8) he speaks of the final destruction: 'He will swallow up death for ever, and the Lord of hosts shall wipe away the tears from all faces.' This passage is quoted by St Paul (1 *Corinthians* 15:54) as if it referred to the general resurrection, but in its own context it may have meant no more than a vision of victory in this life over the gods of paganism. Still, one may assume that St Paul was here following the teaching he had received from Gamaliel or other rabbis in first-century Jerusalem.

Gehenna, or the valley of the son of Hinnom (*Jeremiah* 7:31), was regarded in Jewish tradition as the entrance to Sheol. Johanan ben Zakkai (circa AD 70) held that it was the gate of Hell for wrongdoers, and the Talmud (*Pesachim* 54a) connected it with the opening of the ground to swallow up Korah and the other rebels (*Numbers* 16:30). It was the valley to the south of Jerusalem which joined up with the Kidron valley and which had been the site of the shrine of Moloch, to whom children were sacrificed. Shammai taught that the wicked were kept there for ever, while the lukewarm stayed until they were purged, but Hillel disagreed; he would have only the informers, the deniers of resurrection and the promulgators of scandal stay there for ever. Other sinners need stay a mere twelve months. Josephus (*Jewish Wars* 2:155) tried to assimilate Jewish belief to Greek when he wrote that Jews believed, as did the sons of the Greeks, that the abode of the blessed was in certain islands beyond the ocean where no snow, no rain or fierce heat came, while the wicked were taken to a darkling cavern that was teeming with everlasting punishments. The separation of good from bad was depicted by Ezekiel (9:4), when those in Jerusalem who had no love for evil were to be marked with the sign of the letter *tav* upon their foreheads and all others doomed to punishment.

The episode recounted in *2 Maccabees* (7:1–23) of the mother and her seven sons put to death by Anticchus (circa 165 BC) gives the clearest picture of Jewish belief in future resurrection then current. The second, third, and fourth sons, and the mother herself, are represented as professing faith in resurrection at the moment of death. When the fourth son says to his executioners, 'For you there will be no resurrection to life', he does not deny them all return to the body, but leaves unsaid the penalty of resurrection to punishment which was the lot of the wicked. The same book (12:44–45) records that Judas Maccabeus, 'made atonement for the dead that they might be loosed from their sin'. This sin was one of weakness, for under the tunics of many who fell in battle were discovered idolatrous tokens, which some had worn through habit, some through fear and some as a second insurance, in case Yahweh did not protect them. The idea of discrimination between punishments here proposed was no doubt developed by Hillel in the manner described above.

A general prohibition of offerings to the dead was given in the Law (*Deuteronomy* 26:14). That so pious a man as Tobias should have gone against this law is hardly credible, yet he is told by his father (*Tobit* 4:17): 'Place your bread on the grave of the righteous, but give none to sinners.' This is puzzling, but it may refer to a funeral feast for the living at the site of the tomb. No other trace of such offerings can be found in the Old Testament, though there was a custom (*2 Samuel* 3:35 and *Jeremiah* 16:7) of offering to mourners at the grave both bread and wine. The text of *Tobit* 4:17 is open to some doubt, for the ancient Latin version has: *Panem tuum et vinum tuum super sepulturam iusti constitue*, and this mention of bread and wine 'set down upon the tomb' would quite naturally suggest the funeral feast.

The Jewish sectaries of Qumran, whether Essene or other, do not seem from their documents in the Dead Sea Scrolls to have had a clear doctrine of resurrection. They certainly looked forward to a Messianic time, but then there had been prophets who expected as much, even when, as in the days of Isaiah (25:8), no such doctrine had been formulated. It has been claimed that one passage in the *Manual of Discipline* (4:6) is decisive: 'God has chosen them for an everlasting covenant and all the glory of Adam shall be theirs.' This is the version of Vermes, but Sutcliffe, who does not think the sectaries believed in resurrection, renders it as: 'They have been chosen by God for an eternal covenant and to them belongs all the glory of men.' He notes that the word 'eternal' means no more than a long period of unknown duration, and that the proper name, Adam, could also be used generally for 'man'. Sutcliffe is willing to accept that other texts speak of a blissful life with the angels, but goes on to urge that the angels are said to be present with the community in battle and at worship and hence the promise of life with them is vague; it might denote the future messianic age, when the sectaries hoped to be alive on earth to enjoy the spoils of their final victory. If they were Essenes, they ought, according to Josephus (cited above) to have believed in the survival of the soul apart from the body in the islands of the blest. But were they Essenes? It is hard to be sure. Essenes were pacific, yet at Qumran was found one document at least which was also in use at Masada at the time of the last stand of the rebels of 67–72 AD. Philo was sure that no weapons were to be found among the Essenes (*Quod omnis probus liber* 78), while the Qumran sectaries were brought up on a War-scroll which described the coming great conflict. Among ancient witnesses Hippolytus (*ref. haer.* 9:27) is quite emphatic that the Essenes believed in resurrection of the body: 'They confess that the flesh will also rise and be immortal as the soul is already immortal . . .' With all this uncertainty, it is best to leave in suspense the question of the Qumran attitude to resurrection.

Christian Ideas on Death and the Hereafter

The great innovation by Christianity on Jewish beliefs about the dead was what the Vatican Council has called 'the paschal character of the death of a Christian' (Decree on liturgy, 81). The argument of St Paul (in 1 *Corinthians* 15: 1–17) was that the resurrection of Christ provided a pledge of the future resurrection of the Christian. Paul did not limit his belief to a resurrection for the just only, since when challenged (*Acts* 20:36) by his enemies he made it clear that he taught a general resurrection of the body for just and unjust. This belief was a development out of the Pharisaic tradition, as may be seen from the encounter of Christ with the Sadducees (*Matthew* 22:23–33) over the case of the woman with seven husbands. The same opposition was encountered by the preaching of the Apostles (*Acts* 4:2), who annoyed the Sadducees, 'because they were teaching the people and proclaiming in Jesus the resurrection from the dead.' At Athens (*Acts* 17:18) Paul was credited with preaching about two foreign divinities, Jesus and Resurrection; the Athenians took anastasis, or resurrection, to be the female consort of Jesus, who was Paul's new god.

As already noted, an idea of the purgation of the lukewarm after death was becoming prevalent among the Jews (2 *Maccabees* 12:39–45) before the time of Christ, and Hillel could reckon the duration of this purgation as a twelvemonth. 'Making atonement for the dead that they might be loosed from their sin', was practised by Judas Maccabeus, and the discovery by Paul at Corinth (1 *Corinthians* 15:29) that some Christians were undergoing a second baptism on behalf of dead relatives shows that the idea of a remedy for the sinner after death was not unknown. Paul neither praised nor condemned this practice, merely using it as an argument *ad hominem*, but elsewhere in the same epistle (chapter 3) he draws out an extended comparison between the work of different evangelists and that of the builders of a town. Should a fire break out, the stout building of stone will survive, the shack will perish, and its occupant may just manage to escape, 'being saved as it were through the fire'; in like manner the lazy evangelist may be saved, but only after a struggle. In a later epistle (2 *Timothy* 1:16) there is this prayer: 'May the Lord grant mercy to the household of Onesiphorus, for he often refreshed me', where the mention of the man's past good works and the preoccupation now with his household imply that Onesiphorus must be dead at the time of writing. Similarly the word of Christ (*Matthew* 12:32) about the sin which cannot be remitted 'either in the present age or in the future age' implies that some sins might be remitted in the future age. The parable in *Luke* (12:59) about the man who is put in ward until he has paid the last farthing has the same intent, though it was taken up by the Gnostic followers of Carpocrates as proposing a doctrine of transmigration of souls who were held to be under the necessity of coming to earth time after time until they had committed all the sins in the catalogue; this bizarre idea was refuted by Irenaeus (I:20:2) and by Tertullian (*de Anima* 45).

From the second century onwards there is plenty of evidence of Christian prayer for the dead. The famous inscription at the tomb of Abercius asked the passer-by to pray for this Asiatic bishop after his death. The *Acts of Paul*, an apocryphal product of circa 160, tells how

Queen Tryphaena was instructed in a dream by her dead daughter to adopt the Christian Thecla: 'that she may pray for me and that I be translated to the place of the righteous.' In the text of *Romans* 12:13 there was made before 160 a change of wording by some scribes, so that the verse read: 'Take part in the commemoration of the faithful', instead of the original exhortation to 'contribute to the needs of the saints'. When the Jerusalem Christian community was broken up in the revolt of 132–35, this instruction to help these 'saints' financially was devoid of all meaning for the scribe; he made of the verse what he could by correcting, as he thought, a single Greek word by altering its two initial letters, and the sense was 'restored'.

'Blessed are the dead who die in the Lord from this time forth', was the message of the *Revelation of St John* (14:13). It is added that they are to rest from their labours. The contemporary *Epistle of Clement* speaks of Peter and Paul 'going to the rightful place of glory' and 'departing from this world and going to the holy place.' The martyrs above all were thought to qualify for this reward, and that without delay, but they were not the only ones. In the letter of the Church of Smyrna about the martyrdom of Polycarp (AD 156), after some words about the martyrs, there is added the wish: 'May it be our lot also to be found partakers and fellow-disciples with them.' These ideas involved as a consequence the notion of a 'particular judgment' (the term is first found in a fragmentary work of Origen recently published from a Bologna papyrus) as distinct from the general judgment of all mankind. The difference between the two can be seen in the prayer of Serapion (circa 356) for one who has died and is about to be carried forth: 'Give rest to his soul in green places, in chambers of rest, with Abraham, Isaac and Jacob and all thy saints; and raise up his body in the day which thou hast ordained, according to thy promises which cannot lie, that thou mayst render to it also the heritage of which it is worthy in thy holy pastures.' The pastoral imagery occurs again in the *Ordo commendationis animae* (of ancient date), which borrows the Virgilian *amoena virecta* when it asks for the Good Shepherd to receive the soul *intra Paradisi sui moena virentia*.

The attempts made to assimilate Christian belief about the resurrection of the dead to the Greek philosophy of the age, which favoured a survival of the soul alone, led to various heresies about this resurrection. Some said that the justified alone would rise again. Thus the *Didache* (16:7) in the early second century recounts the signs of the end: 'First, the sign that will be spread out in the heavens; then the sign of the trumpet-blast; and thirdly the rising of the dead, but not of all. For

Scripture says: "The Lord will come and all His saints with Him".'
Others denied that there would be any bodily resurrection. The apocryphal *Third Epistle to the Corinthians* (from about the middle of the
second century) has Paul reply to Simon and Cleobius, two heretics
who denied that God was all-powerful and that there would be a resurrection: 'Christ Jesus came to raise us up in the flesh from death, even
as he showed by his own example . . . As for those who tell you that
there is no resurrection of the flesh, for them there is no resurrection
who refuse faith to the one who rose thus himself.' This apocryphal
work would thus be in line with the *Didache* in denying a resurrection
of the wicked, but the Latin versions of it bring in the distinction
between a resurrection to life and a resurrection to judgment, in accord
with *John* 5:29. It may be that the Latin versions are here more faithful
to the original than the Greek papyrus (of the third century), for the
contents of the work are in general orthodox. The limitation of
judgment to those who reject the faith is in accord with *John* 12:47,
where according to the best-attested reading Christ says: 'If anyone
hears and keeps My word, I do not judge him, for I did not come
to judge the world . . .' Judgment then becomes the concern of the
wicked.

The interim condition of the just between death and final judgment
exercised the minds of the early Christian theologians. Paul's argument
in 2 *Corinthians* 5:1–10 is very difficult to follow. He is using language
borrowed from the Jewish ritual of the Feast of Tabernacles: 'While we
are still in this tent, we sigh with anxiety; not that we would be un-
clothed, but that we would be further clothed, so that what is mortal
may be swallowed up by life.' The parallel of the Christian's resurrection with that of Christ implied that not everything was restored to the
just soul at once after death, though such a soul was certainly blessed
(*Revelations* 14:13). What *Revelations* calls 'the first resurrection' (20:6)
is for some only, while 'the rest of the dead came not to life until the
thousand years were accomplished'. The vision of this residue, whether
it is to be understood as made up of the wicked only, or of all save the
martyrs of Christ, is hard to interpret, but, as it is followed by the vision
of 'the second death', when the wicked depart from judgment unto
punishment, it might seem more probable that 'the rest of the dead'
covers the wicked only and that they are viewed as being in some state
of suspense from death to judgment. Luther toyed with the idea of a
sleep of the dead until Judgment Day, while the youthful Calvin with
his *Psychopannuchia* challenged him for his speculation. One can escape
such dilemmas by using the device, not unknown to the Hebrew

prophets, of a double perspective to interpret the vision. Those who come to life (*Revelations* 20:4), or do not come to life (20:5), are in the foreground of the life of the Church, while in the background is the vision of judgment. In this view the first resurrection would be the awakening to the grace of Christ.

Justin Martyr wrote a treatise on the resurrection, fragments of which were preserved by John of Damascus. He was fighting against the Platonist view that it is only the soul which survives: 'If Christ came to teach us that, He was no better than Pythagoras or Plato.' The newly recovered *Epistle to Rheginos* (by a Gnostic) speaks of the spiritual resurrection as swallowing up both psychic and fleshly resurrection alike. Rheginos is offered the example of the transfiguration, when Moses and Elias were seen with Christ; this visible presence of Moses is taken to indicate what the 'spiritual resurrection' will be like. Athenagoras, a Christian convert from Platonism, wrote a treatise on the resurrection in which he countered the common objections to its possibility. He then presented three arguments for its likelihood, from the motive of creation, from the nature of man, and from the need for rewards and punishments. A popular parable illustrating this last argument circulated among Christians of the second century to this effect: A blind man and a lame man had been excluded from a banquet given by a king to his courtiers, and in revenge they raided the royal orchard while the banquet was in progress. They were caught and in their defence pleaded that they could not possibly have done the damage. The king caused the lame man to be mounted on the shoulders of the blind man and then had the pair whipped, for it was the sound executive legs of the blind man which had done the deed under the guidance of the eyes of the lame man.

The credal status given to the resurrection of the flesh can be established from the end of the second century. Tertullian had a version of the primitive creed which ended with the words: 'He will come again to judge the living and the dead even by the resurrection of the flesh.' Cyprian had as the third baptismal interrogation: 'Do you believe in remission of sins and eternal life through holy Church?', while the creed of Aquileia, as given by Rufinus, had the words: 'In the Holy Ghost the Church is holy, there is remission of sins and resurrection of the flesh.' Nicetas of Remesiana explained this attribution of the resurrection to the work of the Holy Spirit by saying: 'Just as the grain of wheat is made to come alive by the dew, so are the bodies of the dead by the dew of the Spirit, for Isaiah declared: "Thy dew is a dew of light, and on the land of the shades Thou wilt let it fall".'

At least from the middle of the fourth century the Church had substituted for the pagan feast of the dead (*cara cognatio*) on the twenty-second of February a feast of the Chair of St Peter. This was not a random choice; one of the prayers of the liturgy then used asked: 'Grant rest to the spirits of the faithful departed, that this commemoration of them which their dear ones observe may to them give comfort and to ourselves advancement in virtue.' Peter as the key-bearer was regarded as controlling admission through the gates of heaven. In the *Leonine Sacramentary* one of the prayers for the dead begins: 'God, to whom alone it belongs to afford relief to the soul after death'. Picking up a word (*indulgentia*) that was used by the Roman imperial administration for tax-relief, the Church formulated the concept of a pardon that might be won for the dead by the good works and penance of the living, on the condition that they had died contrite for their sins, even if the penance for them had not been terminated. Greek patristic thought after Origen was familiar with the idea that evil spirits, like so many excise-men, hung about on the confines of the world to search departing souls for what they might claim as belonging to them. Hence, to have an easy passage at the customs was much to be desired. A sermon of John of Jerusalem (from circa 392) depicted the circles of the heavens; first the circle of the seraphim, then the heavenly Jerusalem, then Paradise: 'here are Enoch and Elias, here the good thief, here the second Adam, recovered from the lance, here the second Eve, holy virgin Mary, who by the tree of life gained grace for the world, growing up as a shoot from the root, and upon her rested the Spirit of God.' For these, resurrection of the body was for various reasons held to have been achieved.

Manichaean Beliefs about the Dead

That Mani was a Christian heretic has recently been established beyond a doubt. A papyrus at Cologne gives a biography of him in which he is shown to have belonged to a Christian sect, the Elchasaites, and to have left them in 240, when he was 24 years old. Hence it is as a distortion of Christian belief about the dead that Manichaean ideas have to be considered. The Judgment was said by Mani to be reserved for Christ at His second coming. According to the Manichaean *Homilies* (recovered from the Coptic in 1934),

'those who stand by his right he will justify, and give them the victory, that is, the catechumens whom he has called to the kingdom of light; his just ones [the Elect] and his maidens that he has made into angels. And then the goats that stand on the left will see the hope that he has given to those on the right, and their hearts will rejoice for a moment when they think that the victory of the sheep is to be theirs also. Then will he say to them: "Depart from me . . ."'

In the same *Homilies* there is a prayer which starts with a curse upon the body: 'Thy desire is condemned in thee; the demons enter thee; thou hast caused me fear; thou hast brought me to tears; thou art accurst. Cursed be he who made thee. May I conquer all powers of the body. May I go forth from this world . . . May the Great Light [Jesus] come and illumine the path before me . . . May my way be in peace. May a door open before me at the pillars of majesty . . . May I cross over in the Lightship and come to rest.' The mythology of the Lightship was a central part of Manichaean belief. Souls were lightsome and after death migrated to the moon (which was the Lightship), thence to be transported to the sun after full moon (when the ship was thought to be fully loaded). This was an original feature of Mani's belief, which St Efrem received with the sarcasm that the turn-round of the Lightship was somewhat slow.

The idea found in Origen (see above) of the customs-house at the confines of the world was taken up by Mani. In his *Psalms of Thomas* (12) it is said that three ships voyage in the river of testing; one is laden, one half-freighted and one empty. 'Woe to the empty ship that comes empty to the place of the Customs. It shall be asked, having nothing to give . . . It shall be despoiled evilly as it deserves and sent back to the *metangismos*. It shall suffer what the corpses suffer, for they called unto His ear and He did not hear.' The *metangismos* was a transhipment from vessel to vessel. Mani had picked up the word from the Elchasaites, who used it to denote successive Incarnations of Christ (according to their belief). For Mani it meant the gradual ascent of the soul to the realm of Light. This process is described in a Bema-psalm (227): 'Receive the Holy Seal from the Mind of the Church and fulfil the commandments. The Judge himself that is in the air will give thee his three gifts: 1) the baptism of the gods thou shalt receive in the Perfect Man, 2) the Luminaries [moon and sun] will make thee perfect and take thee to thy kingdom; 3) thy Father, the First Man, will give thee thy life.' Baptism was anathema to Mani, who had rebelled against the Elchasaites' misuse of it. Hence he reserved it for the next life and banished it from this.

In Mani's dualism, the soul was the pearl, the body was the oyster. The Luminaries are the merchants who take the pearls aloft (*Kephalaia,*

83). His ascetic life was planned to release as many particles of light as possible from where they were imprisoned in matter. Thus wine from translucent grapes was forbidden his followers but cider from the opaque apple was allowed. One of the psalms (p. 152) tells of the fetters of the body:

'The care of my poor body has made me drunk in its drunkenness. Its demolitions and its buildings have taken my mind from me. Its plantings and its uprootings, they stir up trouble for me. Its fire, its lust, they trick me daily. Its begetting and its destroying bind to me a recompense. Many are the labours I suffered while I was in this dark house.'

The formula of an abjuration which a Manichee had to accept on becoming a Christian included the sentence: 'Anathema to those who say that human souls are consubstantial with God; that they were swallowed up by matter and that God now sits and draws them up through moon and sun, which they call ships' (PG 1:1465). The Manichee was told in his psalms (p. 193): 'A North wind is our Lord Mani blowing upon us, that we may put out with him and sail to the land of Light.'

Death and the Hereafter in ancient Egypt

Egypt differs from all the other lands which have left records of their civilization in that the Egyptians had a more elaborate ritual care for their dead, burying them in pyramids and painted tombs, and also in the fact that the climate of Egypt has preserved the great papyrus rolls of the *Book of the Dead*, along with the Pyramid Texts which were inscribed on the interior of the pyramids to help the kings buried therein to attain everlasting life. Owing to the abundance of Egyptian records, the chronology of the Egyptian dynasties is so much more exact than any available elsewhere, and developments can be studied, whereas the dumb archaeological remains in so many other lands defy attempts at coherent interpretation.

At the same time the basic philosophy of man among the Egyptians is hard to understand. Each man, besides his body or *khat*, was credited with a *ka* and a *ba*. The *ka* may be taken to be a 'double' of the man, his genius or subconscious self; some would call it his guardian angel. It was born with him and lived on in his tomb, but is sometimes said to be 'in heaven'. In the Pyramid Text from the tomb of Unas, a king of the Fifth Dynasty, one may read that: 'Unas is happy with his *ka*; Unas liveth with his *ka*', yet the underground chamber where the mummified body was preserved was known as the house of the *ka*. The *ba* can more easily be identified with the soul; it was the strength and power of life, and it is sometimes depicted as a bird with a tufted breast, and later as a man-headed hawk which can be seen hovering over the embalmed body. For King Unas, his Pyramid Text claims that he is endowed with a *ba* 'like unto a god'. This threefold division of human realities may not have been without its influence on Philo, the Jew of Alexandria, who postulated in his philosophy a heavenly man alongside the earthly man who consisted of body and soul.

Under the Eleventh and Twelfth Dynasties great wooden sarcophagi came into use instead of the pyramids and stone (or mud-brick) tombs of earlier times. On the inside of these sarcophagi were inscribed what are known as coffin-texts, with prayers of this kind: 'Grant unto Sepi that he may traverse the sky, the earth and the waters. May he meet his father, may he meet his mother, his grown sons and daughters; may he meet his brothers and sisters, his friends male and female; may he meet those who have been as parents to him or have worked for him upon the earth; may he meet the concubine whom he loved and knew.' This prayer does not mention the wife, but she is referred to later in the same text: 'The goddess Hathor surrounds Sepi with the power to protect his life, but it is Gebb [the earth-god] who equips him. The sister-wife of Sepi is the guardian of the wood of the Great Field, and she says to him: "Verily thou shalt come with rejoicing".' Hathor, the cow-goddess, was the helper of the dead; she was thought to have reserved for herself a portion of the underworld (the *Tuat*) as a paradise wherein she received the righteous dead. She was often identified as the wife of the sun-god, Ra. A ritual prayer for the embalmer to say when he was about to start the process of mummification was addressed to her. Herodotus, the inquisitive Greek (who travelled in Egypt circa 450 BC), has left an account of the process of embalming with its three grades of treatment, but he had little to say of its purpose. Somehow the Egyptian seems to have felt that the state of his body in the grave was of importance to his *ka*, though the relationship between the two is still mysterious.

The admonitions which King Khati (of the Ninth Dynasty) wrote for his son speak of a judgment:

'Let it be known to thee that there will be no compassion in them [the gods who judge] at the judgment of the evildoing man, at the hour when the ordinances are being carried into effect. It is an awful thing for the sinner to be made to recognize the sin which he has committed . . . Existence there is for ever. He who putteth from him the memory of this fact is a fool. If the man who attaineth to this hath committed no sins, his existence there is like that of *Neter* and he marcheth on like the Lords who are everlasting.'

The *Neter* who is introduced in this admonition is a name for a divine being of mysterious nature, perhaps a survival from very early times. The admonitions end with the old king assuring his son: 'Thou shalt reach me without having an accuser.' It was one thing for the Pharaohs to have their deeds and destiny blazoned on their tombs, but what did the common people think of it all? Herodotus (*Hist.* 2:78) has the tale that in the banquets of the rich, when they rise from the meal, one of the men carries round a carved image of a corpse in a coffin, showing it to each of the guests and saying: 'Look on this man; drink and rejoice, for when you die you will be like him.' The poor, who had to be content with what Herodotus described as third-class embalming, naturally did not leave extensive records of their beliefs. Amulets and scraps of magical papyri which belonged to them do not convey much clear information.

The concept of rectitude or *Maat* was originally that of the straight line, so that the word came to mean both truth and law, whether moral or physical. It was the very opposite of *Asfet*, which meant untruth, sin, or rebellion. A god named *Ater Asfet* ('destroyer of sin') is mentioned in the Pyramid Texts, though his function is uncertain. Later texts describe the annihilation of the wicked after death. Horus is depicted as commanding his serpent to destroy them: 'My serpent Kheti, thou mighty fire, open thy mouth, distend thy jaws, belch fire on the enemies of my father, Osiris; burn their bodies and consume their souls.' Total destruction of the wicked seems thus to have been envisaged. The advice of Ptahhotep to his son, preserved to us from the Fifth Dynasty, speaks of the high importance of *Maat*. '*Maat* is great, for its appropriateness is lasting; it has not been disturbed since the time of him who made it, while there is punishment for him who passes over its laws. It is the path before him who knows nothing. Wrongdoing has never brought its undertaking to port. It is fraud that gains riches, but the strength of justice is that it lasts . . .'

The cult of Ptah as a supreme deity had been upheld by the kings of Memphis, but with the downfall of the Old Kingdom at the end of the Sixth Dynasty, it gave way to the worship of Ra as practised by the priests of Heliopolis, while the cult of Osiris was gradually spreading southwards from the Delta. The Pyramid Texts make no mention of the judging of the king after death, but with the Theban papyri there appears the device of a pair of scales for the weighing of the heart in judgment. At first the judge appears to be the sun-god, Ra, but soon he is replaced by Osiris. In the papyri of the Book of the Dead the weighing of the heart in the presence of Osiris becomes very elaborate. This succession of deities in the act of judgment does not mean that the whole of Egypt changed its faith at a given time, but that there was never a strict credal uniformity in Egyptian religion and that there might be generally accepted ideas about judgment after death with different divine personnel involved for different believers.

Self-justification in view of a life to come can be found before the spread of the cult of Osiris. Thus a high official of the Sixth Dynasty, Pepi-Nekht, left in his inscription the claim: 'I speak what is good, repeating what is approved. I never uttered anything harmful to a man of power to make him attack any people in order that it might be to my advantage before the great god. I gave bread to the hungry man, and clothing to the naked man. I never decided a case between two brothers in such a way as to strip the son of his father's possessions . . .' When one comes to the weighing of the heart before Osiris this self-justification takes the form of a 'negative confession' in forty-two declarations, to the effect that the dead person has not committed this or that sin. In the Hall of Justice there were forty-two Assessors of the Dead. The scales were held by Anubis (as devil's advocate) and in one pan was placed the feather of *Maat* while the man's heart was placed in the other. The ibis-headed god Thoth sat by the scales with a tablet to record the result of the weighing, while a tripartite monster, Am-mit, waited to devour the heart of the one who was found wanting. In the papyri of the *Book of the Dead*, from the Eighteenth Dynasty onwards, there is some variety in the particulars listed in the declarations to the Assessors within a general pattern. Moral offences such as murder and sodomy are denied along with such matters as 'not extinguishing a fire that should be left to burn', or 'not fishing with bait made from the bodies of fish'. During the hearing Osiris was thought to be completely passive and there was no idea that he was in any sense a redeemer.

The lordship of the other world is ascribed to Osiris in many of the later documents; he is 'lord of the *Tuat*' (or Underworld) and also master of the Boat of the Sun which had formerly belonged to the sun-god, Ra. The papyrus of Ani depicts the justified Ani with his wife and with Thoth accompanying them, seated in a boat containing presents for the gods. He is shown later reaping corn in a paradise of sorts, while oxen tread out the grain. A later section of the papyrus shows a boat with serpent-heads at either end, tethered to a quay. In this Ani could set out for the Western region where Osiris dwelt. The papyrus which tells of the Contending of Horus with Set (Chester Beatty pap. 1) has a passage relevant here: 'When Ptah, the great one, south of his wall, made heaven, did he not say unto the stars which are therein: "Make ye your settings in the Western land every night in the place where Osiris is".'

The priests of Ra at Thebes during the Eighteenth Dynasty compiled a guide to the underworld called the Book *Ami Tuat*. In it they told of the voyage of Ra in his boat through all the realms of the dead. This boat was described as the same one in which he voyaged through the sky in day-time, but now its course was from south-west to north-east. Happiness was for the dead to be allowed to enter the boat and to be refreshed with the light of Ra. The first region traversed was full of the souls of the dead waiting for a chance to come on board. This region was not the equivalent of a purgatory, for no cleansing process was carried out there; simply acceptance into the boat or rejection takes place, and the boat passes on. The regions traversed are twelve, to correspond with the hours of the night. In the eleventh region are the fire-pits where the wicked are annihilated; how they get there is left to the imagination.

A second book was compiled about the same time, the *Book of the Gates*, which by contrast gives primacy to Osiris, who had been passed over in the former book. There are twelve regions of the *Tuat*, as before, but now the fifth region is the abode of the just, divided into four provinces; one is for Egyptians, another for the Syrians and peoples of the east, a third for black Sudanese and a fourth for Libyans. The unity of the human race does not seem to have been cherished as a concept here. In the sixth region is the Judgment Hall of Osiris with all its trappings. The land of the blessed who have come through the judgment is also here, and they are said to be reaping, or tending, a plant named *Maat*, on which they feed. Osiris says to them: 'You are *Maat* of *Maat*. Be at peace, you who have the forms of my followers and who dwell in the house of him whose souls are holy.' *Maat* is not their only food, since they are shown reaping corn which has been ripened by the light of Ra. This is an obvious syncretism of two cults, whereby the old religion of Ra is made to make room for the newer Osiris-cult with its magical plant that somehow imparts to the just the power of Osiris. His body, according to the myth, had been dismembered by enemies and was put together again by Isis and Nephthys, his two 'widows'. The manner of this reconstitution of Osiris was kept secret, being the subject of a Mystery-drama.

The Mysteries of Osiris were performed in the temple-precincts at

Denderah, Edfu and Philae by the priests for the benefit of the initiates. Scenes from the drama were sculptured on the walls and inscriptions have preserved most of the speeches. The whole drama lasted twenty-four hours and was supposed to re-enact the restoration of Osiris. The parts of the body, reassembled, are washed and anointed with long prayers and invocations; various deities are said to visit him; the eye of Horus is brought to him; incense is burnt; various incubations take place. A Lament of Isis (Brit. Mus. papyrus 10188) tells how: 'Thy mother *Nut* cometh to thee with holy offerings. She buildeth thee up with the life of her body. Thou art endowed with soul ...' On the other hand a hymn to Osiris (Brit. Mus. papyrus 9901) says: 'Thoth hath brought unto thee sweet air for thy nose, and life and strength for thy beautiful face, and the north wind for thy nostrils ...' In all this there seems to be no trace of a plant of immortality such as is fed to the blessed. Attempts to reduce these Mysteries to a consistent theology are not likely to succeed. The wise summing-up of Sir E. Wallis Budge may be cited: 'Osiris was raised from the dead, and his mortal body reconstituted and revivified by magic, and those who wished to live with him in felicity ... could attain their wish by employing the means which had been used on his behalf by the gods. Myriads of Egyptians died believing in Osirian magic, but there is no evidence that they regarded Osiris as a saviour ...' Herodotus knew more than he chronicled about the Mysteries (*Hist.* 2:170); he equated Isis with Demeter, and claimed that the Greeks had learnt her Mysteries from the daughters of Danaos. It cannot be said that there is much evidence for a direct passage of the Mysteries from Egypt to Eleusis, but some influence via Minoan Crete is possible; it was claimed (by Diodorus Siculus) that the labyrinth of Crete was made on an Egyptian model.

When Egypt became Hellenized after the time of Alexander the Great, Egyptian beliefs about the dead became articles for export. Isis quite eclipsed Osiris as the giver of immortality. In the famous Invocation of Isis (Oxyrhynchus papyri, 1380), composed in the first century AD, she is said to have conferred immortality on Osiris and Horus, thus supporting the claim of Diodorus Siculus (1:25) that she had discovered the drug of immortality. The Invocation identifies Isis with other goddesses; at Sidon, Astarte; in the Cyclades, Artemis, and so on. To the Christian Hippolytus she was the great sorceress with magical remedies, and it was in that capacity that she was known by so many Greeks and Romans. What impressed the Hellenic visitor to Egypt, however, was the contrast between the houses of the living and the tombs of the dead. 'They call the dwellings of the living "staging-posts",' wrote Diodorus

(1:51): 'for we are to dwell but little time in them, while the tombs of the dead they call everlasting houses, as they are to dwell in Hades an endless age.' This language might seem to be Christian, but one should not fall into the trap set by the clumsy forger of a letter supposed to have been sent by the emperor Hadrian to the consul Servianus, where it is said that in Egypt the worshippers of Sarapis are Christian and that those who call themselves Christian bishops are devotees of Sarapis. The language was approximate, but the realities stayed far apart.

7

Islamic Society

M. S. Seale

●

Arab concern with the after-life has passed through three well-defined stages. In the earliest, or the pre-Islamic pagan period, Arabs grieved at the loss of blood relations and friends and sought comfort in the thought that the deceased were not really far away. They believed that the departed lived a life of their own and enjoyed a conscious existence in the grave. A similar belief was nurtured by the ancient Hebrews, who knew the abode of the dead as Sheol, or Hades. Job says:

'If only thou wouldst hide me in Sheol
and conceal me till thy anger turns aside,
if thou wouldst fix a limit for my time there, and then remember me!
Then I would not lose hope, however long my service,
waiting for my relief to come.
Thou wouldst summon me, and I would answer thee;
thou wouldst long to see the creature thou hast made.' (*Job* 14:13-15)

Pagan Arabs cared for their dead and supplied them with food and drink, which was also the practice of the ancient Hebrews until it was banned by the Mosaic law (*Deuteronomy* 26:14). In Arab society, friends and relatives kept in touch with the deceased, lingered at the burial place, and even pitched a tent at the graveside; they could not tear themselves away. Coming upon the grave of an acquaintance, they would call his name and greet him: the deceased was believed to return the greeting. Owls fluttering around were thought to be the spirits of the departed, and their screeching was taken to be the moaning of the dead. The spirit was also referred to as 'echo', 'skull', or 'soul'.

Layla al-Ahyaliya, the poetess, on a visit to the graveside of her poet-lover, dared question the belief that the deceased returned one's salutation, despite the fact that her lover had himself said so in one of his poems. At this bold denial, an owl appeared and flew straight into her face. Layla dropped dead (Al-Aghani, x, 82; Hamasa 576).

The pagan Arab refused to allow death to sever the ties of blood or friendship: following the bier, he would cry: 'Do not be far away!' Besides food, he would also provide the deceased with a riding camel which was tethered at the graveside and left there to die without food or water. In later Islamic times, after this practice was officially banned, its occasional continued observance was justified by the need to provide the deceased with a riding camel at the Resurrection. However, while the pagan pre-Islamic Arabs believed in survival, they knew nothing of the resurrection of the body.

In the second stage, that is to say after the emergence of Islam, Arabs continued to believe that the departed lived their own life in the tomb, but interest now centred on man's destiny and ultimate condition. The two articles of faith that the prophet Muhammad tried to convince his fellow Arabs of were, first, that there was going to be a Day of Resurrection; the pagan Arab found it difficult to believe that God would 'gather his bones', and 'shape again his fingers' (Qur'an 75:4); 'They shall say, "What, are we being restored as we were before? What, when we are bones old and decayed?"' (79:10). Muhammad's second article was that there was going to be a Day of Judgment; that man was accountable to a sovereign creator who had 'not created the heavens and the earth and whatever is between them in sport . . . but for a serious end' (Qur'an 44:38). The free-living Arab, be he nomad or sedentary, boggled at the thought of being called upon to give an account of his faith and deeds.

The pagan Arab spoke unashamedly of the things that for him made life worth living: to spring upon his favourite mare on an early morning raid; to outmanoeuvre his complaining women folk and quaff sparkling red wine with boon companions; to bet in a game of chance; and to be closeted with a girl on a rainy day (see Tarafa's *Golden Ode* for three out of the four just mentioned). This accountability must have been as unpalatable as was the alms tax, prescribed in the Qur'an, which had to be reimposed on the Arabs by force of arms after the prophet's death.

The underworld, as revealed by Muhammad in the Qur'an, was no longer the habitat of beings who were mere shadows of their former selves; it was now full of life and movement: a sad place for some, a happy one for others, depending on the life they had lived above, and the God they had believed in or denied. However, Muhammad's moral tone was not lost on the Arabs. The Qur'an speaks of the great divide between the 'people of the right hand' and the 'people of the left':

'What! have we not made him eyes,
and tongue and lips,
and guided him to the two highways?
Yet he attempted not the steep.
And who shall teach thee what the steep is?
It is to ransom the captive,
or to feed in the day of famine
the orphan who is near of kin, or the poor that lieth in the dust,
Beside this, to be of those who believe, and enjoin steadfastness on
    each other, and enjoin compassion on each other.
These shall be the people of the right hand:
while they who disbelieve our signs,
shall be the people of the left.
Around them the fire shall close.' (90:10–20)[1]

The Qur'an is the best source for the second stage of the Arab's concern with life after death. Dalton Galloway ('The Resurrection and Judgment in the Qur'an')[2] affirms that the last day, or the day of resurrection and judgment, was always in Muhammad's mind and on his tongue, so much so that he coupled the belief in the last day with the belief in Allah, and it was this 'obsession' which he communicated to his followers and companions. The term al-'akhira, the 'hereafter' occurs one hundred and thirteen times in the Qur'an. The great day is called by many names and locations including 'the day when the leg shall be bared', implying that on that day people will cast dignity to the winds and tuck up their ample outer garment to run faster. The happenings of the great and terrible day will begin with a shout and a blast of the trumpet. This summons to judgment will bring together not only all humans but also the jinn and the animal creation. Every creature's work will then be placed on the scales to be weighed. He whose balance is heaped up with good works will be admitted to the Garden, but he who shows a light balance and few merits will be sent down to the Pit. Hell will be full to overflowing as more and more people are thrust into it, and no pleading will be permitted.

'No! I swear by the Day of Resurrection . . .
What, does man reckon We shall not gather his bones?
Yes indeed: We are able to shape again his fingers,
Nay, but man desires to continue on as a libertine,
asking, "When shall be the Day of Resurrection?"' (Qur'an, 75)

'The Blow! What is the Blow?
The day that men shall be like scattered moths,
and the mountains shall be like plucked wool-tufts.
Then he whose deeds weigh heavy in the Balance
    shall inherit a pleasing life;
but he whose deeds weigh light in the Balance
    shall plunge in the womb of the Pit.
And what shall teach thee what is the Pit?
A blazing Fire!' (Qur'an 90:10–20)

Galloway rightly says that 'no revivalist preacher has excelled the Prophet in dangling an audience over the terrors of the future torments.' It appears, however, that as Islamic *sunna* ('tradition') grew and expanded in the centuries that followed Muhammad's death, new horrors were added which the Prophet never conceived. I am referring to the interrogation in the grave and the torments that follow. There were now to be two trials: one in the grave when a person died, the other at the end of the world. The underworld was peopled with angels and demons of various kinds. The angel of death, whose work it was to extract the soul from the dead body, had two eyes, one in his face, the other in the nape of the neck. He showed himself to the dying, seized their soul without a moment's respite and left the house amidst the piteous cries of the family. Islamic tradition has a good deal to say about the interrogation in the tomb and the resulting treatment meted out to believers, and infidels. The virtuous man is welcomed by angels 'with faces like the sun', the unbeliever is received by angels that are ugly and revolting. There is silk and musk for the believer, sackcloth and live coals for the infidel. The believer's tomb automatically turns into a verdant garden, the infidel's tomb is full of seven-headed snakes.

Al-Ghazali faced critics who questioned the existence of such snakes in the tomb. It was plain, they said, from an examination of an infidel's tomb that there were no snakes there, much less the seven-headed variety. 'We are dealing,' retorted al-Ghazali,

'with the unseen, divine world. The snakes and scorpions of the tomb are not of the same species as the snakes and scorpions of our lower world; they belong to a different species and are perceived by a different sense and not by our sense of sight. Muhammad's companions failed to see the angel of revelation who came to him, yet they believed the truth of the revelation. We also know that suffering may be of the mind, as is the case when one dreams that he has been stung and cries out in his sleep. Then again, a man may be tormented by the loss of his worldly goods to which he is much attached. These forms of torment are possible and real. The mind, unlike the body, suffers no change at death and the deceased retains consciousness; he may therefore suffer pain or enjoy felicity, as the case may be.'³

The Two Examining Angels

Tradition has much to say about Munkar and Nakir, the two black angels who interrogate the dead regarding their faith and works. The believer's answer works miracles, causing his dark and narrow tomb to become spacious and full of light. The infidel's answer has the reverse effect: the tomb closes in on him so as to bruise his ribs. He is put in the charge of a brute that can neither see, hear nor speak; it wields its iron whip and never pities its victim.

A tradition which goes back to the Prophet's favourite wife, A'ishah, says that the tombs of Zaynab, the Prophet's daughter, and that of Sa'd b. Mu'adh, a prominent companion, were miraculously widened and made comfortable. This gratified the Prophet and lit up his face.

The Great Day of Judgment

At the blast of the trumpet, the graves will open and the dead will rise. They will be led naked to the great meeting-place – a vast plateau in a depressed desert plain, unlike any place on earth because the earth itself will have been changed beyond recognition. The crowded mass of creatures, gathered from the seven heavens and the seven earths, together with angels, jinn and devils, will stand in the blazing sun, finding no shade anywhere. Sweat pouring out of them will flow like so much water reaching up to the knee, the hip, and even higher. There they will stand for God knows how long.

The Portents

On that day, Tradition relates, the heavens will be rent, the stars scattered, the twinkling luminaries murky, the sun veiled, the mountains levelled. Camels, ten months gone with young, will remain unattended, while the seas boil and Hell stokes its fires. On that day each soul will see what it sent forward and what it kept back. Balances will be set up, books opened and Hell brought near. The fire will crackle and the infidels will despair. At the interrogation, people will be questioned about both great and trivial things. Prophets and apostles will be asked if they delivered the message. Hell will boil and seethe finally to engulf those who dared disobey the Most High.

The Bridge (Qur'an 37:23)

The bridge that stretches across the fiery Pit is sharper than a sword's edge and finer than a hair. The upright will run across in safety. Some will walk across, others will just manage to crawl across, still others, labouring under a load of guilt, will slip and fall into the Pit. The Prophet will be the first to reach the other side. His prayer will be: 'Preserve us, Oh Lord!' Angels will rescue believers who are too frightened to step onto the bridge, and will help them make their way across through the leaping flames.

The Intercession (Qur'an 93:5b)

In one Tradition, the Prophet is reported to have said: 'Five things were given to me alone out of all God's prophets: I was feared by people who lived as far as a month's journey from where I was. I was allowed to keep the spoils when others were not. My people were allowed to worship anywhere and everywhere. I was sent not to one people but all peoples. I was given the prerogative of interceding for others.' When all intercessors fail them, they will come to Muhammad and ask him to intercede for them in their plight. The Prophet will approach the throne and bow down before the Most High. God will then say what he has not said to anyone before. 'Rise, Oh Muhammad, ask and you will receive, plead and your pleading will be accepted.' The Prophet will say: 'My people, I pray for them.' The best of them will then enter a door on the right, while others will enter by a common door. The good folk and the learned will be allowed to intercede for their own tribe and their household. If one of God's people was in life given a cup of cold water, he will be allowed to plead for his benefactor, rescuing him from Hell. Another Tradition runs: some of the Prophet's companions spoke with admiration of Abraham, the friend of God, of Moses, who conversed with God, of Jesus, God's Word and spirit. Muhammad said: 'All you say is true, and I, without boasting, am the beloved of God whose intercession will be accepted on the Day of Judgment.'

The Pool (Qur'an 108)

Kawthar is a river of Paradise, its water is whiter than milk, sweeter than honey and more fragrant than musk. Its banks are of gold, the river bed is of pearls and coral. One tradition says that the domes on each side of the river are of hollow pearls. The Prophet's pool, which is a part of the river, is supplied with water from Paradise. To drink of this water is never to thirst again.

Hell

The Qur'an and the Traditions refer repeatedly to the Pit. The Qur'an says:

> 'Not one of you there is, but he
> shall go down to it; that for the Lord
> is a thing decreed, determined.
> Then we shall deliver those that were
> Godfearing; and the evil-doers We shall
> leave there, hobbling on their knees.' (19:73, 74)

The condemned will cry out to Malik, their keeper, but in vain. There they will lie, manacled, with fire above them and fire below them, fire on their right and fire on their left; their clothing is fire and so is their bedding. Pierced by many sword thrusts, their foreheads broken, their livers ruined, their flesh, skin and hair gone, they will be given new skins periodically for their torments to begin all over again.

> 'Surely those that disbelieve in our signs –
> We shall certainly roast them at a fire; as often
> as their skins are wholly burned, We shall
> give them in exchange other skins, that they
> may taste the chastisement. '(Qur'an 4:56)

Gehenna is the highest of Hell's several compartments; the others follow in descending order: Hell-Fire, the Flame, the Scorcher, the Blazes, the Inferno and the Abyss, which is bottomless. Muhammad's companions, startled on one occasion by a terrific crash, were told that it was the sound of a falling rock which had been let down into the Pit seventy years earlier and had only then touched bottom.

The vehemence of the fire is described in these words: God, the Most High, ordered the fire to burn for a thousand years till it turned red, then another thousand till it turned white, and yet another thousand till it turned black, its present colour. When the fire complained that it was being consumed, the Lord gave it two natures: in the summer it is boiling hot, in the winter it is freezing cold The Qur'an speaks of the drink offered to the wicked:

> . . . then was disappointed
> every forward tyrant – beyond him Gehenna,
> and he is given to drink of oozing pus,
> the which he gulps, and scarcely swallows,
> and death comes upon him from every side:
> and still beyond him is a harsh chastisement. (14:19, 20)

Punishment, however, will be in proportion to a person's wrong-doing: 'God shall not wrong so much as the weight of an ant.' (Qur'an 4:44a)

Heaven

Al-Ghazali exhorts believers to meditate in fear on the terrors of Hell, and likewise recollect and look forward to the promised blessedness of Heaven. The radiant citizens of Heaven sit on thrones beside rivers flowing with wine and honey, and are refreshed with perfumed wine. They have for companions youths and wide-eyed houris untouched by men or *jinn*. Here the citizens are kings, denied no pleasure. At the daily audience round the throne, the inmates will be rapturous over the beatific vision.

Al-Ghazali says: 'If Heaven were nothing more than a life without accidents and privations, without sickness or death, that would be reason enough for giving up this world for the sake of the next.'[4]

A Tradition traced back to the Prophet says: 'If you want to enjoy wine in the hereafter, abstain here and now. This applies equally to gold and silver ornaments and silk garments: shun them in this life and you will have them in abundance in your eternal home. The clothes of the citizens of Heaven never wear out and the person himself never grows old. We shall experience what eye has not seen, what ear has not heard and what has not entered the mind of man.'

When the Prophet was asked if the clothes above were hand-woven or created, he replied that they grew on trees. The food of Heaven is manna, fattened birds, quails, milk, and honey. One will only have to look at a bird in the sky and desire it, for it to drop at one's feet, roasted and ready for the table. The main dish will be the flesh of the bull that has been grazing in the Gardens of Eden. The organism will dispose of body wastes by means of perspiration exhaled like musk.

The Traditions explain Quranic verses relating to life in Heaven: for example, the meaning of 'wide-eyed houris, restrained in tents' (55:72) is that these females are never angry and never go away. They are spoken of as 'pure spouses' (Qur'an 3:13), because they are free from excretions of any kind. The expression 'occupied rejoycing' (36:5b) means that men above will be occupied deflowering virgins (*Ihya'*, vol. iv, p. 508). We learn that the inhabitants of the Garden will be fair, beardless, curly-headed, eye-lids darkened with antimony, thirty-three years of age and ninety feet tall.

A Tradition found in both Al-Bukhari and Muslim declares that the greatest delight awaiting the citizens of Heaven will be to look on the face of God. This is named the 'surplus' (Qur'an 10:27), as it will be granted the virtuous over and above their reward. Jarir b. Abdallah said: 'We were sitting with God's Messenger (May the blessing and peace of God rest upon him) when he saw the full moon. He said: 'You will see your Lord as you see this moon and will come to no harm. This beatific vision is dearer than all else.''

Statistics

The Qur'an refers to 'charming abodes in the Gardens of Eden' (61:12). These abodes, Tradition affirms, are pearly palaces: each palace contains seventy courts, each court seventy houses, and each house seventy couches, with a houri on each couch. There is a tree in the Garden through whose shade one may ride for a hundred years without crossing it. The smallest house in the Garden has a thousand servants, each going about his appointed task. Finally, everyone in the Garden will marry five hundred houris, four thousand virgins and eight thousand non-virgins.

Notes

(1) *The Koran*, trans. J. M. Rodwell (1909).

(2) Dalton Galloway, 'The Resurrection and Judgment in the Qur'an', in *Moslem World*, vol. 17 (1922), 348.

(3) Virginia Cobb's trans. Al-Ghazali, *Dhikr Al-Mawt Wa-Ma Ba'duh Kitab Al-Aghani*.

(4) Al-Ghazali, *Ihya, Ulum al-Din*, Cairo ed., vol. iv.

8

Some Christian Imagery
Renée Haynes

•

The Christian's concern with survival is rooted in his concern with God, whose Being illuminates 'the communion of saints and the life everlasting'. To reiterate in another sphere or in a thousand reincarnations the pattern of daily existence is not his aim. It is a pattern of intense significance while it is being lived, yielding matter for choice and decision now, and imagery for always; but it is neither for endless repetition nor for final repudiation. He is not preoccupied either with the theme of the Buddhist wheel of things whose successive revolutions must be endured until the last remnants of love, free will and identity have been scoured away from the impassive soul, or with the belief that all material things – lions and breaking waves, stars and fruit and dragonflies – are *maya*, illusion, at best irrelevant to the life of the spirit, at worst its contradiction. For him the self, loving and aware, is real, and created things are real, and both can glow with God.

This is true in two contexts, that of creed and that of living imagination. The first states for the Christian that the Divinity made with joy everything that is, from the interrelated universes to the minute jewelled lights of tropical fish, and gradually brought into being entities with ever-increasing potentialities of consciousness, initiative and choice; blue tits learning to remove the tops of milk bottles, dogs that can be taught to herd sheep, intelligent elephants, humans themselves. It states too that when these potentialities had been wrongly used and the whole network of being quivered with pain, God entered creation from within. To quote Geoffrey Riddehough's remarkable translation of a twelfth-century poem by Adam of St Victor:

'Measureless and infinite
Whom no scope of human wit
Nor the bounds of space contain,
Measureless and timeless, He
Now in space and time shall be
Making all things new again.'

His developing unborn body recapitulated, as all human foetuses do, early stages in the lives of animals in the particular evolutionary stem that led to man. It must have retained, as all human bodies do, such vestigial evolutionary remains as for instance the vermiform appendix. He suffered the full consequences of the wrong use of consciousness, initiative, and choice, in all their repercussions, and set humans free once more from the long monotony of evil into which they had been conditioned; and more than free, renewed. He left them the vision of death as the means to life; not only bodily death, though that too, and always at the last, but death to old habits, old reflexes, old sins, death to the clutching part of the self, the self that was to be renewed, reborn, transformed.

He left them too, as well as prayer and meditation and right action, a means of communication with Him based on the most commonplace material things; water, oil, bread and wine, 'fruit of the vine, that God has given and human hands have made', objective and significant.

In the context of the living imagination we are touched by the implicit statements made by created things in being themselves; the skein of geese flying southwards through the autumn afternoon, the moon beyond black branches, the sun descending into endless waves. All these exist – however transiently – whether we see them or not; yet when we do see them they transmit a sense of hidden but intense meaning. This sense is sometimes stronger still when in a person, a glance, a smile, a gesture suddenly seems to express the invisible self within.

The invisible self is real and the body through which we always recognize it and sometimes become intensely aware of it is real; what happens when the self no longer informs the body, and the body is resolved into its physical components?

We cannot know in detail while we are alive; but the Christian grasps at the fact that his dead live, as he does, in relationship to God. However much their death may tear him apart – as it does us all – he cannot immerse himself in attempts to recall them, to switch on as it were a shadowy film in whose production remembrance and telepathy must play an incalculably powerful role; as must the personality, vocabulary and associations of the medium. He can – he must – pray for them as he prays for himself; but not that the past should return and that everything should be as before, the call at the gate, the feet on the steps, the evening peace by the fire. They are gone on to something unimaginably new, and though sometimes he may be comforted by a totally unexpected 'sense of presence', or a few inaudible words out of nowhere, he cannot cling to them. Here as in so many other situations

'He who clutches at a joy
Doth the wingéd life destroy
He who kisses the joy as it flies
Lives in eternity's sunrise.'

For his dead then, as for himself, he must pray knowing that they are alive, that their lives, like his own, only have final meaning in so far as they are orientated to God; and that they are praying for him too. This sounds cold comfort – and it often feels so – but to realize it can carry something of the sense of unity that glows in a crowd of people singing, a crowd so large that its members cannot all see one another, though they know they are together in the song.

Those brought up in the oldest traditional form of Christianity will have learned young to consider two things from which many of their contemporaries have been conditioned to turn away: the fact of mystery and the fact of death. The whole basis of scientific thought over the last century or so has been the assumption that one day human beings will know in precise detail how everything works, and that from this knowledge will flow a complete explanation of our coming as conscious selves . . .

'into this Universe, and why not knowing
Nor whence, like water willy nilly flowing
And out of it, like wind along the waste
We know not whither, willy nilly blowing.'

Until scientific understanding has reached perfection, then, it is usually thought to be time-wasting, as well as uncomfortable, to brood over the ultimate mystery, *Mysterium tremendum et fascinans* though it may be; and it is almost always considered morbid to envisage death.

Meditation on the Four Last Things – Death, the Judgment, Hell and Heaven – has on the contrary been recommended to the Christian, who is to look steadily at the fact that he must one day die, however far or near that death may be, slow in a geriatric ward or sudden in a car crash; that at death the kind of being he has become will be crystallized, will determine absolutely the way in which he perceives, and feels, and reacts – as it does relatively here and now; that he may render himself incapable of eternal happiness, the Beatific Vision (unless some blessed last-minute lightning should destroy his defences) by withdrawing, proud, avaricious, self-centred, from God and man into a cell whose mirroring walls reflect the owner's face alone: or that he may yield to the forces of growth and transformation and grace and be enabled to 'love and serve God and to enjoy Him for ever', perhaps not immediately but after a period of seeing the consequences of his actions and enduring some process in which as it were conditioned reflexes are broken down, stiff muscles are re-educated and full perception returns in wonder.

In this connection St Catherine of Genoa remarked that the love of God, which renews in joy the gentle, the humble and the loving may be intolerable to egotists. What is springtime light to those grown fit to know it, is fire, intolerable intrusive heat to those interested only in their sole selves.

These are all images – the cell the light, the fire – and the use of images, even the most general, is as dangerous as it is inevitable, since images convey different impressions to different people. Images can moreover mean different things to the same people at different times. At its most potent an image is no more than a means of communicating something indescribable but *there*. It is at best like a window 'whereon', as the seventeenth-century poet wrote, 'a man may stay his eye/Or look right through,' seeing his own reflection, or a stained glass picture, or the light beyond. A great deal of misunderstanding has been – and still is – caused by concentrating on the reflection, and even more by taking the image to be the thing in itself, the picture to be what it is meant to convey.

This holds good of ideas of the life to come, as of everything else. How many nineteenth-century children were filled with the dread of eternal boredom rather than with any longing for heaven by the vision of vast crowds of people in white nightgowns endlessly playing harps when they were not 'casting down their golden crowns upon the crystal sea'? Did they bounce back or roll away and have to be picked up? Was the sea frozen perhaps? And why did the Bible say elsewhere the sad words that 'there shall be no more sea'?

What is more, however good an image may be in some contexts, it will be useless and even repellent in others. Thus, the vivid, alien, terrible pictures of Revelation were lit up for the first, the Jewish, Christians by the fact that they were based on familiar Old Testament modes of writing. But the celestial horsemen, the child-devouring dragon, even the jewelled city are very far remote from Western peoples living in industrial civilization today.

For our time the imagery is different. If we look to the end of the world it is in the intolerable white explosions of nuclear war; if to the end of our own lives here it is perhaps to blackness, perhaps to clarity, always to the unknown; if to the end of other lives, it is at best in terms of an aeroplane flying farther and farther away diminishing into the sunset, at worst as the piece of paper blowing down the dusty stairs outside the Bureau of Missing Persons where Black Orpheus has gone in vain to find his lost Eurydice.

I do not say that these images are useful or adequate or true; only that they come naturally to us in our time and place and surroundings.

It would be safest to rest in the evocative familiar words, 'Eye hath not seen, ear hath not heard, nor has it entered into the heart of man to conceive what God has laid up for those who love Him'. But imagine most of us must, unless we belong to the small group of people whose intuitions are formless, and almost incommunicable except in a sense of awe and numinous peace.

The more detailed pictures of life after death are, the less acceptable they seem to be as such (though they may make noble poetry on another level). Dante's explorations of Hell and Purgatory and Heaven are full of beautiful echoing sounds, clear pictures, piercing phrases, but they do not often carry any kind of living, immediate conviction, except as works of art. Where he rings true is when he writes contemplatively. The rest is too temporal, too dated, too solid; though not so solid, so heavy, so marmoreal as Milton peopling both Paradise Lost and Paradise Regained with enormous mobile baroque statues seen against a background of classical landscape. Perhaps the fact is that epic poetry cannot sustain an impetus not of this world. Only a lyric, or a flash of prose can enable the reader to 'trace within this earthly dresse/Bright *shootes* of everlastingnesse'.

The sight of Augustine and Monica, standing together by the window and drawn from considering the works of God to contemplate God Himself, is perhaps the most telling example of what survival must ultimately imply; real selves, in one another's loved and loving company, absorbed in wonder and adoration. With them stand Thomas Aquinas, rejoicing in the divine 'Torrent of Being' and Francis de Sales reflecting on the Source of Joy.

Some have longed for death, so that they might see God the sooner, crying out with St Teresa of Avila and St John of the Cross, 'I die because I cannot die'; but have later been content to live dedicated to His will and to serving His creatures in this world as long as might be required of them.

There have been those who carefully worked out, on intellectual grounds, what they thought to be useful concepts of the after-life. There was, for instance, a mathematician among the early Fathers who argued that as the sphere is the perfect mathematical form, men would arise at the last day as spheres; Thomas Aquinas, who tended towards the spherical in this life – they had to cut out a place at the community table to accommodate his round belly – thought it probable that, at whatever age people died, each would be about thirty years old, the peak of physical perfection, in the life to come.

The Christian emphasis on death has of course changed from epoch to epoch. In the Dark Ages, after the order of the Roman Empire had been broken down by its own heavy, over-centralized complexity, by endemic malaria and by barbarian invasions, it was almost a temptation to bypass living and concentrate on dying, forgetting Christ's promise that He had come that His followers should have life, and have it more abundantly. Though the image of the City of God coming down from heaven like a bride adorned for her husband in itself gave glory both to the idea of a city where men co-operated with one another and to the sacrament of marriage, the instinctive reaction to the chaos and misery and unpredictability of the times was to devalue these things. They began to glow again with meaning when the medievals dedicated different kinds of work to God and man, and saw the King, the embodiment of order, ruling all, the ploughman feeding all, the soldier defending all, the monk praying for all, living and dead.

The contemplative, who had retreated, like the Desert Fathers and the early English hermits from the distracting dangerous world to pray alone or in some small dedicated group, found himself pulled eventually into that world again, interceding for innumerable people, transmitting an awareness of God to them by his very presence. The French St Hugh of Lincoln was drawn from silent adoration in the Grande Chartreuse remote in the mountains successfully to re-establish a community in the Somerset marshes; to serve, with notable efficiency, an enormous diocese; to begin rebuilding a cathedral with his own hands among the other workmen; and to tackle about the cruel forest laws a King who had already inspired the murder of an archbishop and was subject to terrifying fits of fury. The Spanish St Teresa was taken from ecstatic prayer to interminable travels in intense heat, intense cold, jolting carts and complete uncertainty to set up new Carmels. Edith Stein, the distinguished German philosopher who became one of her nuns in our own century, was swept from her convent into a Nazi concentration camp for Jews for whom and with whom she died in a gas chamber, very calm, full of peace and strength for them as well as in herself.

The contemplative, then, might first seek for 'mortification' (the means of death not only to actual sin, the desire to be independent of God, but also to preoccupation with the wants and worries and distractions of every day) and later even long for physical death, as the way to the vision of God. He might be granted 'mystical' death to his own egotism. But whatever its joy, he would not in this life be withdrawn into a lasting Nirvana, or into a continuing state of what the medievals called 'spiritual drunkenness', sought for its own sake. He would be used in prayer or work or both for the living and the dead.

Mors janua vitae, the ancient maxim that death is the gate of life, carries more than one implication. *Mors* means not only the death of the body, but the repeated death and rebirth of the self renewed, the same identity transformed. In our own century C. J. Jung has shown this archetypal pattern shining through innumerable human situations and mythologies. It appears clearly enough, moreover, in every life, as a person grows from one stage of development to another. The egg on the leaf must hatch into a caterpillar, the caterpillar must repeatedly shed its constricting protective skin, and at the last weave its own shroud and submit to passive transmutation in the chrysalis before the newly formed butterfly breaks out to all appearance totally different, and yet continuous with its earlier being. In many societies the transitions are recognized and celebrated by *rites de passage*. These have been given a new dimension among Christians by the sacraments of Confirmation, Marriage, Holy Orders and Extreme Unction. But for much of Western civilization they survive only in such diminished forms as wedding receptions and rationalist wakes with sherry and a spate of speeches.

All the same these lesser deaths and rebirths recur in all ordinary individual lives; and it was to ordinary individual lives that attention swung as feudalism and functionalism declined. Every man began again to become more than a second-class citizen of Christendom content simply to be and to do what he was told by his masters temporal and spiritual who respectively ruled all and prayed for all. He took on responsibility, he prayed without retiring from the world. His life and the way in which he lived it continually made him fitter or less fit for the Kingdom of Heaven, whose beginnings are here and now, as Piers Plowman urged so passionately. Pictures of life after death were drawn to his way of seeing; the pop art of the mystery play, the great Doom and the carved misericord began.

One set of images was shadowed, others were illuminated piecemeal in different parts of Europe. St Thomas More, drawn young to the austere contemplative life of the Charterhouse, the *via negativa*, emerged as the most brilliant layman of his time, who considered life in this world so important that he worked out in his *Utopia* plans for a perfect society. In all the complications of responsible power he dedicated to God his life, public and private, and in the end his death, trusting that he and his family and his executioners might all 'merrily meet in heaven'; which sounds like a party, a simile whose various forms ('the shout of them that triumph/The song of them that feast') have sometimes shocked introverts as much as 'Neti, Neti – not this, not this' has shocked other temperaments.

Thomas More however, like John Bunyan later, wrote more about how to get to Heaven (whither he warned 'we must not look to go . . . on feather beds') than about Heaven itself.

Pictures of it quiver, though, in songs and hymns and poems, like sunrise reflected in rippling water. Thus:

'O Jesus Lord, my heal and weal, my bliss complete
Make thou my heart thy garden plot, true, fair and neat
That I may hear
The music clear
Harp, dulcimer and lute
With cymbal
And timbrel
And the gentle sounding flute'

and again

'Jerusalem, my happy home
When shall I come to thee . . .
Thy gardens and thy gallant walks
Continually are green
There grow such sweet and pleasant flowers
As nowhere else are seen
All through the streets, with silver sound
The flood of life doth flow
Upon whose banks on every side
The wood of life doth grow . . .
And there they live in such delight

> Such pleasure and such play
> A thousand years, it seems to them
> Are but as yesterday . . .'

But first came the journey of the Lyke Wake dirge, with its frightening refrain:

> 'This ae night, this ae night
> Every night and all
> Fire and sleet and candlelight
> And Christ receive thy saule.'

From the glimmering room the dead pass through the dark to Whinnymuir (where the gorse pricks 'to the bare bane' those who have never given away 'hosen and shoon') and inexorably onward to cross the Brig o' Dread, and thence to Purgatory where

> 'If ever thou gavest meat and drink
> Every night and all
> The fire shall never make thee shrink
> And Christ receive thy saule.'

The three chief ways of looking at what lies beyond death are the general: that known to the bereaved: and that in which every man awaits his own experience. Though they are interdependent they can be as different as a map, a wound, and a still sense of awe. Here for instance is the poet mourning:

> 'They are all gone into a world of light
> And I alone sit lingering here . . .
> . . . I see them walking in an Air of glory . . .
> . . . Dear beauteous Death, the Jewel of the Just
> Shining nowhere but in the dark
> What mysteries do lie beyond thy dust
> Could man outlook that mark!
> He that hath found some fledged bird's nest may know
> At first sight if the bird be flown
> But what fair Well, or Grove he sings in now
> That is to him unknown.'

So Henry Vaughan, longing for his dead friends; but for himself amazed with peace when

> 'I saw Eternity the other night
> Like a great Ring of pure and endless Light
> All calm, as it was bright.'

And again, changing his imagery but deepening his desire:

> 'There is in God, some say
> A deep and dazzling darkness; as men here
> Say it is late and dusky because they
> See not all clear.
> O for that Night, that I in Him
> Might live invisible and dim.'

Here is Donne, dying:

> 'Since I am coming to that Holy room
> Where with thy Quire of Saints for evermore
> I shall be made Thy Music: As I come
> I tune the instrument here at the Door
> And what I must do then, think here before . . .
>
> We think that Paradise and Calvary
> Christ's Cross and Adam's tree, stood in one place
> Look Lord and find both Adams met in me;
> As the first Adam's sweat surrounds my face
> May the last Adam's blood my soul embrace.'

and Donne looking beyond death:

'Bring us O Lord at our last awakening into the house and gate of heaven to enter into that gate and dwell in that house where there shall be no darkness nor dazzling but one equal light, no noise or silence but one equal music, no fears or hopes but one equal possession, no ends or beginnings but one equal eternity . . .'

Sir Thomas Browne is less specific, asking only to be awake and aware of the Divine:

> 'Howe'er I rest, great God let me
> Awake again at last with Thee
> . . . O come that hour when I may never
> Sleep again but wake for ever.'

Did he realize, as a doctor, what a small proportion of our potential perceptions we use; did he anticipate the present longing for what are called 'altered states of consciousness'?

By the time these lines were written Reformation doctrines had severed the primeval threads of continuity between the living and the dead. The idea of Purgatory, where they could be linked in prayer for one another was fading away from the general imagination in England, and with it another idea, held among Christians quite certainly from the time of St Augustine of Hippo onwards, that departed souls might sometimes come back unasked to comfort the bereaved or to set some matter straight. There was no more prayer to the saints, dead humans who in their holiness could still love and help living ones. No spirit would wish to return from heaven, it was said; so any apparition recognized as a person once known must be either a demon who had assumed his likeness or a lost soul. Any benevolent apparition must be an angel, and an angel was by definition non-human despite the confusion implied in such words on the after-life as:

'And with the morn those Angel faces smile
Whom we have loved long since and lost awhile.'

The mercy of God to each man stopped at death. By then he had made himself all bad, or had been totally redeemed; and would 'go to his own place'. The imagination boggled, and the visions fell to pieces. What images remained were 'hymnages', alien to ordinary experience; wings, crowns, thrones, harps, white robes. Sometimes these were accepted literally, as when a Seventh-Day Adventist father, poor as he was, insisted that each of his seven children must have a clean white robe ready for Judgment Day (and had unexpected dress rehearsals in the middle of the night). But for the most part they became increasingly unreal. Many of the Victorians looked away, convincing themselves that death ended all consciousness, which was no more than an epiphenomenon of physical existence. Others discharged feeling without examining faith. Though they could not pray for the dead they could keep their memory green (and black) with elaborate mourning, enormous tombstones, and even on occasion the manufacture of life-sized figures of dead children dressed in their clothes and kept in the nursery so that their brothers and sisters should not forget them.

Spiritualism developed, redressing the psychological balance with pictures of a Summerland where the dead lived in simulacra of their earthly surroundings. But *The Dream of Gerontius*, sometimes almost hidden in its heavy music, seems to have been the first poem written for centuries by an English Christian on the experience of the departing and departed soul on its way to God.

The most illuminating words for me in our own time occur at the end of C. S. Lewis's *The Screwtape Letters*, and concern a man killed in an air raid:

'There was a sudden clearing of his eyes . . . he saw Them . . . The dim consciousness of friends about him which had haunted his solitudes from infancy was now at last explained; that central music in every pure experience which had always just evaded memory was now at last recovered . . . He saw not only Them, he saw Him . . . cool light . . . clarity itself.'

9

Resurrection in a
post-religious age

Ulrich Simon

●

Having read most of the contributions to this volume I feel more puzzled
than before, and I am sure the reader shares my perplexity. How can
the human brain make sense of such an immensity of information?
There are perspectives of survival, absorption, reincarnation, of bliss
and anguish, heaven and hell, geographical and cultural distinctions,
of scientific considerations and paranormal claims, all of which present a
kaleidoscope which defies our powers of understanding. I cannot attempt
to evaluate the various approaches nor verify the evidence offered here
and there. I do not even know whether to come to the quest with an open
mind or with no mind at all. Unamuno in his great book *The Tragic
Sense of Life* (1921), which may be regarded as a classic on the subject,
pleads passionately for the exercise of the reason of the heart (Pascal) as
against the cold logic of science. I think he is right: even in the face of
the evidence included since his day, we do not reach the ecstatic affirmation 'I shall rise from the dead' by drawing upon an argument composed
of sense data. Even if it were proved that a disembodied life were verified after death, we should know nothing of its state. Would 'it' be good,
eternal, enjoyable, continuous? The view remains barred, as Goethe's
Faust states, before his death and resurrection.

The view remains barred not only because we depend upon the
scientific-logical methods of reasoning, but also because life after death
has lost its appeal for those who no longer reason with the heart. There
has been an internal shrinking away from the risen life. Ever since
Spinoza the educated have concentrated their wills on *this* world. They
regard a post-mortem hope as cheap. They disdain to buy comfort at
the price of dishonesty. The vulgar make play of the inevitable boredom

of a prolonged existence. Who wants to live for ever? Take away the pleasures of the flesh and most men would prefer not to be.

These strictures on life after death overlap and give support to the official political veto on a religious hope. The plain materialism of philosophy feeds the socialist dialectic which imposes a dogmatic unbelief on the ants of the communal heap. Marx and Lenin chide all mystical claims as monstrous weapons of the bourgeoisie. No class-conscious worker can accept the 'pie in the sky' baits. In the peoples' democracies no otherworldly consolations are necessary or permitted. The power structure of the proletarian dictatorship cannot tolerate mystical expectations, since these would introduce a dimension of values which must contradict the planned economy of the monolithic state. The collective does not *need* another life.

It should at once be admitted that any doctrine favourable to life after death must be considered dangerous from a collectivist point of view. To begin with, it cannot enhance production. Next, it detracts from the present glory of the state. Lastly, it raises the question of the meaning of the individual's life which of all questions is the most heretical to be whispered in a collectivist dictatorship. The collective, it is alleged, is continuous and the death of its individual members is made up by the births.

The socialist defence reacts predictably against all empirical claims for survival. They cannot be admitted. They are either fraudulent, paid for by capitalist agents, or the uncultured have allowed themselves to be deceived. Paranormal phenomena are safely in the hands of state observers; thus ESP is a safe subject within Soviet control. If anyone were to appear after death the state's regulations would silence such an appearance. But the socialist case rests with the scientific norm that life ends with physical death, even if the problem of the moment of death may still bear investigation in medical circles and under supervision.

The secularization of death hits all religious traditions with an immense force. Its main strength lies in its implicit power of persuasion. 'We shall be dead', is the secular creed. For the Christians it is not simple to reply 'We shall all be alive', since the tradition, from antiquity until now, is highly complex, if not contradictory. To the rational mind it must look vulnerable in the extreme. How, for example, can we assert that the body is raised when we also commit it to the earth? How can we posit an immortality of the soul when at the same time many Christian theologians allow no independent existence to the soul? More important, what are we to make of a continuity of the self, when the Christian preaching from the earliest days gloried in change, a kind of transformation in which the original seed bears fruit but is hardly recognized? Even more searchingly, how can the Christian denounce the secular affirmation of total and universal death, when Christians used to hold the view that the mass of humanity is lost in death, since only faith and union in Christ vouchsafe the miraculous passage from death to life?

Now the variegated and paradoxical intimations of life after death were not always a source of weakness. On the contrary, there was the bedrock conviction as expressed in the classical creeds, and even the apparent distinction between the resurrection of the individual and the final general resurrection of all mankind, which coincided with the end of history, lent additional strength to the believers. These 'two resurrections' provided a twofold buttress to the faith by combining the individual's destiny with the cosmic unfolding of events. Similarly the threefold expectation – of Hell, Purgatory, and Heaven – agreed with the experience of damnation, reformation, and bliss which the world around us seemed to suggest in daily life. But these orderly and systematized schemata have not weathered the storm of the secularization of death. Not only socialist and collectivist opposition to them, but the whole vista of industrialism and the spoliation of the world, in war and in peace, have nipped the bud of hope. The burden of our history no longer favours the triumphant and self-explanatory cry: *Et Resurrexit*! The emotional link has gone and mankind is not naturally drawn to identify with the risen Christ.

Even more enticing and destructive appears the so-called ecumenical perspective. Christians are invited to mix their belief (highly complex as it is) with other faiths (whose complexity is no less), and the result is not surprisingly a hotch-potch of symbols of after-death states. You can hear or read the upshot of these attempts quite frequently: we (who are 'we'?) are said to be absorbed into a total nothing, which is a cosmic immensity of Being, of which Christ (or Buddha or anyone else) is the source, or the exponent, or the goal. Again 'we' are said to be remembered by God as pure spirit in an ocean of Christ-like memories. It is very easy to parody these well-meant but meaningless substitutes for the incisive pictures of Christian doctrines and traditions.

The authentic and undiluted assurance of life after death cannot be taken out of the context of God, Christ, and the Holy Spirit. 'God is the God of the living, and not of the dead': thus we reach the faith of the after-life not through the study of man, not even through sympathy with his aspirations, but with the revelation of God himself. Without God we die . . . it is as simple as that. With God we live, but not outside the dialectic of human experience. What we expect after death fills us with hope and fear, for there is the incontrovertible Either–Or which corresponds to the evidence gathered in our hearts. Heaven or Hell symbolize the *Pro* and *Contra* of this experience.

At this stage I can hear my editor groan and my reader turn away with dismay. And both are right: the Christian after-life should not need such difficult language, as Either–Or. Why list the Pros for life, and the Contras against it, when in former ages the after-life was sweetly continuous with the embodied life? Then a lover could greet his beloved, now departed, with a warm 'good-bye', and look forward to the time when both would again be together, not in sleep but in a restful life, a return to the garden of innocence. There are among us still many simple folk who have never seen the pictures in the Roman catacombs and yet look forward to this kind of happy consummation. I have known almost illiterate parishioners who greeted their departure with a serenity derived from this confidence, which merely repeats the Pauline 'I shall know as I shall be known'. The eternalization of love is here taken for granted, apart from the drama of Pro and Contra.

Nevertheless, we die and cannot be content with peaceful continuity. The dead man is represented by Lazarus, whom Jesus calls out of the tomb. He is deathless after having been in death, cut off, and hopeless, 'stinking' after initial decomposition. This stench is not only physical, but also, and perhaps more strikingly, spiritual. Lazarus, tied up with grave-clothes, symbolizes our dying humanity, alienated, isolated, fit for the scrap-heap. Nothing, not even medicine, can rescue him, and yet he ought not to perish. There cries out a nucleus of life, a person, not a mask. But this Ego is lost in self and therefore cannot live. Mankind is fit for neither life nor death, but for the great trial, the accusation first, the hearing of the defence next, and the pleas and counter-pleas, until the verdict be given and sentence pronounced.

The Christian tradition cannot treat of the after-life apart from this trial of Man, the ordeal of the Son of Man, who is killed and whom God raises up in order to vindicate himself and the whole creation. God ends the hopeless ambiguity of our existence. Left to ourselves we have no alternative to despair. As Dostoevsky concluded in his magisterial Pro and Contra (in *The Brothers Karamazov*) the rational man (Ivan) must 'return his ticket' in view of all the frightfulness and the suffering on earth. Only the loving man (Alyosha) can travel on this ticket, for it takes him on a journey of faith where God vindicates his servants.

Eternal life is the cosmic framework of personal vindication. In biblical terms it is the culmination of human history, the conquest of human history by the Kingdom of God. Hence the element of drama in eternal life, a paradox indeed! The temporal experience of conflict, of intense expectation, endurance, the attainment of the decisive turning-point, contrast with the tranquil timelessness of the unchangeable Deity. Unamuno is right when he therefore considers our tragic existence and its claim for eternalization as an anti-rational necessity. This stance beyond reason is precisely true of our earthly experience which longs to be undone in order to be reclothed. The tragic heroes no less than the Christian martyrs testify to this 'pressing on' towards the eternal reward, for life is a kind of reward after death when it is viewed in this way. The tragic hero – Oedipus, Orestes, Antigone, Philoctetus, Prometheus – is always alone; he or she suffers uniquely; the world or fate or the gods subdue the sufferer. But in the end the pollution is washed away, death is achieved, reconciliation reached. The tragedy intimates the immortality of man in and after his ordeal. The martyr testifies to the hope that the sacred cause, the truth, will live through his sacrifice and that he himself will live because of, and in, the truth. Thus the eternal future 'crowns' the disastrous present.

This stress on struggle and triumph may seem to accord with the experience of the giants of faith, but not with the routine existence of average men. Christians have always had this problem of the mediocre, who neither sin too much nor excel in virtue. The New Testament does not make much contact with sheep who simply graze on earth and are then transferred to heavenly pastures, although the early iconography seems to cherish this picture. The answer may lie in an estimation of 'average' men as not being what they think they are. They are made for eternal life, and if their triviality excludes them they suffer from an inner defect which testifies against them. They also will stand the trial, though they would opt out. On the other hand the great sinners, who boast of their originality and stride the earth like a colossus, may in reality measure up to nothing more than trivial dust. Ibsen ends his *Peer Gynt* on this masterly note, when Peer, approaching death as the great sinner, turns out to be so insignificant that he is only fit to be melted down by the button-moulder. We cannot be certain of our status, of our motivations, and of our expectations. Hamlet is made to realize this: the choice is not simply between 'to be or not to be', for there is the threat of the unknown country, from which no traveller has yet returned. There is the rub: we may have dreams, may become dreams. Our consciousness may linger on, with ourselves exposed to what we really are.

This self-exposure is not voluntary. Dante's unsurpassed achievement in the *Divina Commedia* lies partly in his insistence on the enforcement of the truth on the infernal spirits. Far from being transformed at all they have no wish to be other than they are and have been. They will not repent. They exist, not in the sense of standing outside themselves, but in their isolation. They are totally wrapped up in themselves and with voracious appetites they would eat others to maintain their own raving selves. They are self-condemned and act as their own executioners. They are their own hell, but they also are in Hell. They would break the divine order, if they could, in order to end their ordeal which is now pointless. They lack the power to do this, as Milton's Satan has to admit at the end. Their state is neither eternal life nor elimination.

The grotesque paintings of Hieronymus Bosch translate this nightmarish world where wolf eats wolf, leopard jabs at leopard, and man hates man. But the pandemonium may deceive the unwary with elegance and wit. The seducer Don Juan embraces damnation as his due as Mozart leads him to the final refusal after the shattering laughter in the cemetery. The d-minor scales above, and the trombones below, seal the doom of the proud nihilist.

You may protest against this conception of eternal punishment. But 'fear and trembling' is precisely the note which a modern treatment must give to this theme. Without it we arrive at a resort of bourgeois cosiness, a hotel with two stars. But as Sartre has shown in *Huis Clos* we are our own hell, and our neighbours are the devils who torment us and whom we torment, locked in for evermore by closed doors. When the doors are open the damned still remain stuck. The secularists do not suppress this truth which Christians often find too disturbing. Dante really saw this, his, hopeless state, shared by the careless, the indifferent, and the vicious, treacherous, brutal butchers, tyrants, and popes. Verdi – after Mozart – sketched their immortal regress and descent in the *Requiem*. There is no rest for them in the *Dies Irae*: down they go, down they are hurtled, and in the abyss they find themselves where they belong. But there is a difference between us and the beatific vision of earlier centuries. We no longer satisfy our thirst for vengeance as we look at them: for we wonder of our share in their condemnation. It is a very secular Requiem.

I consider this the most problematic aspect of our quest. We are not dealing with verses and paintings and liturgies, when we deal with real men and women as we open, for example, the annals of the war-time trials. There are the facts: what some have suffered, and the sufferings which some devils have inflicted. Can there be an end to this, or must eternity sanction the concentration camp as 'real'? Neither eternal punishment nor universal restoration answer to our predicament any more, for we see only too clearly that these empty, banal self-seekers are faceless, or, as we would say, 'dead'. Yet who would be so bold as to deny that the disembodied Hitlers and Stalins, with their vast entourage, still operate in the demonic realm of the spheres? We cannot speak of life after death without firmly expressing our horror and anguish at their death after life, which still kills in our earthly perversions and distortions of the truth. The faceless, divorced from God himself, encapsulate their emptiness in the impersonal power which drags this world to its final collapse. But this triumph of the lie, which Solzhenitsyn so brilliantly describes, has no future beyond its own cancerous growth.

The secular age almost succeeds in stamping out a hope beyond this total collapse, but the Christian clings to the optimistic consummation, to the divine comedy. Not only does the theme of vindication still ring powerfully, in as much as we, like the prophet Ezekiel (ch. 37), look to the restoration of the great army of innocent sufferers; even more authentic sounds the music of the Resurrection, which (in Pauline thought) spells out the defeat of death itself. Music, rather than verbal articulation, reasserts the joys of those endless sabbaths, as celebrated in the hymn *O quanta qualia sabbata*. Unamuno denies that peace and glory can come together – 'and may God deny you peace, but give you glory!' is his final benediction. But the Christian expectation looks for the impossible, where change gives stability, power enhances form, and our humanity ascends in and through God himself. Words certainly fail to describe this, except in the rarest mystical texts. Dante remains the master of these affirmations, and it should be noted that only he who has come out of the stink of Hell can deploy all the shades of light to be guided, and to guide us, on the upward ascent. This ascent is not uniform, but graded dimensionally, always in proportion to Grace, election, love, and obedience. Here the question is no longer about life-after-death, but the healing beyond death in repentance and the ecstatic approach to the Creator.

The nagging question 'how are the dead raised?' no longer casts its spell when, following Dante, we deny that the dead are dead. The dead bury their dead, but the living die to live. The identity of Christ in the Christian guarantees this dying and rising as a continuous process. We are being transformed, and life on earth is the record of this ordeal of transformation. If we ask 'how are we being transformed?' we may draw upon our experience of resurrection on earth. But we are not often conscious of this transformation, and the process seems to vary from individual to individual. It certainly stands outside the categories of economics and social behaviour. Transformation is the personal answer to, and against, the world around us. Yet there are certain common features which Christians regard as mandatory.

Baptism, church membership, sacramental practice, marital fidelity and chastity, stewardship of goods and talents, acts of compassion, and prayer sound almost too abstract and narrowly ecclesiastical to serve as milestones to Heaven in the secular age. Yet they cannot be circumvented, for the transformation depends upon an active – passive participation in the life of God. The purgatorial progress in love is quite simply prayer itself. Dante's friends in Purgatory always ask to be prayed for and their courtesy of interceding for him is always assumed. In prayer the eternal energy of charity widens and spirals.

Nothing could stand in a greater conflict with the outlook of the secular age than this direction of the will in prayer. If we take Dr Faustus as the classical exponent of the modern will we understand that he cannot pray, except to himself and for himself. His vast energy anticipates the scope of modern technology and industry. He would take the world by storm and transform it. He must sell his soul for total dominion. Even Helen of Troy must come to him who strives to marry the past with the present in an exploration on the cosmic scale. But can he live for ever? In the traditional treatment he is 'damned'. Goethe, however, brings to his end the finest irony: when the earth-movers shovel away to reclaim the ground from the sea and the innocent old couple are removed by force from their ancient home to make room for the new, Faust, though blind, thinks he sees the brave new world in the making. This he greets as his heaven to which he would say 'Stay, abide!', but what he takes to be eternal bliss is the preparation of his grave. Yet Goethe saves the dead Faust from the devil and opens the 'Catholic' Heaven to his soul, for 'those who strive earnestly we can redeem'. Defended by angelic rose petals, in the company of innocent babes, and at the intercession of the penitent and wronged Margaret, Faust rises, snatched from Mephistopheles, united soon with the highest saints and contemplatives.

Yet despite the poetry and allegory we have our doubts about the salvation of Faust the secular superman. Our worries do not concern his pagan self-confidence nor even his outrages. We cannot believe that he would allow himself to be transformed and broken, so as to enter the bliss which he has not made himself. The modern secularist must reach the immortal spheres by his own efforts. As Goethe said about his own future: destiny owes him a further entelechy. But perhaps destiny owes him nothing at all, except total oblivion. When Thomas Mann, a true son of everything Goethe stood for, took up the parable of Dr Faustus during the Second World War he could no longer subscribe to the optimistic climax of the redeemed secular titan. On the contrary, his Adrian Leverkuehn, a musician who also signs the pact with his devil, reaches the heights of inspiration, gains new ground in composition, attains to the apocalyptic vision, only to collapse and to head for nothingness. He dies, insane and harmless, in 1940 as the German armies in true Faustian manner crash through the defences of the West. Thus, the individual tragedy and the corporate destiny do not end in rose petals and the ascent through Purgatory, but in final death.

Again I hear the voice of my editor and of my reader in some despair: 'Never mind literary allusions. Tell us what happens to us? Tell us what happens to me?' I cannot tell. I refuse to regard myself in isolation, for in isolation, out of context, I am not only lost, but I want to be lost. Who would want to live on in the emptiness of self? Who would want to perpetuate the little family? Who could tolerate an eternalization of our rubbishy civilization? Either you broaden the perspective, and take in not only the Scriptures, but also Dante and Shakespeare, Milton and Goethe, the great painters of Resurrections and Ascensions (Raphael, Michelangelo, El Greco), or you get lost in the petty verbal polemics which are the death of everything. I accept the structure of Purgatory, because transformation under the stars argues strongly for metamorphosis above the stars. I long for Purgatory, because I do not want to remain what I am. I affirm Purgatory because nothing can be left as it is, and yet, when all is burnt away which is dross, there is a nucleus of true worth on which is built the eternal, radiant, Christ-like face, which wants to reflect its light which it has received in a cosmic harmony of exchange or love.

But here on earth only music can give a foretaste of this *Paradiso*. Trumpets and drums traditionally accompany the opening of the tombs. The great *Et Resurrexit* choruses, followed by those of *Expecto Resurrectionem Mortuorum* and *Vitam Venturi Saeculi* speak more eloquently of Heaven than words, since only polyphonic music can begin to evoke the endless facets of our goal. Perhaps music alone is the enduring property, the direct continuum which we have here and shall have there, which enwraps us here (though we make it), and will clothe us there. Bach again and again expresses the joy of death, the satisfaction of dying, the consolation of 'You are with me', as the culmination of life, and I can only ask the reader to hear Cantatas 8, 21, 26, 38, 82 among the many. Karl Barth spoke again and again of Mozart's music among the angels, and though Mozart is deeply disturbing, as one who has been 'on the other side' of death, his music takes us through the fire and water of the great ordeal. Mozart, more than any other, sounds the deeply threatening notes of demonic seduction, of the descent to the meaningless through obsessional d-minor triplets and syncopations. He does not preach at us, nor does he elegantly alter the scenario with eighteenth-century niceties. Rather he takes us through the depth to the *Gloria* which is in the depth. Whatever death is, it can only be met by God with glory and light.

Glory is a concept which has been abused for centuries. It has been identified with triumph and success, especially in politics and war. Yet there is no other concept which can accommodate all the different shades and dimensions, which this book has shown to point to life after death. The Christians do not think of this glory as impersonal or vague; rather it summarizes all the weight of existential anguish, of intellectual striving, of sacrificial self-giving, and of ecstatic pleasure, in the face of Jesus Christ. St Paul in II Corinthians sets forth the amazing progress from glory to glory, an ascent of total being in Christ, which retains all the marks of earthly dying. The Cross of living is not annulled in the life to come but 'glorified', or seen in the light of God's truth. This process of glorification – 'glorify thou me, as I have glorified thee' – is the experience of the 'hour' of death.

Without music, polyphonous in fugal richness, this claim to glory cannot be substantiated. Therefore no adult Christian (pity the truly deaf whose hope must be deferred) can claim to have access to this glory without singing and playing, and listening to, the *Glorias* of our liturgies. There, and there only, are incarnate the strains of eternal glory, which mediate the depth of dying and the height of living. The secular age will recover its belief not through theological words but through the trumpets of the *Gloria*.

The nature of eternal life: A mystical consideration

Martin Israel

●

If we are to consider the nature of the eternal life to which the higher religions point, we should first think about the life we lead on earth and its ultimate meaning. If our present life is that of a sleep-walker – and this assessment is unfortunately true of many people who have walked the face of the earth from the beginning of time – we can hardly expect the life beyond the grave to be more than an empty dream. But if we have, even during a brief span of years in this world, been able to effect some understanding of ourselves, then we have a solid basis of future development to anticipate. If personal life has any real meaning at all, it points to a time when we shall grow into something of the measure of the stature of the fullness of a complete person, such as were the great representatives of the human race in other times and places. These were the saints of all the world's higher religions, for it is to them that the aspiring person looks in warmest approbation and deepest longing.

The meaning we place on life is an indication of our status in the realm of eternal life, and eternal life is in turn a function of the knowledge we have of the immortal principle that is part of our own personality. 'For where your treasure is, there will your heart be also' (*Luke* 12:34). If our treasure is a worldly one, whether riches, power and prestige, pleasure, or intellectual supremacy, our heart will be immured in the realm of material life, and will have little that is real to look forward to when the things of this world are surrendered. But if our treasure is the pearl of great price within, known as the Kingdom of God, for which every outer thing we possess is sacrificed, then our true life will flower into real radiance when we have moved beyond the incarceration of the mortal body. It follows from this that our great work while on earth is self-knowledge, for only when we know and love ourselves as we have been made by God can we begin to understand and love others also. Furthermore, a concern for life after death is then a natural extension of the understanding of personal identity, and far from being a pathetic wish-fulfilling fantasy to escape from the painful fact of mortal annihilation at death, it becomes the rational and ethical growth of consciousness into ever-widening realms of reality and meaning.

He who cannot envisage discarnate existence is lacking in something much more than a healthy imagination; he is deficient in a full appreciation of himself. The identification of the material world alone with the fully real is the great error of modern man; it is as serious as the pseudo-mystical heresy of identifying the world of matter as merely an illusory appearance in a spiritually based reality, a view that has been justly attacked by a scientifically orientated generation. In fact, there is only one reality, and that is the place of action where the aspiring person finds himself at any time and in any place. Armed with these considerations, let us consider the constitution of the person in terms of immortality.

The Immortal Principle in Man

In the precision of Greek thought man was considered a duality of mortal flesh and immortal soul. While Hebrew thought saw man more as a unity of body and soul, there can be no doubt that it is the immaterial principle of soul that is the durable part of our personality. The very concept of soul has been frequently derided in modern times, but current trends in transpersonal psychology have served to re-instate this aspect of human personality. Indeed, the barrenness of behaviouristic psychology has brought in its train an awakened appreciation of values as the most durable part of human experience while on earth. Nowadays the soul is described as the transpersonal self or the spiritual self. It is the true focus of identity of each person, for by its unique judgments both on a moral level and especially in moments of existential crisis we begin to know ourselves as distinct and distinctive members of creation. This true self is to be distinguished from the unstable flitting centre of consciousness, by which we show ourselves in everyday life. This aspect of personality is heavily conditioned by past education and experience, and it tends to fluctuate according to outer circumstances and the need to conform to prevailing attitudes. It is unfortunately true that most people spend their whole lives at this level of the changing, self-centred personality, and identify themselves completely with such outer attributes as wealth, physical appearance, intellectual endowment, or social eminence. Now while all these characteristics are real enough, and of considerable importance in terms of the world's needs, none can be regarded as permanent. Not only does our worldly fortune alter according to outer and inner events in our lives, but physical attractiveness and intellectual prowess tend to diminish as one grows older. It is a truly terrible thing to find oneself bereft of those things to which one had previously clung as objects of ultimate stability. Those who identify themselves with anything outside their true self, or soul, will be shattered as life cruelly, yet beneficially, takes away from them all false objects of attachment and identification.

It is in this context that the redemptive role of suffering becomes clear. No matter how unpleasant such things as illness, frustration, and loss are, they do at least teach us what is durable in our lives and what is transient and meretricious. In the story of Job one can see how he had to lose everything outside himself before he could find himself in God, so vast as to make all human complaint irrelevant, and yet his true self shone through in the divine encounter. Jesus asks, 'What does a man gain by winning the whole world at the cost of his true self?' (*Mark* 8:36). He also says, 'Whoever cares for his own safety is lost; but if a man will let himself be lost for my sake and for the Gospel, that man is safe' (*Mark* 8:35). The other higher religions, especially Hinduism and Buddhism, are equally explicit in stressing the need to lose concern for personal craving before the true, spiritual self, which is immortal, can be known and acknowledged.

The true self is acknowledged when one makes a deep choice following a moral decision of great magnitude. Whatever one decides is bound to cause much pain both to oneself and to one's family and friends. Here the decision is beyond such considerations as conformity or ease, but is rather an active movement of the true self to freedom, the freedom of self-expression. One can also begin to discover the inner true self during periods of rapt meditation and prayer, when one's attention enters the greater stillness, where in the void, the voice of God can be heard.

The True Self and the Person

A full understanding of personality requires something more than merely the spiritual centre of integration; it needs the flesh and bones of the physical body, the thoughts of the rational mind, the drives and emotional response of the feeling nature, and the will based on aspiration towards completeness as a person. A real person is rare to find. He is one in whom the body, reasoning mind, emotional nature, and personal will are fully integrated around the spiritual centre which we call the soul, or true self. The typical man of the world has only the faintest grasp of the nobility of a real person. It is our life's work to achieve personality. A real person is alive in the world, capable of independent moral choice, able to work harmoniously yet as an individual in whatever circumstances he finds himself, and able to adapt himself to the needs of other people around him without surrendering his own identity. Neither the spineless conformist nor the obsessive anarchist are full persons, for both, in contrary ways, identify themselves in terms of the world around them, and not in relation to the centre of their own being. As one grows into mature personality, so one becomes increasingly detached from one's outer circumstances and even one's inner conditioning, and functions instead in a larger world of universal concern and moral choice. To be a person is to experience that service to the highest one knows which is true freedom – freedom from selfish demands, from envy of others, and from the need for constant support from others. A person can be himself in all circumstances, for being integrated in himself, he is unmoved, at least in the depths of his own being, in no matter what difficulties or dangers he may find himself. Such a person is living consciously in eternity at this very moment, for the seat of his awareness is detached from the exigency of the moment to the eternity of which every moment of time is an outer sacrament. In other words, the present ceases to be merely a period of meaningless suffering but becomes instead invested with the radiance of eternal meaning, a meaning that testifies to a state of ultimate completeness of being, when the wisdom of the true self will have penetrated to the very core of the personality, and lifted it from the mortality of selfish desire to the immortality of universal concern. When we consider that this is the work of each living person, it becomes fearfully obvious how little of this labour is carried out in any one life on earth with its limitations, disappointments, and final physical disintegration. For completion to be realized, life in the world to come is inevitable.

Patterns of Survival

The belief in survival hinges on the acceptance of a dualism of mind and body. If the physical body alone is real, and what we call mind is merely an emanation from the brain, or an epiphenomenon of cerebral activity, it follows that there can be no survival of death. But the data of psychical research strongly suggest that mental activity can occur outside the orbit of the brain, even during mortal life, and spontaneous communication with the deceased, and also the more contentious material evoked by mediums build up a fairly strong case for post-mortem survival of the mental and spiritual component of personality. In our present state of knowledge (and disbelief) none of this bears the imprint of absolute truth, and I personally doubt whether survival of death can ever be scientifically proved until man generally reaches a new level of spiritual receptivity and can communicate more effectively not only with the discarnate beyond the grave, but also, and of even greater importance, with his fellows in his present life.

If one accepts, on the basis of religious faith, the probability of survival, and if one has been fortunate enough to be given direct communication with those who have passed on – which to me is the ultimate subjective proof of survival, though, being a private experience, it cannot be transmitted to sceptics and therefore will never prove survival to others besides oneself – a definite pattern of persisting personality presents itself to the recipient. In the instance of thoroughly selfish people, those who have never been able to make any sort of relationship except on the basis of using others and taking advantage of them, the surviving part is a blurred assortment of memories and past conditioning without any central stabilizing focus. Such a person relied on bodily sensation and gratification for his awareness of identity when he was still alive in the world, and when divested of physical consciousness, he is in a state of literal darkness and confusion. This type of survival has little to recommend it, and is part of the traditional hell portrayed in religious doctrine. Such a person is certainly not functioning at the level of the true self, the existence of which he knew and knows nothing. The main feature of this disastrous type of post-mortem experience is a separation of personal identity, in its most rudimentary form, from the greater body of living things. This type of existence is simply a continuation of the selfish life the person enjoyed while on earth, but now he has lost the comforting presence of the physical body. Such an entity may haunt a particular environment for some time.

The type of existence in store for those of broader sympathies, who have been able to forge real relationships while on earth, is rather more promising. The making of an enduring relationship needs self-sacrifice and the willingness to serve others, at least to the extent of giving oneself to the other in steadfast attention. As a result there is a penetration of the enclosure of the selfish personality, and an awareness of corporate unity, even beyond the limitation of the flesh. Here the surviving part of the personality is a much better organized mental and emotional component with even the true self, or soul, partly laid bare. It is this type of discarnate personality that is most likely to communicate purposefully and lovingly with those on earth, either spontaneously or (less perfectly) through a medium. This type of survival, which we surely are all to experience in one form or another, is more inspiring than the life we led on earth, for our range of psychic vision is much greater, but it is still essentially selfish and restricted to a personal view of immortality. The personality may grow in stature through the accumulation of arcane knowledge on the other side of death, but there is no growth in fullness of being, in becoming a more rounded person. The communication that such a source may effect, and the knowledge he may attempt to provide, is often of a rather mundane type, and it may seem at times remote from the past personality of the communicator while he was on earth. Postmortem communication can trivialize a previously rewarding relationship while on earth, and the matter is better left alone until such time as the bereaved spontaneously receives an authentic message from the departed.

The limitation of spiritualistic communication lies in its tendency to exalt the personality of the recipient, and to stress the personality of the deceased. But it is probable that the trend of post-mortem existence has been fairly accurately charted by spiritualism. This type of survival, while no doubt part of the evolution of human consciousness beyond the grave, has little to teach us about the eternal life aspired to in higher religious thought. It is doubtful whether a discarnate person can grow into full personality when devoid of some body of limitation. Growth is not a function of increased intellectual knowledge, but of suffering and sacrifice in a world of limitation. It is for this reason that the spiritualistic view of survival, while probably true, is finally inadequate. Its importance lies in the bridge it provides for linking the present life of the person, with all his inadequacies, with the glorious day in which he may be so fully himself, in union with God, that death is finally conquered in victory. To me the immediate period of post-mortem existence is a time of rest, recuperation, and preparation in which the soul can prepare for further trials ahead.

Rebirth Sequences

The surviving elements of personality would, according to this scheme, include the true self of the individual and such mental experience and emotional development as he had achieved in the previous life on earth. Communication with those still in the flesh introduces recognizable aspects of the old personality, at least soon after its death. But it would seem that later there is an incorporation of all past conditioning into a broadened, more comprehensive self, which is then better equipped to continue its journey towards completion. Certainly most progressive religions accept an intermediate state, or purgatory as it is sometimes called, as the way of growth of the soul to its ultimate fulfilment in God. The rather more exclusive view, based to some extent on scriptural fundamentalism, that the soul either goes to a blissful heaven if it is 'saved' or else suffers the eternal torments of hell and damnation if not, is so clearly unjust and unloving that it has repelled many thinking people against religion and caused much neurotic ill-health amongst those who believe. Indeed, there are some aspects of survivalistic belief that are even more harmful than a categorical denial of survival of death or even of meaning in life.

In the purgatorial scheme, growth of the soul, enshrouded in its spiritual body afforded by the mind-stuff of its past life on earth, takes place by successive experiences of limitation, in which suffering and self-sacrifice would be the means of development. One can only speculate about the nature of this growth into full personality, but one possible way is by the process of re-incarnation. This implies the adoption of a fresh human body by the soul on successive occasions, each earth life helping to bring the true self into greater reality and unity with other selves. This is the way of rebirth envisaged by Hinduism and Buddhism, the latter taking a negative view of the existence of the individual soul. Western theistic religion is generally opposed to the re-incarnational scheme, both because in its more popular and fundamentalistic forms it looks forward to a literal resurrection of the physical body, and because it sees life in the world to come in terms of a linear progression rather than a cyclical movement such as bodily rebirth would seem to imply. Furthermore, the Christian would look to the atoning sacrifice of Christ as rendering the scheme of painful development in the life hereafter unnecessary, at least for the believer, who might be expected to enter the realm of blissful heaven when he dies. The data of psychical research – largely the early, corroborated memories of past lives of very young children – do seem to bear out the possibility of the re-incarnational hypothesis in the instance of some individuals, but it is much less certain whether this is a universal, or even common way of personal growth. Popular re-incarnational teaching is often very loveless, and is more concerned about the repayment of past debts and old scores than about the growth of the soul into the unity of God. In other words, it boosts separate personality at the expense of corporate unity, and people heavily addicted to alleged re-incarnational memories are seldom satisfactory in their personal relationships with others. Considering the number of past lives they claim to be aware of, in some of which they were allegedly important personages, their poor degree of spiritual development in the present life, as is witnessed in their unsatisfactory responses to the world they live in, makes one wonder about the value of their memory of re-incarnation, if indeed it is a fact and not merely part of a system of delusions built up by an inadequate personality.

The truth probably lies somewhere in the middle between the claims of the ardent re-incarnationalists and those who discountenance any type of intermediate state after physical death. Re-incarnation could be one of the 'many mansions' promised by Jesus in his Father's house. Provided the personal punitive aspect of rebirth is rejected, and the growth of the aspiring soul into fullness of being is seen to be the overriding factor, a scheme of rebirth, which may involve a return to this world or else to some other world of limitation, is both just and merciful. Spiritual growth is always essentially by experience, not by intellectual knowledge. And the experience which is at the heart of reality is always love. An understanding of the unitive love that binds creator and creature together, a love that has no conditions attached to it from the creator's point of view and one that looks for no benefits other than the fact of eternal union from the creature's point of view, is an understanding of the nature of eternal life. Such an understanding is the path of man towards his final consummation in God. His life is in fact an exploration of the means and nature of selfless love, and when he has finally acquired that understanding, his life as a separate unit is transmuted into a corporate unity with all creation and with God also. It seems likely that this wisdom is the fruit of much experience in many forms and in many different 'worlds', all of which are really aspects of the same world, for there is only one world and that is the life of eternity.

Our present earthly experience is a reflection in microcosm of the splendour of God, which is inevitably marred by the perverted action of his creatures, especially man, who have, through his grace, been given absolute free will, even to the extent of repudiating the creator entirely, and thereby destroying the earth over which they have been given charge and dominion. Fortunately the fact of survival of personality, even after a terrible repudiation of responsibility in this life, makes the future growth of the person at least a possibility. If the soul continually repudiates the higher good, which means in effect the common good rather than mere self interest, it is conceivable that it might finally forfeit its identity and disintegrate into nonentity. But personally I hope for the redemption of all corrupt beings in the greater love of God. This does not mean a spineless type of universalism in which there is an automatic, or magical salvation, but rather a long, painful working out of inner difficulties, and their transmutation in the light of God's love. When one considers the great social injustices under which most people have to work out even this earthly life, and the severe psychological handicaps under which they labour, it becomes increasingly difficult to condemn any person, and ever more pressing to lend assistance to the forces of love and compassion in the world. Indeed, Jesus' injunction against judging others lest we ourselves are judged becomes the very heart of creative living. It would be humbling to reflect on the extent of our own blame for the delinquencies of other people, not so much by positive actions against them as by our habitually negative attitude towards them through our lack of concern in our daily lives.

The Experience of Eternal Life

Eternal life is not a state of existence we should dimly anticipate in the world beyond death. It is, at least potentially, with us now. Its attainment depends on our attitude to the world and the people among whom we live. Earthly man starts his long pilgrimage as a self-centred being, and the self of which he is aware is merely his physical body with its innate desires and the drives accruing from them, chief of which are those of survival and self-gratification. Such a simple view of life cannot transcend bodily annihilation. But there is in all human beings an inner principle, the soul, that looks towards immortality, and the more abundantly the person lives in the world, the more his true self blossoms and integrates his personality from its central position. The discovery of the true self is a product of self-giving relationships with those whom we love – and as the personality becomes better integrated so the intensity and the range of that love increases. As I lose my self-centred concern, so I grow more into identity with others, and I become a very part of them without at any time losing awareness of my unique identity. On the contrary, as I sacrifice my selfish concerns and attitudes in serving those around me, I discover what is permanent and indestructible in me. And this principle that cannot be destroyed is not confined to me, but is one with the creative centre of the universe. To experience the being of God, who is immanent in the soul as its most exalted point, is the way of eternal life. In this experience the self is swept off its pinnacle of isolated fearfulness; indeed, it ceases to exist as a separate entity, and is one with the creative power of God. The experience is one of ineffable love, a love that is both personal in terms of each individual, and also transpersonal, in that it embraces all created things in equality of love. Thus in the divine mind all creatures are equally cared for, because God made them, and not because of their intrinsic merit. Once this great understanding comes to the person, his whole attitude to the world and to his fellows changes. He ceases to war against others or treat them as mere instruments for his own survival and satisfaction, but instead cares for them with a love that is the same love that God has for him, and he learns to have even for himself. For we can never love our neighbour properly, by which I mean with unclinging, detached regard, if we are unable to accept ourselves as we now stand. This does not mean that we are to disregard our defects or pretend they do not really exist, but rather to accept them with the love a parent has for its child so that they may be redeemed in that love which is primarily divine.

Once we have learned to accept ourselves, others, and the world we live in with real joy and love, we have passed beyond the thraldom of death and decay to a new life. Well did St John write, 'We know that we have passed from death to life because we love the brethren.' This new life is the old life lived in new awareness. Every moment is invested in a splendour of meaning, and each present activity and relationship is bathed in the radiance of recognition. Eternal life can be experienced even now if only we can put self-concern behind us, and can give of our whole personalities to the demands of the present moment. Eternal life is, in fact, nothing more than living constructively and in full awareness as each moment passes us by. The past can never be changed, and the future is outside our understanding until it merges into the present, but the present moment, fully lived, is our experience of reality, and it is also the experience of God in a point of time and space. To live in this way is a gift of God's grace, for it is a mystical experience of ultimate reality even while incarcerated in the matter of the earth. But to live this way for ever is man's ultimate end, and as such is the life of the incarnate Christ. In this life the coarse corruptibility of matter itself is transmuted into a spiritual essence that can never perish. Thus the body itself can be resurrected from the corruption of the flesh to the eternity of the spirit, and yet it is the same body but in a different form.

It is evident that this scheme of redemption and resurrection is visionary when applied to man in his present state of spiritual awareness. There was indeed only one, the incarnate Christ, who was able to demonstrate this resurrection, but it is the promise that we shall all be like him in the fullness of self-giving. Until that time, which is para-doxically both outside the sequence of time and a very possible gift even now, there must continue to be a sequence of physical death with its attendant discomforts and a growth of the mind-soul complex into greater knowledge and understanding in the world beyond the grave, a world punctuated with repeated episodes of limitation in a rebirth situation. This may take a cyclical earthly form or perhaps be consum-mated in some other form of life. Through suffering and the experience of God's everlasting love, which is most available to us when we are humble enough to receive it, the soul ceases to appear remote from the totality of the personality, but instead becomes the very centre of a resurrected person in whom body and soul function as a composite unit. The Hebraic view of personality as a complete union of body and soul is indeed the right one, but its essential truth will only be demonstrated as we grow into full personality and become real persons, in the image of the incarnate Christ, in whom the Godhead dwelt bodily. As we exist at present, this union is at most only partial, and often non-existent, especially in those who are completely earth-bound in selfish imagination.

It follows from all this that a really self-actualizing person is not afraid of death, and looks forward to its advent when his earthly mission has been completed. He can say, albeit less certainly than Jesus, 'It is finished' and 'Into thy hands I commend my spirit.' Being in this frame of mind of complete self-dedication to the Most High he can look for-ward to the onward passage of time with quiet confidence. Yet para-doxically, such a person, being at one with both life and death, ceases to think very much about death, or dwell a great deal on the after-life state. He has passed beyond the duality of life and death, mind and body, past and future, and lives wholly in the present moment, which is also the moment of eternity, the point of intersection of time and time-lessness. Thus it comes about that concern about life after death and rebirth sequences occupies a self-realized person's attention less and less, and the fact of eternity now is his constant realization. It is, in fact, in this frame of mind that St Paul's injunction, 'Pray without ceasing' becomes both possible and inevitable. Each act of work in the world is consummated to God's glory no less than to the well-being of our fellow creatures, and the perfection that accrues thereby is our gift to posterity, who may see the divine nature speaking through man's highest gift to the world, a gift bestowed in self-giving love.

All considerations of life after death can thus be seen to be related to the perfection of human nature. This is to partake increasingly of the divine nature also, and no matter how bitter may be the trials that it must undergo, all is in the final act consummated in fullness of being. The faith that is deeply embedded in the concealed soul of the undeveloped man leads him through hope to the experience of God's love. This love so infuses him that he grows progressively into the stature of a real person, a reflection of the person of God.

Part III

•

The idea of the hereafter:
the future

II

Life, death, awareness, and concern: a progression

Doris F. Jonas

●

Life unfolds from its birth in the chemical elements that formed our earth to its present seemingly miraculous complexity, and here I hope to find a context within which we may place our awareness of death and our concern about the continuation of individual existence.

When life first emerged from inorganic matter it reproduced itself by fission so that the earliest life forms, so long as they were not separated from nutrient material, were quasi immortal.[1] We do not know the form of the earliest and simplest life, but the closer we study living unicellular forms the greater is the complexity we find. Indeed we then understand why it was that it took as long from the time of the formation of our planet until the first organic cells evolved upon it, as it has taken for the whole of organic evolution to unfold from that single cell to man. It took some two to two-and-a-half billion years for chemical material to evolve a self-reproductive cell and has taken two to two-and-a-half billions of years for the forces of nature to evolve our species from that original life.

The tendency inherent in the chemical properties of carbon compounds in solution to polymerize results in long chains that eventually, because of their length, are prone to break up. This simple fact ultimately underlies the processes of vegetative or asexual reproduction. Thus unicellular life, nourished by chemicals of the solution in which it took form and provided with energy by the radiations of the sun, regenerated itself by constantly splitting itself into two parts in the process of meiosis and was, as we have said, quasi immortal.

One outcome of regeneration by this means, however, is that the daughter cells of a dividing parent cell frequently remain close to each other and form clusters. Among these clusters it eventually happens that by chance or accident some of them merge. Their genetic material thus combined, a groundwork is laid for further evolutionary change that forms the basis for sexual reproduction. Here lies the origin of mortality.

Sexual reproduction by fusion as contrasted with vegetative reproduction by fission is so much more efficient in evolutionary terms that its products gain advantage in competition for available nutrient resources and therefore are preserved by the pressures of natural selection. The continuing evolution of ever more complex forms is speeded at a geometric rate as individual beings are, so to speak, recycled, and only their genes continue existence in a constant reshuffling that perpetually refines the creature's form and function and renders it increasingly adapted to its environment. Thus only the genes retain life's original immortality while the rest of the organism becomes mortal.

As this process continues and gains momentum, and natural selection operates on breeding populations to the end of their adaptation to their environment, we see emerging certain lines of development that we come to recognize as species. It is precisely in this scheme that we can see death as an essential part of the processes of life, since the stage of life at which an individual creature dies is also a factor that is worked upon by the pressure of natural selection, so that death inevitably occurs at that point in the individual life when it serves the viability of the breeding group and thus the species. The species, like the gene, also has a quasi immortal life. Albert Gaudry, in 1888, defined species as 'transitory modes of types which pursue their evolution across the immensity of the ages.'[2] Like cells sloughed off by a human body and constantly renewed, individuals within a species also are sloughed off and renewed in order to sustain the viability of the species as a whole.

One can illustrate this process most clearly by looking at the life cycles of other creatures. The natural order of things might be said to frown upon the wasteful use of biological material. Each phase of the existence of each individual serves a purpose in the perpetuation of its kind, and when the individual comes to the end of its reproductive usefulness and can serve no further purpose for its species, it dies, so that its bodily material may aid in the maintenance of life in other species and thus be quickly reabsorbed into the total cycle of nature.

Perhaps the best examples of economy of means are to be found in the insect world, where males of many species die in the act of mating or very soon after and the females live only long enough to lay their eggs.[3]

Female spiders,[4] mantises and beetles, for example, are, so to speak, programmed for what we might consider the rather unpleasant habit of eating their consorts either during or soon after their fertilization, thus keeping the bodily matter of the male in the service of his species as food for his mate when his other functions are fulfilled. Clearly courting and mating are dangerous occupations for males of these and many other species, but hardly less so than giving birth for many of the females. The presence of the new generation renders both of them superfluous.

Among fishes it is not the destiny of males to render a final service to their species by becoming food for their mates, but the pattern of death for the parents soon after their reproductive mission is completed is found in many. The sockeye salmon, for instance, after spending three or four years grazing on plankton in the Pacific, find their way back, against all kinds of difficulties, to the particular gravel beds in the rivers where they were born some five years previously. At the time the salmon enter the fresh water they become sexually mature and they are in peak condition, but from that moment on they cease to feed. When their destination is reached, the nest is dug by the female. With her tail she digs a hollow about three feet wide and lays part of her eggs in it. She then moves a little upstream and digs another for more of them, continuing the process until a total of three-and-a-half to five thousand eggs have been housed and deposited. The male passes over the eggs as they are laid and fertilizes them, after which the loosened gravel and sand slip back over them to protect them. By this time the parent fish, their bodies stripped of all their reserves of fat by their prolonged fast (some eighteen days since they entered the river) – their eggs deposited, fertilized, and protected and the future of their race assured – then die, the male usually first. The female digs her fins into the gravel so that her body forms a protective roof over her nest until the last flicker of life.[5]

Of course, not all insects nor all fish die at the end of their first breeding season. Nevertheless, so far as we know, none of them lives on to a post-reproductive old age, nor would such a phase of life be functional until we come to the level of the mammals in the course of evolutionary development.

While it is impossible to make any statement that allows for no exception when one is speaking of the countless species of all forms of life, nevertheless some generalizations are possible. On the whole most insects, fish, amphibians and reptiles ensure the survival of their kinds by producing eggs in such large numbers that some small percentage of them are bound to survive and be viable. In these circumstances selection is unnecessary for parents that would live to provide care for the newly hatched young, beyond having laid their eggs in a suitable place. As the processes of evolution refine this prodigality of offspring to less wasteful methods, we find in birds and among mammals species that survive by producing fewer offspring per individual female. This reduction in the number of offspring, however, enforces greater care for those that are produced, and hence a longer life for the parent that must care for them.

At the levels developed earlier on the ladder of life than the mammals, the most vulnerable periods of any creature's life cycle are when it is in the egg stage and the time immediately after it emerges from the egg. In those stages it is an easily available food for a great variety of predaters. By retaining the young for the entire foetal phase within the body of the mother, mammals achieved a very great advance in the protection of their young at these most crucial times. And once the mother's life has been prolonged enough for her to afford her body as an ultimate protection to the embryo so that she is present at and takes part in its emergence, other functions justifying her continued existence become immediately apparent: the nurture, continued protection, and training of the extremely helpless newborn.

Among groups of individuals making up any species, their natural variability ensures that among them there are some that have shorter lives and some that have longer ones. When it is adaptive to the survival of a group that their individuals have short lives and, so to speak, get out of the way of the new generation, then the short-lived individuals prove to have a selective advantage and their lines survive. However, when it is of advantage to the survival of a population for individuals to live longer, then the long-lived survive in greater proportion and pass this propensity on to their posterity. This is what happened increasingly among the higher mammals. The reason for drawing attention to this rather self-evident fact is to point out that longer life in an animal group is not a thing that just happens, but is a circumstance that occurs only when there is a functional need for it.

In mammals, then, evolutionary processes achieved forms that lived to be able to reproduce a limited number of young in successive seasons and to take care of them. But even in most mammals there is no need for a further phase, a state of old age, after that of the prime of life.

There are several ways in which a mammal that is approaching the end of its useful life can be eliminated from its group, and incidentally this also applies to many birds. Animals may lose their dominant and privileged positions to younger and stronger newcomers, as is the case, for instance, among the deer or the seals. They may be weakened by injury and lose their physical capacity to forage for food or to hunt and they may then get edged to the periphery of their groups where they are more easily picked off by predators, as in many herd animals, or they may continue hunting until they succumb to their disabilities, like the hyena, the wild-dog, or the wolf. For some the shock of loss of status alone is sufficient to precipitate their death.

The life of an individual animal is by no means an absolute. Both the nature of its life and the time at which it dies are determined by the needs of its group. The process of natural selection does not operate to preserve an individual but to maintain a breeding group as a whole at its highest level of function. Indeed, adaptive selection depends upon a high death-rate and encourages competition.

From all this it is apparent that the function of life is to perpetuate life. Like leaves falling off the tree each autumn to conserve the energy available to the whole organism during the winter, and renewed again in the spring to capture the sunlight and convert it to new energy, each leaf playing its part in the overall fitness-for-life of the tree, so each individual is a part of the ongoing life of its species.

Among all these species death is neither sought nor feared. It is *experienced*, as are all the other phases of life, when its time comes. Among mammals this attitude (if we may call it that) is usually mediated by the very nature of the animals' perception. Much of their social interrelationship is governed by the olfactory sense, so that a dead creature, smelling different from a live one, is no longer identified as a conspecific by most animals.

This leads us to a few higher animals that have a long life and among which we begin to see a concern being shown for the wellbeing of their fellows.

'A sick dolphin, for example, cannot afford to go into a coma. It cannot afford even to go to sleep for more than about six minutes. If it falls asleep for longer than this it is in great danger of dying – asleep too deeply, its respiration stops. Because of this particular peculiarity of the dolphins, a sick dolphin must be attended twenty-four hours a day. One dolphin will do this for another dolphin.'[6]

Dr John Cunningham Lilly, in the process of establishing an experiment in interspecies communication in which a young woman and a bottle-nose dolphin lived together for a year mutually exchanging learning and teaching, recorded that again and again at his Institute they had seen dolphins tend one another twenty-four hours a day until recovery took place several days or even weeks later.

African elephants present us with another striking parallel with human cultural practices. Sylvia Sikes, a consultant zoologist in Nigeria, saw and recorded mourning rituals among them. She recorded a typical one as follows:

'In a case where an animal is mortally wounded and cannot rise, the other members of the herd . . . circle it disconsolately several times, and if it is still motionless they come to an uncertain halt. They then face outward, their trunks hanging limply to the ground. After a while they may prod and circle again, and then again stand, facing outward. Eventually, if the fallen animal is dead, they move aside and just hang around . . . for several hours, or until nightfall, when they may tear out branches and grass clumps from the surrounding vegetation and drop these on and around the carcass, the younger elephants also taking part in this behaviour. They also scrape soil toward the carcass and then stand by, weaving restlessly from side to side. Eventually they move away from the area.'[7]

David Attenborough of BBC fame has also recorded photographically the behaviour of elephants burying their dead under leafy branches.

Coming closer to man, chimpanzees have not been observed to carry out any proto-funerary rites, but among them social friendships and individual attachments are formed. Jane Goodall has recorded that a chimpanzee mother will sometimes carry around a dead infant for days although, if nothing else, her sense of smell must inform her at least as well as ours does that the infant has ceased to be a living creature. Nevertheless in these animals the evolving neocortex seems to be accompanied by a dawning of self-awareness. In addition, their lengthy infancy (they do not reach sexual maturity until they are about eight or full social maturity until they are about twelve years old) imposes a necessity for attachment behaviour between mother and young that is sufficiently strong for such incidents of a mother being unwilling to cease carrying her dead infant to occur.

This leads us directly to emerging man. Beginning with the highest non-human mammals, we see increased development of neocortex accompanied by an emergence of an awareness of the self – a necessary prerequisite to concern about death.

Until very recently it used to be thought that very early man (and, for that matter, also contemporary tribal man) had little concept of death and was unconcerned about it. The 11th Edition of the *Encyclopaedia Britannica*, published in 1910, has this to say on the matter:

'To the savage, death from natural causes is inexplicable. At all times and in all lands, if he reflects upon death at all, he fails to understand it as a natural phenomenon, nor in its presence is he awed or curious. Man in a primitive state has had for his dead an almost animal indifference. The researches of archaeologists prove that Quaternary man cared little what became of his fellow creature's body ...'

Such a tone of contemptuous superiority, along with the information itself, would now be hard to sustain, especially since the series of expeditions led by Dr Ralph Solecki from 1951 to 1960 to the Shanidar cave in the Kurdistan area of northern Irak.[8] There they discovered the skeletons of a large number of Neanderthals. The first they uncovered, and that they named Shanidar I for identification, had been killed by a rockfall, but among his remains were small concentrations of mammal bones that suggested they had been dropped there as part of a funeral feast. The most interesting aspect of this particular skeleton was that although his right shoulder blade, collarbone and upper arm were undeveloped from birth, and the useless right arm appeared to have been amputated early in life, it was nevertheless about forty years old at the time of death, a very old man for a Neanderthal. Moreover he must have been blind in his left eye, since he had extensive bone scar tissue on the left side of his face. And, as if this were not enough, the top right side of his head had received some damage that had healed before the time of his death. In short, Shanidar I was at a distinct disadvantage in an environment where men, even in the best condition, lived hard lives. Yet he had been allowed to live. That he had made himself useful around the hearth (two hearths were found close to him) is evidenced by his unusually worn front teeth – which he had apparently used for grasping in lieu of his right arm. But since he could hardly have foraged or fended for himself, one must assume that he was accepted and supported by his people to the day he died. The stone heap found over his skeleton and the near-by mammal food remains show that even in death he was an object of some regard.

A second man had been killed by a relatively minor rockfall and his demise had obviously not gone unnoticed by his companions. Some time after the tumult of the crashing rocks, when the dust had subsided, they had returned to see what had happened. A small collection of stones was placed over the body and a fire lit above it. In the hearth there, too, split and broken small mammal bones look like the remains of a funeral feast. When the ceremony was at an end, the hearth appears to have been covered over with soil while the fire was still burning. Six more skeletons were uncovered, several showing healed wounds. Of these, Shanidar IV was found to be lying on pollen remains. Under the microscope of Mme. Arlette Leroi-Gourhan, a Paris paleobotanist, these pollens were shown to be not only the usual kinds of trees and grasses, but also pollen from at least eight species of flowers, apparently woven into branches of a pine-like shrub. No accident of nature could have deposited such remains so deep in the cave. As Solecki writes:

'Someone in the Last Ice Age must have ranged the mountainside in the mournful task of collecting flowers for the dead ... It seems logical to us today that pretty things like flowers should be placed with the cherished dead, but to find flowers in a Neanderthal burial that took place about 60,000 years ago is another matter ... In the millions of years of evolution that began with ape-like hominids in Africa, it is among the Neanderthals that we have evidence of the first stirrings of social and religious sense and feelings: the obvious care with which the lame and crippled were treated, the burials – and the flowers.'

In view of the refinement of ceremonial connected with death among the Neanderthals, we are obliged to assume that some concern with and about death began to emerge even earlier and, indeed, if all the data were available to us, that we should probably find continuities from forms that preceded the Neanderthal. We have to try to put ourselves into the skin of the earliest men. Life was all they knew and understood. They had no way of conceptualizing death, but the evidence is clear that they thought about it. As human cultures developed we find several themes emerging. One is the death and rebirth theme. Arnold van Gennep[9] in 1909 saw 'regeneration' as a law of life and of the universe: the energy which is found in any system gradually becomes spent and must be renewed at intervals. For him, regeneration is accomplished in the social world by what he called the 'rites of passage' – given expression from earliest times in the rites, among others, of death and rebirth. We find skeletal remains of bodies of Cro-Magnon man buried in the foetal position and are able to interpret this (from the myths of those peoples where the practice survived until recently) as a desire to facilitate the rebirth of the departed into a new life. The practice of wrapping the body in shrouds also echoes the covering of the foetus by membranes, and the cleansing of the body of the dead is a ritualistic equivalent (perhaps magical) of the cleansing of the newborn. This magical theme is associated with hunting and foraging peoples.

Another theme, associated with patriarchal and stock-raising groups, has to do with the idea that in death a person would continue to lead the same kind of existence that he or she had led during life, and so food and implements and weapons were left with the deceased to take with them and to be of use to them in a continuing existence.

At some time in the developing self-awareness of our forerunners an animistic theme arose, primarily among matriarchal and agricultural peoples. These primitive men explained the processes of inanimate nature by assuming that living spirits, possessed of capacities similar to their own, are within the inanimate object, and in parallel fashion explained to themselves the phenomenon of human life, believing that each man has within himself a mannikin or animal that dictates his activities – this miniature man is the primitive's soul. Sometimes the soul was conceived of as a bird. The Bororos of Brazil, still today, fancy that in that shape the soul of a sleeper passes out of his body at nighttime and returns when he awakens.

Lastly the soul is pictured as being a man's breath (*anima*). Right into modern times the 'last breath' has meant more than a mere metaphor. It expresses the belief that there departs from the dying in the final expiration something tangible, capable of separate existence – the soul. Among the ancient Romans custom imposed a sacred duty on the nearest relative to inhale the 'last breath' of the dying. This idea persists in the sanctity attached to the last kiss.

But to return to early man, the idea, as it evolves, of the spirit leaving the body at death in one form or another became the source of intense fears. Rites of all kinds became established that were designed to speed the spirit away from the living group, to make sure that it stayed away and would not return to harm the survivors. The rationale was that the spirit would resent having been deprived of its body in death and would return to harass the living either from revenge or to find a new body to house it – or alternatively to take the living with it for company in the afterworld.

If a man died without being wounded it came to be thought that he must have been a victim of witches or sorcerers who associated with malevolent spirits. Until contact with Europeans, throughout Africa tribes still ascribed death to the magicians of a hostile tribe or to the malicious act of a neighbour, so that revenge was called for and blood feuds initiated. In Australia it was the same. Andrew Lang wrote, 'Whenever a native dies, no matter how evident it may be that death has been a result of natural causes, it is at once set down that the defunct was bewitched.'

From the inability to comprehend death there results a tendency to personify it, and myths are invented to account for its origin. Sometimes it is a taboo that has been broken. In New Zealand, Mani, the divine hero of Polynesia, was not properly baptized. In Australia a woman was told not to go near a certain tree where a bat lived; she infringed the prohibition, the bat fluttered out, and death resulted. The Ningphoos (of China) were dismissed from paradise and became mortal because one of them bathed in water that had been tabooed; Greek Pandora opened the forbidden box; biblical Eve ate the forbidden apple. These myths indicate that among many peoples death came to be seen as a punishment for wrongdoing, and this idea eventually led to rites of propitiation and then to those of repentance and atonement that developed into a line leading towards modern Western religions.

The rest comes into historical times, where we can see two streams in apparent opposition to each other. On the one hand ancestor worship, the honouring of the dead, and the regarding of the dead as permanently a part of the existing family – as in ancient Rome where the *genius* of the Roman house-father and the *inno* of the house-mother were worshipped. These were not the 'souls' of ancestors in our sense, but rather the male and female forms of a family or clan's powers of continuing itself by reproduction. Something of these feelings still exists in modern societies where the honoured dead of a family become a part of that family's social heritage.

It is a universal law of nature that functionless traits, functionless organs, and functionless individuals tend to be eliminated, and there has been no exception to this rule in the social groups of man until very modern times. In mentioning some of the practices that dealt with this aspect of life we have to remind ourselves that evolving customs all had meaning within the terms of the lives and cultures of early man, and we cannot place our own value judgments on them.

Almost universally among the groups of early tribal man even the revered elder was put aside if and when he was no longer capable of performing his role, or if his physical disabilities outweighed his social worth. These customs were carried out in some groups with the co-operation of the elders themselves and in others without it, and the customs themselves were compassionate in some tribes and in others less so, frequently depending upon the external circumstances of the tribe. Nomadic groups, on the whole, and those living in the most rigorous extremes of climate in the arctic or in deserts, were simply not able to carry the burden of any nonproductive person and were obliged to dispose of them promptly.

Among some Eskimo tribes it was the practice for an old person who could no longer perform any tasks (an old woman, say, who had lost her teeth and could no longer chew leather to soften it for making boots, or an old man who had become decrepit) 'voluntarily' to leave the shelter of the family's hut and expose himself to death by freezing on the ice. In a nomadic tribe of central Africa, when old age made a person a burden to his group, at the time when the group moved on it left him behind with a piece of meat and the egg-shell of an ostrich filled with water, so that he could survive only as long as these meagre supplies lasted. Among the Yakuts of Siberia old people begged their children to end their lives and a funeral feast was held for three days. Then the children led their parents into a forest and prepared a grave in which they buried them alive with arms, utensils, and provisions. The Yerkla-mining of Australia left the dying comfortably near a fire and abandoned them; the Baumanas of (formerly) French Sudan abandoned their dying with loud cries intended to frighten away the spirits; the Selung of the Mergui archipelago off the coast of Burma took the dying to an uninhabited island and left them there; the Dorachos of Central America took the dying to a forest; the natives of Natilevu in Fiji placed the dying into a grave with food and water – as long as they could make use of these the grave remained open; the Hottentots buried their moribund alive or left them in a cleft in the mountains.

Stable groups in more benevolent environments were able to, and usually did, ease the senile out of their councils and lives more kindly. In the folklore of all parts of the world, and in many customs that survived in rural areas right into this century, we have abundant evidence that remains to attest to these practices. In rural Norway, in South Germany, and in parts of the Punjab, to this day it is a practice for the father and mother to retire to a kind of dower house on their property when their oldest son marries and is able to manage their land. This symbolic stepping aside is a relic of more drastic earlier practices.

If we now pick up the thread again at the beginning, we can see that all the beliefs and practices we have referred to are extensions – perhaps we might call them ultimate byproducts – of the vastly increased complexity of the brain that marked the emergence of mankind, and of the quality of the enlarged neocortex that impelled our species to seek causes for events and purposes or meaning for life. But this same brain had other extensions and other ultimate byproducts that included the use and then the making of tools, and this extension (as well as the one leading from primate sociality and primate communication to human groups and languages) like almost everything else in nature had an accelerating feedback effect. It promoted changes in the social systems from gathering and, probably, scavenging, economies, to hunting, and in turn to agricultural and then industrial ones.

Now we are standing at the frontier of a new technological stage. In Western societies we see this involving a break-up of traditional family patterns. The requirements of technology speed the flow of information and at the same time facilitate it, increasing the gap between generations and decreasing the value of the knowledge accumulated in the minds of the elders. Attitudes towards death are, and have always of necessity been, closely intertwined with attitudes towards the family or clan. The recent diminution of the value of the elder to his society has gone hand-in-hand with a loss of respect in general – a loss of the attitude of respect – and with a loss of a sense of attachment to the social unit, a loss of reverence for death and of concern with the hereafter. Present attitudes in technological societies show concern only with the here and now, and with an individual life as and for itself, disconnecting it from its place in a family lineage and from its social group. For this reason, because it is believed to be all that there is, every moment of an individual's life seems to be very important and is clutched at. Where hope of future existence and faith in remaining an eternal part of a family's life is lost, all our ingenuity becomes focused on extending the life we have for as long as we can and filling it with as much experience as possible.

Thus at the present time many find themselves emotionally back with those primitive peoples who could conceive no life but the one they knew and who provided their dead with artifacts to enable them to continue it. The contemporary version is an almost obsessive concern with the prolongation of an individual's life by all available means, including the wilder excesses of heroic surgical technology and even the freezing of bodies for future resuscitation.

It would seem that we have come to a point where we have a need for education towards an understanding of life as a whole and of death as a biological function. Surveying the panorama of the evolution of life on earth in its totality, we may discern a continuum arising in inorganic matter and progressing from the simplest forms to increasing complexity, ultimately achieving self-awareness and a sense of concern about individual destiny. But whether we hold life to be a divine gift or an inevitable consequence of the chemical properties of matter, death is in either case an inherent part of it, and indeed essential for its continuation.

Notes

(1) A. I. Oparin, *The Chemical Origin of Life* (1964).
(2) A. Gaudry, *Les ancêtres de nos animaux dans les temps géologiques* (1888).
(3) J. H. Fabre, *Social Life in the Insect World* (1937).
(4) Ann Moreton, 'Spiders', in *Smithsonian* 2, 5 (1971).
(5) Betty Carter, 'Salmon', in *Smithsonian* 2, 7 (1971).
(6) John C. Lilly, *The Mind of the Dolphin* (1967).
(7) Sylvia Sikes, *The African Elephant* (1970).
(8) Ralph Solecki, *Shanidar* (1971).
(9) Arnold van Gennep, *The Rites of Passage*, trans. Monique Vizedom and Gabrielle Gaffee (1960).

12

Psychedelics and the experience of death

Stanislav Grof and Joan Halifax-Grof

•

If we consider the relevance of death to human life, it is surprising to see the denial and avoidance to which death and dying have been subjected in Western societies. Terminal disease and death are not regarded as a meaningful part of life, but as an unpleasant reminder of man's inability to master and control nature. A dying person is someone who has nothing more to contribute. Very few people believe that there is a lesson to be learned from the encounter with dying and death.

The contemporary approach to a dying person is dominated by an effort to delay death by all means available. Most individuals die in hospital wards or nursing homes surrounded by life-maintaining technology. The companions of such dying people are infusion bottles and tubes, electric pace-makers, artificial kidneys, and monitors of vital functions. This intensive concern with the mechanical prolongation of life has suppressed the concern with the quality of a dying individual's remaining days and the relevance of death itself. Contemporary medical care generally excludes the emotional, philosophical and spiritual needs of the dying. Religion offers little help. We have been deprived of the opportunity to participate in the death of others or prepare ourselves for this ultimate experience. Many dying people are thus facing a profound crisis; basic and total since it affects simultaneously the biological, emotional, psychological, and spiritual aspects. Yet psychiatrists, psychologists, and other members of the helping professions have not until recently identified this area as one where sensitive help is urgently needed. There has also been a lack of interest in important related issues such as personality changes in dying individuals, subjective experiences associated with the process of dying, the effect of near-death experiences on survivors, and the psychological, philosophical, and spiritual implications of the death–rebirth experience.

Western attitudes contrast sharply with those found in less technologically developed societies, particularly ancient and Eastern cultures where death is treated as an important part of the life process. Learning to die was considered an integral aspect of living. Emphasis is placed on understanding dying as a means of comprehending living. In various mystery religions, temple mysteries, and rites of passage performed over millenniums in many different cultures of the world, disciples are guided to experience death and rebirth. This is believed to result in spiritual enlightenment. At the same time, this symbolic death prepares the human being for the actual experience. The ancient books of the dead, such as those of Egypt and Tibet, were considered manuals preparing a person for ritual death and rebirth, as well as for the actual experience of death. In many pre-modern cultures, elaborate religious and social rituals were developed in order to give effective support to a person facing impending death.

The increasing psychological and academic awareness of the enormous practical and theoretical importance of death has only taken place in the last decade. Here we would like to focus on psychedelic therapy with dying individuals, an approach that we consider on the basis of our clinical experiences to be of great practical and theoretical relevance for the problem of dying and death. In our own research, LSD-assisted psychotherapy with persons dying of cancer proved to be a powerful therapeutic technique that can not only alleviate the emotional and physical suffering associated with dying, but also, often dramatically, transform the individual's concept of death and his attitude towards it. In addition, the observations and data obtained in this research have important theoretical implications for understanding the process of dying.

Although psychedelic therapy represents a relatively recent development, its roots reach far back into the prehistory of mankind. Since time immemorial man has known and used various mind-altering substances that can break through the membrane of everyday consciousness. Such compounds with psychedelic properties are usually extracts from various plants, less frequently materials of animal origin. Reports about hallucinogenic drugs can be found in Chinese scriptures as early as 2700 BC.[1] The legendary divine potion soma of the ancient Indian Vedas was used by the Indo-Iranian tribes several millenniums ago; according to Gordon Wasson,[2] soma was the mushroom *Amanita muscaria*, or fly agaric. Preparations from Indian hemp have been used in oriental countries for many centuries in folk medicine, meditational practices, and religious ceremonies, as well as for recreation and pleasure. In the Middle Ages, potions and ointments containing psychoactive plants, such as the deadly nightshade, thorn-apple, henbane and mandrake, were reputed to be used in the witches' Sabbath and in Black Mass rituals. Psychedelic plants have a long history in Pre-Columbian Indian cultures among the Aztecs, Olmecs, Mayans, and Incas. The most famous of these plants are the Mexican cactus *Lophophora williamsii* (peyote), the sacred mushroom *Psilocybe mexicana* (teonanacatl), several varieties of the morning glory (ololiuqui), and yage. A number of additional hallucinogenic plants have been used by tribes in Africa, South America, and Asia.

The long history of use of psychedelic drugs contrasts sharply with a relatively short history of scientific study of these substances. Although mescaline and bulbocapnine were studied in the early decades of this century, real interest did not develop until the early 1950s. Explosive development ensued on the discovery of LSD-25, accidentally made by the Swiss chemist, Albert Hofmann, in Sandoz laboratories. Since then, chemists have succeeded in identifying the active principles from the most famous psychedelic plants and preparing them in pure form for laboratory and clinical use. In the last two decades, these substances have been given to tens of thousands of psychiatric patients, mental health professionals, scientists, and artists.

Among those for whom psychedelic experiences had a profound and life-transforming influence was Aldous Huxley. His experiences with mescaline and LSD influenced in a decisive way his world view and his work. The inhabitants of his *Brave New World* ingest a chemical substance for relaxation and recreation; Huxley calls it 'soma', which is the name of the deified potion described in the ancient Vedas. In his novel, *Island*, he writes of 'moksha' medicine which gives the inhabitants of the island a mystical vision. This experience frees them from their fear of death and enables them to live more fully during their everyday life. Huxley himself was very deeply interested in this. When his first wife, Maria, was dying of cancer, he used during her final hours a hypnotic technique to remind her of mystical experiences she had had during her lifetime. In *Island* he describes a similar scene during the death of the character Lakshmi.

Through his psychedelic experiments, Huxley arrived at the conclusion that LSD experiences can make dying easier and raise man's final physiological act to the level of consciousness and perhaps even spirituality. In a letter that Huxley wrote in 1958 to Humphrey Osmond, a pioneer in LSD research who introduced him to psychedelic drugs, he specifically recommended the administration of LSD to dying cancer patients. Huxley was able to prove the seriousness of his proposal. In 1963, a few hours before he himself died of cancer, he asked his second wife, Laura, to give him 100 mcg of LSD. In her book *This Timeless Moment*[3] she gives a moving description of this event.

In 1963, Eric Kast of Chicago Medical School conducted his first experiments using LSD with cancer patients. His primary interest was in analgesia, and his approach was purely pharmacological. He found that LSD had a significant analgesic effect superior to dihydromorphinone (morphine) and meperidine (Demerol).[4,5] In addition, he observed in many patients relief from depression, improved sleep, and lessened fear of death.[6,7] Subsequently, Sidney Cohen,[8] inspired by his personal friendship with Aldous Huxley and stimulated by Kast's positive results, was able to confirm Kast's findings.

The potential of psychedelic therapy was systematically tested in a study conducted by a group of psychiatrists and psychologists at Spring Grove in Baltimore. The attention of this group was first focused on the needs of cancer patients in an unforeseen and tragic manner. In 1965, when this group was studying the effect of psychedelic therapy on alcoholic and neurotic patients, a middle-aged female staff member developed carcinoma of the breast accompanied by marked physical and emotional distress. A member of the psychotherapeutic team, Sidney Wolf, suggested that she might benefit from LSD-assisted psychotherapy. The outcome of this pioneering experiment was so encouraging that it was decided to investigate further. Connections were made with Sinai Hospital in Baltimore, where a group of surgeons headed by Louis Goodman offered their co-operation. In 1967, Walter Pahnke joined the Spring Grove group, initiated a research programme in this area, and became its principal investigator. After his tragic death in 1971, the first author took over the medical responsibility for this project. As of now, more than one hundred cancer patients have been treated by the Spring Grove group with psychedelic therapy. The psychoactive substances used as adjuncts to psychotherapy were diethylamide of lysergic acid (LSD-25) and dipropyltryptamine (DPT), a short-acting psychedelic compound with effects similar to LSD.

The findings and implications of this research can be divided into two major categories: (1) practical significance of alleviating the emotional and physical suffering of dying people; (2) theoretical significance, exploring the nature of the actual death process and the meaning of the symbolic death–rebirth experience for the living.

The study was conducted in co-operation between the Maryland Psychiatric Research Centre and Sinai Hospital in Baltimore.[9,10] Several primary criteria were used for the selection of the cancer patients for the program. The patient with malignancy should show signs of marked emotional distress, such as depression, anxiety, insomnia, tension, and psychological isolation. Another indication was a high degree of physical pain that did not readily respond to analgesic or narcotic medication. Since follow-up was an important part of the study, a reasonable survival expectancy of at least three months was an important condition. Serious cardiovascular problems, organic brain damage, and cerebral metastases were considered contra-indications for psychedelic psychotherapy. From the psychiatric point of view, there was a tendency to screen out patients with gross psychopathology, such as psychosis or borderline symptomatology.

The treatment procedure consisted of three mutually interrelated phases: a series of drug-free interviews with the patient and members of his family, the psychedelic session, and several drug-free interviews for the integration of the session experiences.

The preparation period usually lasted from eight to fifteen hours with an average of ten hours. The potential benefits and risks inherent in this form of therapy were openly discussed with the patient and his family; an informed consent was, of course, a necessary prerequisite. In the psychotherapeutic work, the primary focus was on the present situation, such as problems of facing and accepting the diagnosis, prognosis, and death; we did not confront the patient as a matter of routine with the fatal outcome of his illness. The therapists would discuss issues of diagnosis and prognosis when the patient was ready. Reliance was always placed on the intuitive sensitivity of the therapists. Although important intrapsychic conflicts were dealt with when they emerged during psychotherapeutic work, no sustained attempts were made to probe into deep conflict material or childhood traumas, as has been the case in the work with alcoholics, heroin addicts, and neurotics.

Many of the discussions with such patients revolved around philosophical and religious issues. An important goal of the preparation period was to establish close contact with the dying individual.

When we came to the patients' social background, much attention was paid to unresolved issues between the dying and family members, and to distortions of communication between the patient, family, and

hospital staff. Every possible effort was made to clarify personal interactions, introduce honesty into the situation, and open new channels of
understanding. Families were seen both with and without the patient
and encouraged to discuss their own feelings about death. There was a
general tendency to increase communication as much as possible in
order to overcome the psychological isolation that is so typical for
cancer patients.

When the major issues were explored and a relationship of trust
established between the patient and therapists, plans were made for the
actual psychedelic session. In a special interview on the day immediately
preceding the drug session, the patient received specific and comprehensive information and instructions concerning the unusual states of
consciousness induced by LSD (or DPT) and the best way of using
them constructively. This induction period was particularly interesting
from the anthropological point of view as it had many parallels with the
information an initiate would receive before entering into an arduous
rite of passage.

On the day of the session, the patient was given a dose of LSD,
ranging between 200 and 500 micrograms, or an intramuscular injection
of 90 to 120 mg of DPT, depending on which study he was participating
in. Most of the sessions were run in private rooms of Sinai Hospital;
however, when the physical condition of the patient allowed it, the
session was conducted in one of the two special treatment suites at the
Maryland Psychiatric Research Centre or in the patient's home. During
the drug session itself, the patient was encouraged to stay in a reclining
position, keep his eyes covered with eyeshades, and listen to selected
stereophonic music. According to our observations, such internalization
of the LSD session was conducive to the most profound and beneficial
experiences.

A male and female therapist stayed with the patient for the whole
period of drug action, which was between ten and fifteen hours in the
case of LSD and four to six hours in the case of DPT. When necessary
or appropriate, emotional support was given to the patient such as
reassuring touches, holding the patient's hand, or cradling him;
according to our experience this is more effective than talking. Whenever words were used in the first few hours of the session, it was usually
to encourage the patient to go deeper into the experience, confront all
the material that was emerging, and express his feelings freely. After
several hours of the session, when the major issues were resolved, the
patient was asked to talk about the experience if he cared to. Later, in the
termination period, family members were introduced into the situation;

not infrequently, this time spent together was found very valuable, and significant progress was made in family relationships.

On the following day and during the next week, the therapists helped the patient to integrate the LSD experience into his everyday life. In most cases, the contact with the patient and his family continued beyond this time. If necessary, the LSD session was repeated; some patients who survived a long period of time had up to six sessions over a period of several years. In some instances, we have followed the patient to the day of his death and then worked with surviving family members.

The changes observed in dying cancer patients in the course of psychedelic therapy were often dramatic and have occurred in various areas. Most frequent was the relief of depression, anxiety, tension, psychological isolation, and insomnia. This was not so surprising since similar results were previously observed in different categories of psychiatric patients. Rather unexpected was alleviation or even disappearance of severe physical pain in some patients. In the most dramatic cases, pain that could not be controlled by high dosages of narcotics disappeared for weeks or months after a single LSD session. But the most remarkable effect of psychedelic therapy has been a dramatic transformation of the concept of death. Some patients became open to such ideas as the primacy of mind over matter, the continuity of consciousness after dying, the soul's survival of death, or the concept of reincarnation.

Another consequence of psychedelic therapy that made the encounter with death easier was the specific changes in value judgments. These involved a shift from the rumination on the past and apprehension about the future towards greater emphasis on the here and now. There was also a definite trend towards losing interest in status, money, possessions, and ambitions and an increased appreciation of the simple things in life.

We cannot here discuss in detail the methodology of the cancer study and its results. We will give only in a brief summary of the data obtained in a group of thirty-one cancer patients treated by LSD-assisted psychotherapy. Interested readers can find more information and statistical data in several previous publications.[11,12]

According to the original research design, each patient was expected to complete selected psychological tests before and after treatment. This, however, turned out to be a rather unrealistic expectation as such tests require a degree of concentration that for many cancer patients is almost impossible because of physical pain and exhaustion. As a result, primary emphasis had to be placed on ratings by external observers, rather than on psychological tests. For this purpose a special rating scale was developed by Pahnke and Richards. This instrument made it possible to obtain values ranging from −6 to +6 reflecting the degree of the patient's depression, psychological isolation, anxiety, difficulty in management, fear of death, preoccupation with pain, and, since its recent revision, denial of the imminence of death. Ratings with the use of this instrument were made one day before and three days after treatment by attending physicians, nurses, family members, therapists, and co-therapists.

We then performed statistical tests on the pre- and post-session assessments as reflected by the values assigned to the patients by those who operated on the rating scale. The computations of the ratings were done separately for each of the individual subscales and also for representatives of the six categories of raters.

In addition, a composite index was obtained for each of the categories of distress by pooling the ratings of all the raters. Therapeutic improvement then was assessed by comparing the composite indexes from pre- to post-treatment. For gross assessment of the degree of improvement, one global index of the clinical condition was developed for each patient by collapsing the data from all individual raters for all the clinical categories measured.

The use of the global index made it possible to estimate the percentage of therapeutic success. 'Dramatic improvement' can be defined as increase of the global index of four or more points, and 'moderate improvement' as a gain of between two and four points; patients who show an increase of less than two points, or an equivalent decrease, can be considered as 'essentially unchanged'. According to this definition nine patients (29·0%) showed dramatic improvement following psychedelic therapy, thirteen (41·9%) were moderately improved, and nine (29·0%) were essentially unchanged. Only two patients had a lower global index in the post-treatment period; in both of these patients, the decrease was negligible (−0·21 and −0·51 points respectively).

The significance of psychedelic therapy with cancer patients transcends the narrow framework of the short-lived help to the patient. Times of death are times of crisis in any family. It seems that the bereavement period is affected by the degree and nature of conflicts in the relationship with the dying person that have preceded it. Relatives may have ambiguous feelings about the appropriateness of their decisions at that particular moment. There has been very little study of the relationship between the situation at the time when a relative was dying and the nature of the subsequent grief reaction. Practising psychiatrists are, however, well acquainted with the crucial importance of how a person copes with the death of a relevant emotional figure. Psychedelic therapy with cancer patients that includes the family members thus offers a unique opportunity to practise preventive medicine. By adequate therapeutic intervention, we have the opportunity to ease the agony of death for the one who dies and, at the same time, to help those who must continue their lives to absorb this deep trauma in a healthy manner.

In spite of their therapeutic potential, the wide non-medical use of psychedelic substances and restrictive legislature make the future of this treatment modality uncertain. Whatever the future fate of psychedelic therapy will be, the research described above introduced more optimism into an area which was viewed with much anxiety and despair. There is now hope that one day it will be possible to transform radically the experience of dying, by chemical means or by some powerful non-drug techniques.

Few ideas and beliefs have occurred in the history of mankind with the same degree of constancy and frequency as those related to the continuation of existence beyond the moment of biological demise. The concept of afterlife has taken many specific forms, but the basic underlying idea is the same: death does not terminate human existence entirely and in one way or another life or consciousness will continue. Sometimes the image of the afterworld is very concrete and real, not dissimilar to earthly existence. More frequently, the realms of the world beyond have special characteristics distinguishing them from anything known on earth. Many peoples have developed a concept of the posthumous journey of the soul, where the deceased has to undergo a complicated process of transitions through various levels and realms of the other world.

In psychiatric and psychological literature, the concept of after-life and of the spiritual journey after death has usually been treated as a manifestation of primitive magical thinking, or as an expression of reluctance and inability to accept the fact of human impermanence. Until recently it was hardly ever considered that the descriptions of ancient and aboriginal cultures concerning the posthumous adventures of the soul could reflect experiential reality. Reports of experiences of individuals who survived clinical death indicate that the concepts of such a journey represents actual maps of altered states of consciousness experienced by dying individuals. Psychedelic research has brought important additional data of a phenomenological and neurophysiological nature indicating that experiences involving complicated mythological, religious, and mystical sequences before, during, and after death might well be a clinical reality. The possibility of extricating this area from superstition and fantasy and subjecting it to scientific scrutiny is so intriguing that it deserves a systematic discussion.

Comparative studies of the concepts of after-life and of the posthumous journey of the soul reveal striking similarities between cultures and ethnic groups separated historically and geographically. The recurrence of certain motifs and themes in different time periods and remote countries is quite remarkable. The idea of the final home for the righteous after death, heaven or paradise, appears in many different cultures.

The concept of hell or purgatory, a place where the departed will be exposed to inhuman tortures, is as ubiquitous as that of heaven or paradise. Similarly to the various paradises, it is not a place where the deceased stay for ever; it is merely a transitional stage in the cycle of birth, death, and rebirth.

Another recurrent theme in escatological mythology is the judgment of the dead. Christian art abounds in images where devils and angels are fighting for the soul of the deceased, or in depictions of the Last Judgment with the just ascending into heaven and the damned devoured by the mouth of hell. The Moslem tradition speaks about a bridge over hell which all departed must cross. Believers are able to keep their balance and cross successfully; unbelievers will slip and plunge into the infernal abyss. A similar ordeal in the Zoroastrian religion involved the 'Bridge of the Separator'. Those who are found just easily pass across to eternal bliss; those who are found wicked are seized by the demon Vizarsh. In the oldest version of the Judgment of the Dead found in the Egyptian Book of the Dead dating back to about 2400 BC, the psychostasis takes place in the Hall of the Two Truths. The heart of the deceased is weighed against the feather of the goddess Maat symbolizing truth and justice. The balance is attended by the jackal-headed god Anubis, while the ibis-headed god Thoth records the verdict as an impartial judge. The triform monster Amemet, Devourer of the Souls, stands by ready to swallow those who have fallen through at the trial. The just are introduced by Horus to Osiris who accepts them into the pleasures of his kingdom. In the Tibetan version of the judgment scene found in the Bardo Thödol, the administrator of truth and justice is called Dharma-Raja, the King of Truth, or Yama Raja, the King of the Dead. He is adorned with human skulls and holds the mirror of karma that reflects every good and evil act of the dead. From the court lead six karmic pathways to separate lokas, realms in which the deceased will be reborn according to his credits and debits.

The fate of the departed is often represented as a path, a journey, or a specific sequence of events. Some of the descriptions appear to be primitive and naïve, others represent a complicated and sophisticated cartography of experience. There exist deep parallels between the basic characteristics of the posthumous journey of the soul as represented in various cultures and the experiences characterizing the shaman's journey, initiation in temple mysteries, or rites of passage.

The descriptions of the spiritual adventures of the dying and dead, whether presented in the form of aboriginal mythologies or in more sophisticated versions, such as in Tibetan Buddhism, have attracted very little attention from Western scientists. Eschatological mythology has been treated as an expression of a massive denial of man's impermanence and an attempt to overcome his fear of death and the unknown. This situation was not noticeably influenced by the fact that accounts of death and near-death experiences, and death-bed observations by physicians and nurses, showed great similarity to the ancient and aboriginal descriptions of the phenomenology of death. At least two exceptions should be mentioned in this context. Carl Gustav Jung, as a result of his extensive studies in comparative mythology, unusual intuitive capacity, and his own near-death experience recognized the extraordinary value of the Bardo Thödol and similar texts describing the post-mortem experiences for the understanding of the human mind. He saw them as manifestations of archetypes, transindividual matrices in our unconscious, that form an integral part of the human psyche and can under some conditions find expression in powerful individual experiences. Aldous Huxley suggested that such concepts as hell and heaven represent subjective realities that are experienced very convincingly in the states of mind induced by drugs or other techniques.

Systematic clinical research with LSD has brought ample evidence supporting the ideas of Jung and Huxley. Subjects unsophisticated in anthropology and mythology experience images, episodes, and even entire thematic sequences that bear a striking similarity to the description of the posthumous journey of the soul and the death–rebirth mysteries of various cultures. Psychedelic drugs have made it possible to study the deep parallels and unusual interrelations among actual near-death and death experiences, maps of the post-mortem journey developed by various cultures, psychological events occurring in rites of passage, temple mysteries, and other rituals focusing on death and rebirth, drug-induced states, and other instances of altered states of consciousness. The extended map of the human unconscious developed on the basis of observations from LSD research is applicable to all the related states described above.

Detailed phenomenological analysis of the content of LSD sessions of a larger number of individuals reveals a fascinating fact. These sessions not only contain general experiential matrices and sequences that are identical with those found in eschatological mythologies but are frequently expressed in terms of specific symbolisms of culture areas basically alien to the experiencer. Thus, the experience of heaven, hell, or judgment of the dead in European and American subjects do not necessarily follow the Judeo-Christian tradition, as one would expect. On occasion, unsophisticated subjects described, for example, detailed sequences from Hindu, Buddhist, and Jain mythology, or complex scenes from the little-known Egyptian Book of the Dead depicting the fights of the crew of the solar barge with its specific enemies in the darkness of the Tuat. Parallels of some of the experiences with the Tibetan Bardo Thödol are so striking that in the mid-sixties Leary, Metzner and Alpert,[13] recommended the use of this sacred text as a guide for psychedelic sessions. Similarly, death–rebirth sequences can be experienced by some subjects as identification with Christ's suffering, death on the cross, and resurrection. Others, however, tend to identify at this point with Osiris, Dionysus, Adonis, or the victims sacrificed to the Aztec sun-god. The final blow mediating the ego death can be also experienced as coming from the terrible goddess Kali from Shiva the Destroyer, from the Bacchantes, or the Egyptian god Set. In all this, the specific cultural symbolism can be very detailed and accurate.

The sophisticated structure of such sequences can transcend the educational background and training of the experiencer; the origin and nature of such information remains a mystery. To follow Jung's example and call these phenomena archetypal provides a label but does not solve the problem. Obviously, much more work awaits in the future for all serious researchers.

The far-reaching parallels between the experience of dying (and death) and LSD sessions can be demonstrated by describing an episode from the history of Dean, a 26-year-old black patient with advanced cancer of the colon who participated in our program of psychedelic therapy.

'In an advanced stage of his cancer, Dean suddenly developed severe uremia. Several years earlier, one of his kidneys had to be surgically removed because it was attacked by malignant growth. At this point, the ureter of the remaining kidney became obstructed by infection and Dean was developing symptoms of intoxication by his own waste products. The surgeons kept delaying the operation apparently questioning the meaningfulness of an intervention that would at best prolong Dean's life for several additional weeks.

'After Dean had spent eight days in progressively worsening uremia, we received an urgent telephone call from his wife at five o'clock in the morning. That night, Dean had seen Stan in a dream and wanted to discuss an issue that he considered most important. We arrived at the hospital about an hour later; by that time Dean's condition had deteriorated considerably, and he appeared to be in a coma. He was surrounded by several of his relatives who tried to communicate with him; there was no reaction except for an occasional quite incomprehensible mumbling. It was apparent that Dean's death was imminent. While Stan was comforting Flora and the relatives, trying to help them accept the inevitable, Joan sat down by Dean's side and talked to him gently, using her own westernized version of the instructions from the Bardo Thödol. In essence, she was suggesting that he move toward the light and merge with it, unafraid of its splendour. At a time when everybody in the room seemed to have accepted the situation, a quite unexpected thing happened. In the last moment, the surgical team decided to operate; without forewarning, two male attendants entered the room, transferred Dean to a four-wheeler and took him to the operating room. All the persons in the room were shocked by what appeared to be a brutal intrusion into an intimate and special situation.

'During the operation Dean had two cardiac arrests resulting in clinical death and was resuscitated on both occasions. When we visited him in the afternoon in the Intensive Care Unit (ICU), he was just recovering from anaesthesia. He looked at Joan and surprised us with an unexpected, yet accurate comment: "You changed your dress!" Unwilling to believe that somebody who was apparently comatose correctly observed and remembered such a subtlety, we started inquiring about the nature of his experiences on the morning of that day. It became obvious that he correctly perceived the people present in the room, their actions and conversations. He even noticed that at one point tears rolled down Joan's cheeks. At the same time, however, he was involved in a number of unusual experiences that seemed to be unfolding on at least three levels. He listened to Joan's voice and responded to her suggestions. The initial darkness was replaced by brilliant light, and he was able to approach it and fuse with it. Simultaneously, he saw a movie on the ceiling, a vivid reenactment of all the bad things he had done in his life. He saw a gallery of faces of all the people whom he had killed in the Korean War and all the youngsters he had beaten up as an adolescent hoodlum. He had to suffer the pain and agony of all the people whom he had hurt during his lifetime. While all this was happening, he was aware of the presence of God, who was watching and judging this karmic review. Before we left him that day, he emphasized how glad he was that he had had three LSD sessions. He found the experience of actual dying extremely similar to his psychedelic experiences and considered the latter an excellent training and preparation. "Without the sessions, I would have been terribly scared by what was happening, but knowing these states, I was not afraid at all."'

Dean's experience is very important. It offers more than a simple demonstration of the formal parallels between the situation of dying and the phenomenology of the LSD intoxication. Dean was one of the persons who actually experienced both states and could make a valid comparison between them. His explicit statement about the deep similarity between his experience of dying and the LSD sessions confirmed our own conclusions, based on clinical observations in psychedelic sessions, the study of anthropological and mythological literature, the analysis of accounts of survivors of clinical death, and, last but not least, on several situations similar to Dean's.

All this clearly indicates that the human unconscious contains matrices for a wide variety of experiences that constitute the basic elements of the spiritual journey of the dying. The techniques and circumstances that can activate these matrices and transform their latent content into a vivid conscious experience cover a very wide range. They involve psychedelic substances, sensory isolation as well as overload, sonic and photic driving, hypnosis, monotonous chanting and rhythmic dancing, sleep deprivation, fasting, and various techniques of meditation and spiritual practice. Some pathological states will have a similar effect; this is true for severe emotional and physical stress, exhausting diseases, intoxications, and certain injuries and accidents. For reasons that are not clear at the present state of research, the perinatal and transpersonal levels of the unconscious become activated in naturally occurring psychoses, in particular schizophrenia and melancholia.

In the dying, such unconscious matrices can become activated by many different mechanisms. The specific triggers in individual cases will depend on the personality of the subject, his mental and physical condition, type of illness, and specific organs involved. We will briefly review in this context only the most obvious factors of this kind. The studies of Heim,[14] Noyes, [15,16] Rosen,[17] and others have clearly demonstrated that a sudden confrontation with death can result in an unusual subjective experience even if the organism itself is intact. In this case, the only conceivable mechanism is psychological regression under the influence of severe emotional stress or shock. It is possible that a mitigated version of the same mechanism is also operating in individuals facing a less imminent prospect of death. In dying individuals there exists, however, a variety of deep organismic changes, which can function as triggers of unconscious matrices. Many diseases interfere with proper nutrition and sleep of the patient and are associated with various degrees of starvation and sleep deprivation.

Frequently inundation of the organism by toxic products is responsible for profound psychological changes. This is true especially in the case of hepatic and renal disease, since the liver plays an important role in the detoxification process of various noxious substances and the kidney eliminates the waste products of the organism. Mental changes are particularly profound when the individual suffers from a progressive involvement of the kidneys with subsequent uremia. A high degree of auto-intoxication can also result from disorders that are associated with disintegration of bodily tissues, as in cancer or wasting and degenerative diseases. Psychological concomitants of a physical disease are most easily understandable if the pathological process is affecting the brain; this occurs in patients with meningitis, encephalitis, head injuries, brain tumors, and other types of organic brain damage. Anoxia, insufficient supply of oxygen to the tissues of the body, is of such paramount significance as a trigger of unconscious matrices that it deserves a more detailed discussion. In dying individuals, anoxia is an extremely frequent condition. It can be caused by processes in the lungs reducing the degree of oxygen intake (emphysema, pulmonary tumors, pneumonia, tuberculosis, and others), by inadequate distribution of oxygen such as in the case of anemias and cardiac failure, or by interference with the enzymatic transfer of oxygen on a subcellular level. It is well known from many different sources that a limited supply of oxygen or an excess of carbon dioxide produces abnormal mental states. Experiments with the anoxic chamber have shown that lack of oxygen can produce unusual experiences quite similar to LSD. McFarland[18] has demonstrated that the psychosomatic reaction to anoxia is directly related to the pre-experimental personality of the subject. Neurotic persons have a much lower tolerance to the situation and tend to respond quite early by difficult psychosomatic symptoms. His findings show far-reaching parallels with the results of LSD research. In 1950, Meduna[19] published his book on therapeutic use of carbon dioxide in emotional disorders. The so-called Meduna mixture containing 70 per cent oxygen and 30 per cent carbon dioxide can produce after brief inhalation the whole range of experiences known from LSD sessions. The similarity is so close that this mixture can be used as a prognostic tool before LSD sessions; the nature of the subject's reaction to carbon dioxide predicts quite reliably the response of that person to LSD. It can also be used before the session to acquaint a subject with the unusual states of mind that he will experience under LSD, or after the LSD experience to work through residual problems that remained unresolved in the session. Manoeuvres restricting the supply of oxygen have been widely used through ages in the process of inducing unusual experiences. Thus, certain aboriginal rituals involve suffocation by mechanical means, near drowning, or smoke inhalation. According to some sources, the original form of baptism involved a forced situation of near drowning resulting in a profound death–rebirth experience. An anecdotal description of the interaction between a guru and his disciple can be mentioned in this connection. The guru holds the disciple's head under water for an excessive period of time and lets him surface only after repeated desperate signals. While the disciple, blue in his face and his eyes popping out of his head, is gasping for breath, the guru asks him, 'Do you want knowledge or air?' Indian pranayama uses periods of hyperventilation alternating with prolonged withholding of breath to induce a spiritual experience. Other Indian techniques involve obstruction of the larynx by the tongue twisted backwards, constriction of the carotid arteries, or prolonged suspension by the feet with ensuing long-term congestion of the blood in the head and brain anoxia. The Taoists advocate a technique of breathing during meditation where the intake of air is so slow and inapparent that a tiny feather placed in front of the nostrils remains unmoved.

It is possible that the similarities between LSD experiences and subjective concomitants of anoxia are more than accidental. Many hypotheses have been developed to explain the pharmacological and biochemical effects of LSD. There exists some laboratory evidence indicating that LSD might interfere with the transfer of oxygen on the enzymatic level. Abramson and Evans, who studied the effects of LSD on Siamese fighting fish (Betta splendens), described a variety of specific vegetative, motor, and behavioural responses to the drug. The fish responded by increased pigmentation and caricature-like postures and movements; the authors gave special names to some of these phenomena, such as the 'Cartesian diver', 'barrel-roll', and 'trance-like' effect. In a separate study, Weiss, Abramson, and Baron obtained similar effects using two inhibitors of tissue respiration, potassium cyanide and sodium azide, in nonlethal concentrations; some of these phenomena could also be induced by anoxia and asphyxia. Although direct laboratory evidence concerning the inhibitory effect of LSD on tissue oxidation is controversial and inconclusive, the possibility of such effect is extremely interesting from the point of view of our discussion.

We have already mentioned that anoxia is rather frequent in dying individuals. Thus, in the study conducted by Karlis Osis[20] on deathbed observations of medical doctors and nurses, anoxia was described most frequently by the attending physicians as the explanatory principle accounting for visions, apparitions, and other unusual experiences. If lack of oxygen and excess of carbon dioxide can produce effects similar to LSD, then a combination of these factors could be responsible for some of the unusual experiences accompanying and following clinical death. In those instances where death is caused by the cessation of the heart-beat, the tissues of the body can survive a certain time using the oxygen present in the blood and turning it into carbon dioxide. In the case of brain cells, this situation lasts for about ten minutes before irreversible damage occurs. It is conceivable that the brain processes at this time have their conscious concomitants. If we believe that consciousness is associated with subcortical areas of the central nervous system, then this time period would be of even greater duration, since the cellular elements in more archaic parts of the brain are less sensitive to lack of oxygen and can survive longer.

Under these circumstances, the deceased individual would experience what is called an altered state of consciousness similar to those induced by LSD or Meduna mixture. Activation of psychodynamic, perinatal, and transpersonal matrices in the unconscious could result in experiences of life review, divine judgment, hell, purgatory, heaven, or other elements of the posthumous journey of the soul as depicted in various traditions. Then there is the question of time. The person in an unusual state of consciousness experiences time in a way that is quite different from our everyday perception of clocktime. During several minutes of objective time, LSD subjects can subjectively experience entire lifetimes, centuries, millenniums, even aeons. Similarly, a dying individual can relive his entire life within several seconds and within minutes of clocktime he can experience an entire cosmic journey. Under these circumstances, one hour can be perceived as a second and one split-second can become eternity. Here the psychology of unusual states has to wait for its Einstein to construct the equations that govern these extraordinary transformations between objective and subjective space-time.

The most obvious objection to this concept is the alternative that is usually taken for granted – instant and permanent loss of consciousness at the time of clinical death, comparable to that occurring during general anaesthesia or following a brain concussion. Here the subjective accounts of survivors of clinical death indicate that there might be more than one alternative. Interesting observations regarding general anaesthesia can be mentioned here to show the complexity of the problems involved. In the so-called dissociative anaesthesia induced by ketamine (Ketalar), patients experience a variety of unusual states of mind while they appear to be unconscious to an external observer. The operations performed in this condition are possible not because consciousness is extinguished, but because it is drastically refocused. LSD subjects have occasionally relived all the sensations from operations performed under deep anaesthesia of a conventional type. In other experiments, patients were capable of reconstructing under the influence of hypnosis the conversations during an operation that had been conducted with the help of general anaesthetics.

If there is a reasonable possibility that the experience of dying might be a complex process, at least as complicated and ramified as life itself, the efforts invested in antiquity and in aboriginal cultures to this issue suddenly appear in a new light. In view of the psychological relevance of this event, it certainly makes sense to learn as much as we can about this process, familiarize ourselves with the maps of the posthumous journey, and, if possible, obtain practice and adequate training in the unusual states of consciousness that it entails. Many non-Western cultures have occasions on which their members get acquainted with unusual states of consciousness. In others, the death experience is regularly enacted within the framework of rites of passage. In our world, death takes the individual by surprise and finds him for the most part totally unprepared.

Specific procedures that make it possible to experience profound sequences of psychological death and rebirth and other perinatal and transpersonal phenomena might be, however, more than just training and preparation for the final transition. There are indications that what the individual has undergone during his lifetime actually modifies the way in which he will die. It seems that some of the struggle and agony associated with the process of dying in some persons is due to the fact that the physiological and biochemical changes in the organism activate various difficult unconscious matrices. Thus, at least part of the problem of dying might be related to unresolved conflicts from the individual's history and to the re-enactment of the agony of birth that has not been worked through and consciously integrated. An important observation from LSD psychotherapy can be mentioned to support this possibility. In patients who have had serial LSD sessions, the earlier LSD experiences usually contain much psychodynamic material and dramatic perinatal sequences. If the sessions continue, these areas can be completely worked through and all subsequent sessions are of a transpersonal, religious, and mystical nature. When these patients are given inhalations of Meduna mixture in the course of their LSD therapy, their response to carbon dioxide will change depending on the stage of LSD treatment. In the free intervals between early LSD sessions this mixture will evoke visions of abstract geometrical patterns and reliving of childhood memories. The same combination of gases administered later, at a time when these patients are working on perinatal material, will trigger sequences of the death–rebirth struggle. At the advanced stages of psycholytic treatment when LSD sessions are predominantly transpersonal in nature, the Meduna mixture will induce mystical and religious states, or even past incarnation experiences. Some direct evidence indicating that psychedelic sessions can change not only the concept of death and the attitude towards it, but the very nature and content of the experience of dying, comes from psychedelic therapy of persons dying of cancer. All the observations described above seem to support the point of view so clearly and succinctly expressed by Abraham de Sancta Clara, an Austrian Augustinian monk: 'The man who dies before he dies, does not die when he dies.'

The present difficulties in administering psychedelic therapy naturally raise the question of the practical relevance of the above discussion. Since the major objections against the professional use of LSD and other psychedelics are of an emotional rather than scientific nature, it is difficult at this point to predict the future of LSD therapy. The work with psychedelics has, however, made it possible to map this new territory, realize the nature of the problems involved, and discover certain therapeutic mechanisms applicable to this area. At the present time, many individual researchers are trying to develop non-drug alternatives to psychedelics based on the same general principles.

It is not necessary, however, to wait for relegalization of LSD therapy or development of new powerful non-drug techniques for altering consciousness. Closer examination reveals that unusual states of consciousness, similar to those produced by LSD, occur spontaneously in many dying individuals for reasons of a physiological, biochemical, and psychological nature. At the present state of knowledge, such unusual states are usually considered psychiatric complications and are suppressed by tranquillizers. According to our experience, a sensitive psychologist or psychiatrist can use at least some of these states constructively, in a way not dissimilar to an LSD experience. With adequate support and guidance, such episodes can prove to be very meaningful and beneficial for the dying individual. Such an approach necessitates however, a dramatic shift in our values from emphasis on mechanical prolongation of life to concern about the quality of the death experience.

A few words should now be said about the new relationship between religion and science that seems to be emerging from the study of unusual states of consciousness. At the present time, the prevailing feeling is that the discoveries and developments of science have discredited the validity of religious beliefs, The basic concepts and assumptions of religions if taken literally, appear naïve, childish, and absurd. Astronomers have charted vast areas of the universe and no space is left for celestial spheres, hierarchies of angels, or God himself. Geological and geophysical research established the structure and composition of the crust and core of the earth; hell was not discovered. What was attacked and discarded by contemporary science, however, is a primitive and naïve belief that the basic religious concepts have an objective existence in the three-dimensional physical universe as we experience it in usual states of consciousness. The observations from LSD research clearly indicate that the bliss of paradise, horrors of hell, and ecstatic rapture of salvation can be experienced with a vividness that surpasses our everyday perceptions. The matrices for these experiences appear to be an intrinsic part of the human personality.

Recognition and exploration of these dimensions is vital for a deeper understanding of human nature.

Notes

(1) W. A. Emboden, 'Ritual Use of Cannabis sativa L.: A Historical-Ethnographic Survey', in *Flesh of the Gods*. ed. P. Furst (1972).
(2) R. G. Wasson, *Soma: Divine Mushroom of Immortality*.
(3) L. A. Huxley, *This Timeless Moment* (1968).
(4) E. C. Kast, 'The Analgesic Action of Lysergic Acid Compared with

Dihydromorphinone and Meperidine' in *Bull. of Drug Addiction and Narcotics*, App. 27, 3517 (1963).

(5) *idem*, 'Pain and LSD-25: A Theory of Attenuation of Anticipation', in *LSD: The Consciousness Expanding Drug*, ed. D. Solomon (1964).

(6) *idem*. V. J. Collins, 'A Study of Lysergic Acid Diethylamid As An Analgesic Agent', in *Anaesth. Analg. Curr. Res.* 43, 285 (1964).

(7) *idem*. 'LSD and the Dying Patient' in *Chicago Med. Sch. Quart*, 26, 80 (1966).

(8) S. Cohen, 'LSD and the Anguish of Dying', *Harper's Magazine* 231, 69 (1965) and 231, 77 (1965).

(9) W. N. Pahnke, A. A. Kurland, W. Richards, L. E. Goodman, 'LSD-Assisted Psychotherapy with Terminal Cancer Patients', in *Psychedelic Drugs*, eds., R. E. Hicks, P. J. Fink (1969).

(10) W. Richards, S. Grof, L. E. Goodman, A. A. Kurland, 'LSD-Assisted Psychotherapy and the Human Encounter with Death', in J. Transpers, *Psychol*, 4, 121 (1972).

(11) S. Grof, W. N. Pahnke, A. A. Kurland, L. E. Goodman, 'LSD-Assisted Psychotherapy in Patients with Terminal Cancer', a paper at the Fifth Symposium of the Foundation of Thanatology, New York City (November 1971).

(12) S. Grof, 'LSD and the Human Encounter with Death', *Voices*, 8, 64 (1972).

(13) T. Leary, R. Metzner, R. Albert, *The Psychedelic Experience: A Manual Based on the Tibetan Book of the Dead* (1964).

(14) A. Heim, 'Notizen uber den Tod durch Absturz', in *Jahrbuch des Schweizer Alpenklub*, 27, 327 (1892).

(15) R. Noyes, 'Dying and Mystical Consciousness' in *J. Thanatol*, 1, 25 (1971).

(16) *idem*, 'The Experience of Dying' in *Psychiatry*, 35, 174 (1972).

(17) D. Rosen, in a personal communication.

(18) R. A. McFarland, in *Fatigue and Stress Symposium* (January 1952).

(19) L. J. Meduna, *Carbon Dioxide Therapy* (1950).

(20) K. Osis, *Deathbed Observations of Physicians and Nurses* (1961).

13
Illusion – or what?
Rosalind Heywood

•

I must first make clear the task I have been asked to undertake. It is to consider what, if anything, certain experiences of my own suggest *to me* about the possible nature of life after death. I emphasize 'to me', since I cannot share the experiences with other people. They give private, not public, evidence. Moreover, that evidence causes a sharp conflict within myself. For many years the orthodox scientific view that all our experiences can be explained in terms of physics and chemistry has been conditioning my reasoning side to find the survival of consciousness after death of the body, in whatever form, about as unthinkable as intangible steam or fluid water would be to one who only knew H_2O as solid ice. Yet, as against that, I am driven to ask, 'Is it honest to dismiss one's own real-seeming experiences because other people, however distinguished, assume that they must be illusions due to silly wishful thinking?' And one has to remember Einstein's words that all knowledge of reality starts from experience and ends with it.

In this paper, then, I shall try to convey the impressions made on me *at the time* by my own experiences (other people have had thousands more impressive) rather than by my conditioned analysis of them; in other words I shall be writing, not as an orthodox scientist observing from the outside, but as one of the half-blind travellers who have no choice but to stumble through the dark wood from the Here-and-Now towards the mystery of death. That we have no choice entitles the humblest of us to peer up from the undergrowth for any gleam of light which may hint at the nature of that mystery; and we can remind ourselves that scientific orthodoxy is always changing. 'The existence of most things in the universe,' says Professor Michael Polanyi, 'must be based on principles that are missing from the current scientific world view.'[1]

Six years ago I was asked to write a short note for a symposium, *Man's Concern with Death*, as to whether I felt that consciousness continued beyond the grave, or the end of us all was oblivion. The tentative guesses I then hazarded in favour of survival were prompted in part by a few flashes of altered consciousness, in which I seemed to feel contact being made with me by discarnate sparks of consciousness, which were vivid, purposeful and apparently existing in a wider aspect of reality, and in part by the great physicist Schroedinger's emphatic insistence that 'in no case will there be a loss of personal experience to deplore. Nor will there ever be.'[2] That phrase made a powerful impact on me.

Since then I have had further fleeting intimations of contact with sparks of consciousness, which seem to exist outside the physical world as it is perceived *via* the senses, and Schroedinger's insistence has helped me not entirely to reject them, however strong the conventional materialist pressure to assume that physical world to be the only 'real' one. Such intimations also seem to the experient a little less crazy in the light of discoveries by pioneer physicists that the physical world itself is very different from what our senses tell us. To begin with, it seems that we only get our information about it at second hand. 'When we thought we were studying the external world,' said Sir Herbert Dingle, 'our data were still our observations; the world was an inference from them.'[3]

It is startling to realize the extraordinary inferences drawn by physicists today about the nature of the external world. Take what J. B. Oppenheimer says about one of its basic elements, the electron. The Mad Hatter isn't in it.

'If we ask, for instance, whether the position of the electron remains the same, we must say, "No"; if we ask whether the electron's position changes with time, we must say, "No"; if we ask whether it is at rest, we must say, "No"; if we ask whether it is in motion, we must say, "No".'[4]

Next, take Professor Henry Margenau, another outstanding physicist, on the general situation in physics. He has pointed out that science no longer contains absolute truths; there there are fields which are wholly non-physical; that in ordinary sense perception the conversion of the physiological stimulus into a conscious response is tantamount to a miracle, and that Mach's principle (that the inertia of all objects on the earth is determined by the total mass of the universe around it) is as mysterious as unexplained psychic phenomena.[5,6]

It is worth reading these passages twice. Can one wonder that Eddington says, 'I very much doubt if anyone has the faintest idea of what is meant by the reality of anything but our own egos'.[7]

These are but a small sample of many such statements made by pioneer physicists, and it is interesting that, in spite of them, yesterday's materialism is still widely looked on as the Holy Office which knows all the answers. (It is as if we little men *require* the Universe to be within our comprehension.) But for those whose experience can clash with these answers, it comes as a great relief to hear that the world as experienced *via* the senses is not the basic reality from which all experience must be judged, but merely a man-made abstraction from something wider. Not, of course, that an official habitat for experiences such as mine has yet been found; but pioneer physics does perhaps hint that contact with that something wider may be less *unthinkable* than is now assumed. Einstein, for instance, wrote that when a theoretical physicist told him he was inclined to believe in telepathy, he replied, 'This has probably more relation to physics than to psychology'.[8] One day it may be possible to record such experiences without being credited with exaggerated presuppositions and beliefs which one may not hold.

I will start at the Here-and-Now end of the wood by describing a type of experience which, on the level of a pianist who can just manage chopsticks with one finger, I have quite often, and which seems very like my occasional contacts with what appear to be wider aspects of reality. This resemblance may suggest that certain kinds of relationship are continuous throughout all its aspects. The experience is of relating to other living persons or to distant events by some means other than the *known* senses and it is relatively widespread, though little publicized by many who have it, since some people look on such an idea as weird or uncanny and others dismiss it as impossible nonsense. I should perhaps say that to me the experience of relating in this way seems as normal as sight or hearing. Nowadays it is usually labelled extrasensory perception or ESP, but that term may be misleading as the limits of sensory perception are not known.[9] It has only recently been discovered that rats will remove their progeny from X-rays of which human beings are unconscious, that bees can see by ultra-violet light, and that dolphins and bats can steer by sonar. Moreover, the word extrasensory seems to imply a break in the continuity of perception which it is hard to envisage. Can there be an iron curtain in nature? It is encouraging to find this doubt shared by Professor Margenau. He writes: 'I cannot believe that there are any discrete quantum-like transitions in human experience. There must be an area where wholly inexplicable things merge with those we understand as normal happenings'.[10]

For purposes of study investigators have divided ESP into four categories: precognition, retrocognition, clairvoyance (reaction to physical events) and telepathy (reaction to another person's mental state); but there seems no reason to think that these are not the same capacity functioning in different situations. If so, ESP may have a more fluid relationship than surface consciousness to what we call space and time. But then, says Heisenberg, 'When we get down to the atomic level the objective world of space and time no longer exists.'

As is well known, apparent ESP has been recorded anecdotally throughout the ages, though in classical times it was called divination or magic and in the main was looked on as supernatural. But not all first-class thinkers appear to have held that view. Democritus, for instance, believed that by means of mental images senders could transmit their own states to distant recipients, and he also thought that 'images which leap out from persons in an excited and inflamed condition ... yield especially vivid and significant representation'.[11] It would seem that, like many people today, he looked on ESP as a natural capacity which was stimulated by emotional situations and relationships. This approach brings to mind the warning dreams of Caesar's and Pilate's wives and of Elisha's mental tapping of the king of Syria's military secrets. 'Will ye not show me,' complained the king, 'which of you is for the king of Israel?' 'None, my lord, O King,' replied his servants, 'but Elisha, the Prophet, telleth the king of Israel what thou sayest in thy bedchamber.'

With the onset of the Age of Science ESP (along with all other forms of alleged *psi*) was demoted from its supernatural status; in fact it was not allowed, officially, to exist at all. For one thing, it did not conform to the principles on which the new science was based; for another, throughout the ages it had always been disgustingly contaminated by fraud and superstition. There is a nice story, quoted by Dr George Owen of Trinity College, Cambridge, on BBC television (April 4 1967), which gives an early illustration of most scientists' stern (and continuing) disapproval. In 1695 scholars were showing an interest in a Cambridge building in which poltergeist disturbances were said to be taking place. It is recorded, said Dr Owen, that

'there came by Mr Isaac Newton, a very learned man, Fellow of Trinity College, and seeing several scholars about the door, "Oh ye fools," says he, "will you never have any wit? Know ye not that all such things are mere cheats and imposters? Fie! go Home! For Shame"; and he would not go in.'

Later on, we remember, Newton himself got into trouble with his fellow scientists for having put forward the idea of an 'occult force', gravity!

During the last fifty odd years, however, in spite of this continuing official disapproval, increasingly coercive experimental evidence for ESP of mundane events has been produced in a number of countries from the USA to the USSR, and, ironically enough, research into it has of late been encouraged in some orthodox high places on account of the fear that an enemy might learn to repeat Elisha's gift of probing military secrets by telepathy. This research and the apparent dematerialization of the basic elements of the physical world by pioneer physics has slightly softened the scientific mental climate. For instance, the American Association for the Advancement of Science has admitted the Parapsychological Association to affiliation, the British Journals *Nature* and the *New Scientist* have published descriptions of experiments in it, and during the last few years the late Professors Sir Cyril Burt and C. D. Broad, Professors Sir Alister Hardy and H. H. Price, Mr Arthur Koestler and Dr John Beloff, among others, have discussed it in print in relation to physics and psychology.

But they are in a minority. Such weakening among members of the intellectual élite causes the majority of orthodox scientists, who still believe that all human experience can be explained in terms of physics and chemistry, to recoil in horror. In July, 1973, I heard Dr Bronowski lament on the air:

'I am infinitely saddened to find myself surrounded by a terrible loss of nerve, a retreat from knowledge into ... extrasensory perception and mystery. They do not lie along the line of what we are now able to know if we devote ourselves to it: an understanding of man himself.'

In the following September I also heard a professor of mathematics, Dr John Taylor, say in a broadcast: 'I would, *as a scientist* [my italics], try to take the position that I can completely describe all of reality by one aspect of it, "the physical".' And in a letter to *The Times* of 6 December, Mr James Friday, archivist of the Royal Institution, dismissed 'ESP and other psychic phenomena as the pure fiction they, in fact, are.' These three quotations represent the many serious scientists who still endorse the majestic dismissal, in the words of one of them, of 'all forms of ... ESP-ism' as 'spurious sentimental substitutes, filling the vacuum created by the loss of effete theological superstitions'.

I will now do my tiny bit towards filling that vacuum by considering some of my own ESP-type experiences, which range from telepathy between the living to an apparent awareness of the invisible, yet purposeful, presence of my recently departed friends – and, on a few occasions, even beyond.

My invisible friends are quite different from ordinary aimless hallucinations, for which a number of explanations can be put forward, just because they are *purposeful*. They are also so 'real-seeming' that at the time my intuitive side cannot help welcoming them as the friends they purport to be, whatever doubts my reasoning side feels afterwards. One cannot cut one's friends. Nor is it honest to *assume* that the faint hints they appear to provide about other aspects of reality are spurious. When writing about them I shall cut down the use of such safeguarding words as purported, ostensible, apparent and so on, for simplicity's sake; but this does not mean that I feel I *know* them to be what they seem to be. Neither does anyone else *know* that they are not.

The incapacity of my reasoning side to accept these invisible presences as anything but illusions was slightly weakened three years ago by a fleeting altered state of consciousness which left a double effect. To some extent it released me from looking at the physical world solely from the point of view of an outside observer, as modern man has been conditioned to do – even though contemporary physicists have shown this to be impossible. It also seemed to bring that physical world itself within the inter-related whole, which hitherto I had only appeared to glimpse in terms of consciousness. William James once said that an experience cannot be conveyed to those who have not had one similar, and I am only too well aware that this experience, expressed in words designed to deal with the so-called objective world as revealed through the senses, will sound childish. But as it modified my outlook it must be told.

One sunny morning I stepped onto my balcony to look at my pampered flowers. Suddenly. Like a bullet, the awareness struck me: *physically*, they and I were one, *physically* they and I and the trees and the grass and the soil in the garden – and everything on earth – were made of that earth, were part of it. And the earth was part of the solar system, and so on, right up to the whole universe. All, however diverse, was one. I did not think it; I experienced it.

This, of course, is what physicists today are telling us: that they have de-materialized the fundamentals of the physical world into a *network of inter-relationships* so mysterious that the only known way to describe them is by mathematical models. Bertrand Russell once wrote that 'physics is mathematical not because we know so much about the physical world but because we know so little. It is only its mathematical properties that we can discover.' And Einstein went further. 'As far as the laws of mathematics refer to reality they are not certain; as far as they are certain they do not refer to reality.'

But that is an intellectual approach, and an intellectual approach by itself differs from that magnificent sense of belonging as much as knowing that a fire burns differs from putting one's hand in it. Donne knew what it felt like. 'No man is an island entire of itself; every man is an island, a peece of the maine.' And yet – though in one's everyday state of mind this seems a paradox – within that unity diversity remained. Sparrows were still sparrows and men, men. And like were specially related to like.

'The world is like one great animal,' said Plotinus, '. . . Like parts may be discontinuous, yet have a sympathy in virtue of their likeness, so that the action of an element spatially isolated cannot fail to reach its remotest counterpart.' (*Plotinus Enn* 4.4.)

Nowadays, since Kammerer and Jung, serious thinkers are once more pondering the mystery of like to like within the whole. Perhaps it may turn out to be as basic a law as that of causality.

Since I wrote tentatively in 1969 about the possibility of contact with discarnate consciousness, existing in other aspects of reality, my balcony experience, and also an increasing sense of like being drawn to like within a total inter-relationship, have helped to make the idea of such consciousness less unthinkable. So, as I said, has further reading about the demolition by physics of our commonsense assumption that matter, time and space *as we perceive them* are the basis of, rather than an abstraction from, reality. Recently, too, it has been borne in on me how much these apparent discarnate contacts resemble my lifelong telepathic interaction, which I do not doubt, with living persons whom I love, or who need my help, or with whom I am linked by common interests. From now on, then, I shall write on the frankly speculative hypothesis that there may be continuity between 'physical' and 'ultra-physical' and that what seems to be my contact with the latter may possibly contain hints as to the nature of discarnate existence, or at least as to the barriers which prevent our awareness of it.

In the hope of conveying this apparent continuity of relationships, I will first describe a very recent telepathic interaction with my husband, with whom I relate in this way most frequently, before going on to other interactions which seem to be with the discarnate. Such mundane interaction has the advantage which, even if genuine, meetings across the apparent divide cannot have, of being as watertight evidentially as any spontaneous occurrence of the kind can ever be, seeing that chance, hoaxing or what you will can always be invoked to explain away any single event. The following account was written at the time.

On Tuesday, 11 September 1973, a car from the BBC was due at 4.30 p.m. to fetch me from my home in Wimbledon to take part in a radio programme. It being a beautiful evening, at 4.25 I went out and sat down on the step at the lefthand end of our doorstep, to enjoy the sunlight through the copper beech and tall shrubs which divide our half-moon drive from the road. To keep clean I sat on the brown envelope containing my BBC script on which I had made some notes.

A big bay-window juts out to the left of the doorstep with, in front of it, tall luxuriant berberis. To the left of these, set farther back, is the garage, facing the road. My husband had also come out of the house just before I sat down on the step and I heard him start up his car in the garage to go for some golf on our local course, which is a mile or so away. I could not see him from where I sat but he tells me that, when he drove forward into the road, from *outside* our lefthand exit he saw the BBC car reverse and stop for me outside our righthand exit. When driving out, he could have seen nothing low down to the right *within* the exit, even had I already got up, not only because the window and berberis blocked part of the view, but also because our daughter-in-law's parked car blocked the rest. From the road outside the trees and shrubs along our boundary wall make the doorstep invisible.

As I hurried out to the BBC car to save time (it was approaching rush hour) I called a last goodbye to my husband, but getting no answer and seeing no car, I realized he had gone. About five to ten minutes later I also realized that I had forgotten the envelope on which I had been sitting. At this I felt a spurt of emotion on account of my notes on the script, and told the driver, adding that there was no time to go back for it. Thereafter I was worried by a mental picture of my husband, who is eighty-three, dashing into London with it during the rush hour when this was not necessary. I told myself not to be silly as I should have time to telephone home on arrival at the BBC before he got back from golf, but I continued to worry in spite of scolding myself. On arrival at the BBC I hastened to the reception desk to telephone, only to be told that a message had already come from my husband that he was on his way with the envelope. He arrived, astonishingly soon, at 5.28. During his drive he had scribbled the following message on the back of my envelope on his knee whenever he was stopped by a red light.

'When I got to the golf course, "Orders" said, "Don't play, go home." I did so and put the car in the garage. I was about to go in by the side door when "Orders" said, "No, go in by the front door", and there I found this envelope which you had obviously meant to take with you.' (Signed) F.

'Orders' is the name my husband and I give to apparently irrational impulses to action. On returning home I told him that Professor John Taylor, who had chaired our programme and to whom I had jokingly shown his message, had said that he must have seen the envelope on the doorstep. My husband commented on this that he had felt annoyed at being 'ordered' to go into the house by the front door, because our daughter-in-law's car was parked so close to the upright bricks edging the gravel that he had had to step gingerly along them against the bushes, which was trying on account of his artificial hip. This, he said, confirmed that his view low down to the right had been blocked earlier.

There seem to us to be only three alternatives to Professor Taylor's view that my husband had seen the envelope: that his impulse to go home when he wanted to play golf may have tallied by chance with my shock at forgetting my notes; that he and I had planned a hoax beforehand, or that telepathic interaction had occurred between us. We prefer the last, since the incident follows a pattern we have come to know well after fifty-two years of marriage. He is liable to respond to a sudden spurt of emotion on my part, and at times I appear to be affected by his perilous situation or impetuous action.

Such cases of *useful* telepathic interaction with my husband have occurred so often that to ascribe everyone of them to chance would seem to us more credulous than to accept the reality of ESP. As I have said, in the end the experient comes to regard such interaction as a means of communication as natural as sight or hearing, though less precise or frequent, and not available to order at the conscious level. I would like to consider this interaction a little further, in the hope that it may throw some light on difficulties involved in possible communication with the discarnate.

Our telepathic impressions crop up out of the blue, usually when there is emotional need for them and when no ordinary means of communication is at hand. This tallies, not only with traditional tales and with incidents related by primitive people who have no artificial means of contact, but with Democritus' observations. Eventually one finds oneself assuming that, although ESP is only observed sporadically, it is not discontinuous; rather that, *beyond the threshold of surface consciousness*, there is a permanent inter-relationship between human beings which is greater or less according to their degree of affinity. Again, like to like.

A buried sense of this inter-relationship may partly account for the deep satisfaction given by joint music-making, dance, ritual, games and so forth. In them we may act out a linkage of which, consciously, we are not aware. But why are we not aware of it? Where is the blockage? One would guess it to lie at the last stage, when bringing subliminal material up to surface consciousness. The feeling is of a censor to be by-passed, a filter to be worked through. This could well cause impressions to emerge – as they do – vaguely, obliquely, symbolically, disguised, distorted, or not at all; though even then behaviour may be affected by them. Take the above telepathic interaction between my husband and myself. Why should he merely feel, 'I must go home', although his conscious intention was to play golf? Why did he feel impelled, for no apparent reason, to enter the house by the less convenient front door? Why could he not become aware of the actual fact: 'Rosalind has left her script on the front doorstep'? And, on my side, why was my reasoning mind, which *insisted* that as I saw him go to the golf course he must be on the golf course, able to overbear the misty, agitated – but correct – impression that he was driving in haste through the rush hour?

Freud and others have produced plenty of reasons for censorship of material from the subliminal, and experiences under psychedelic drugs make it clear enough that floods of unselected impressions pouring into consciousness – particularly if one imagines some of them as possibly coming from other aspects of reality – would scarcely conduce to efficiency when, say, traffic driving. As Bergson put it, nature has arranged for '*attention à la vie*'.

Although I am ignorant of physiology, my experience on the balcony of a Unity, which included both what we call the physical world and consciousness, stimulated my amateur's interest in the part played by the brain in the emergence of ESP.[12] Not long after it I came upon the two following quotations which may be apposite. The first is an abstract of a pilot experiment entitled 'Objective Events in the Brain correlating with Psychic Phenomena' which appeared in a new Canadian Journal, founded by Dr A. R. G. Owen, late of Trinity College, Cambridge. The second is the beginning of an article by Professor R. E. Ornstein, on 'Right and Left Thinking'.

'I A new phenomenon is reported. A pilot experiment, using well-established techniques, is described, in which images transmitted telepathically are found to evoke responses in the EEG which are similar in form, and comparable in magnitude, to those evoked by physical stimuli such as sounds.

Remarkably, in this experiment, although the response is demonstrably present in the cortex, the recipient, though aware of the nature of the experiment, *does not consciously register* the content of the message or consciously recognize when it is sent.'[13] [My italics.]

'II The belief that there are two forms of consciousness has been with us for centuries. Reason versus passion is one of its guises; mind versus intuition another. The feminine, the sacred, the mysterious, historically have lined up against the masculine, the profane, the logical. Medicine argues with art, yin complements yang. In fable and folklore, religion and science, this dualism has recurred with stunning regularity.

What is new is the discovery that the two modes of consciousness have a physiological basis. They are not simply a reflection of culture or philosophy. The evidence accumulates that the human brain has specialized, and that each half of that organ is responsible for a distinct mode of thought.

The differences between the right and left sides of the body gave researchers their main clue to the biological mechanisms of thought. In this regard, other cultures have been ahead of us. The Australian aborigines hold the "male" stick in the right hand and the "female" stick in the left hand. To the Mojave Indians the left hand is the passive, maternal side of the person, while the right hand represents the active father.

Specialities in the Half-Brain. It turns out that such distinctions are not arbitrary. The cerebral cortex of the brain is divided into two hemispheres, joined by a large bundle of interconnecting fibres called the corpus callosum. The right side of the cortex primarily controls the left side of the body, and the left side of the cortex largely controls the right side of the body. The structure and the functions of these two "half-brains" influence the two modes of consciousness. The left hemisphere is predominantly involved with analytic thinking, especially language and logic. This hemisphere seems to process information sequentially, which is necessary for logical thought, since logic depends on sequences and order.

The right hemisphere, by contrast, appears to be primarily responsible for our orientation in space, artistic talents [including musical ability, Ornstein says later in the article], body awareness and the recognition of faces. It processes information more diffusely than the left hemisphere does, and integrates material in a simultaneous, rather than linear, fashion.'[14]

To the experient this is a good description of material which seems first to be acquired subliminally by ESP and then slips up to surface consciousness (*via* the right hemisphere of the brain?) when the boss, the sequential thinker, is asleep, or day-dreaming, or mowing the lawn. 'Precognition occurs,' said Aristotle, 'when the mind is not occupied with thoughts, but is, as it were, deserted and completely emptied.'

It perhaps suggests the normality of ESP that creative thought is inclined to behave in a similar way. As is well-known, poets, artists, musicians, scientists, all tell of the sudden appearance of original ideas 'out of the blue': among many others, for instance, Blake, Stevenson, Mozart, Dirac, Kekulé, Coleridge and even Bertrand Russell. No wonder that the great mathematician, Henri Poincaré, considers that

'... the subliminal self is in no way inferior to the conscious self; it is not purely automatic; it is capable of discernment; it has tact, delicacy; it knows how to choose, to divine ... It knows better how to divine than the conscious self, since it succeeds where that has failed. In a word, is not the subliminal self superior to the conscious self?'[15]

This description by Poincaré of the subliminal self suggests that it may be more capable than the conscious self of sensing other aspects of reality.

Another resemblance between creative thought and ESP is elusiveness; neither can be summoned to order. In *The Art of Scientific Investigation*, Professor W. I. B. Beveridge comments that 'Ideas often make their appearance on the fringe of consciousness', and that 'Messages from the subconscious may never be received at all if the mind is too actively occupied or too fatigued.' He also records that A. N. Whitehead declared himself 'impressed by the inadequacy of our conscious thoughts to express our subconscious ... only at rare moments does that deeper and vaster world come through to conscious thought and expression'.

The following example of my telepathic interaction with a living person seems to me to have been a typical eruption from that deeper and vaster world, because there was a sense of immediate *presence*, though none of solid objects or of activities or boundaries. Perhaps one could call it a momentary lighting up of a continuing relationship. I choose it as an example for three reasons. It was much as occurs with apparent discarnate contacts, except that (i) I could not feel whether the conscious mind of the other person was aware of me as I was of him; (ii) he was a person I loved from whom I had had to separate, which gave rise to the emotional state of mind described by Democritus, and (iii) I had already had a similar experience in connection with him.

In our youth a friend and I had suffered a sharp attack by *Vénus toute entierè à sa proie attachée*, but, being unable to marry, had broken away, very painfully, from her clutches. Some months later I was visiting another friend in a distant city, when, one afternoon, I felt aware of him standing, though invisible, in front of me. He was *there*. The next day I heard from a woman friend that he, too, had happened to go to that city the day before, and she had told him of my visit there, at, so far as I could judge, about the time I had experienced what seemed to be his presence.

This incident leads, at last, to the experience on which these speculations are mainly built. It was also of personal contact with a friend; but this time the friend was a discarnate one, who seemed as aware of me as I was of him. I choose it rather than others similar, because a comment he made suggests that it may be next to impossible for embodied persons, whose awareness of their surroundings comes through the physical senses, to realize the *nature* of discarnate conditions. The following account is taken from a record I wrote in 1963 of some of my ESP-type experiences:

'The meeting was entirely unexpected, and the friend was Vivian Usborne, the naval inventor, who had been kind to me as a youthful V.A.D. in Macedonia, and who was the first person to share my "obstinate questionings of sense and outward things". Since my marriage our lives had scarcely overlapped until, in the early 1950s, nearly thirty years later, we found ourselves living within a stone's throw of each other in London. Then we picked up easily where we had left off; but it was not to be for long as Vivian was soon smitten by a lingering but incurable disease. By now he had come to feel, like me, that at death man snuffed out like a candle, and he lamented bitterly that all the many ideas still simmering in his head would never come to fruition. I had in honesty to agree with him.

At his funeral I felt nothing but profound relief at his escape from frustration and suffering – and selfish relief, too, that I no longer had to witness it; I had no sense of his presence at all. About ten days later I went early one morning to get a painting by him which had been given to me. It is perhaps relevant that I was hastening to another appointment in which I was emotionally involved and felt no nostalgic longing for Vivian. As I hurried into his room to fetch the picture I was shocked by a sickening blast of what I have come to call the smell of death. I am never quite sure whether this is physical or what a sensitive might call border-line – though he would be hard put to it to tell an investigator what he meant by that. Then, in staggering contrast (at the time it seemed almost deliberate, but that idea should probably be written off as imagination), I ran slap into "Vivian" himself, most joyfully and most vividly alive. I pulled up sharply as one would on running into a friend in the street, and then came an experience which it is extremely hard to describe without sounding either flat and meaningless or overdramatic. As with "Julia", I felt "Vivian" communicate "inside my mind", and I shut my eyes and stood very still to attend better.[16] He conveyed in some fashion so intimate that the best word seems to be communion, pretentious though that sounds, that he had been entirely mistaken in expecting extinction at death. On the contrary, he now had scope, freedom and opportunity beyond his wildest dreams. The emphasis was not merely on being alive but on this magnificent expansion of opportunity. Then I too seemed to be caught up into the quality of his situation – but not into its form. I experienced no forms and no images.

For a few moments I stood very still, acutely aware of the striking contrast between the smell of death and "Vivian's" intensity of life – it was as if they were in a different order of things – and then I remembered my duty and "said" to him, "This is wonderful, but you've given me no evidence. What can I say to the S.P.R.?"

(I hope that my attempt to describe the immediacy of the purported Julia's communication with me will have made it clear that "said" is far too remote a word to use for this intimate kind of united awareness. It feels, as Gilbert Murray said of his own telepathic experience, like a kind of co-sensitivity.)

"Vivian's" response to my question was emphatic and immediate. "I cannot give you evidence. You have no concepts for these conditions. I can only give you poetic images."

At that, far, far above me, I saw – with the inner eye – an immense pair of white wings flying in a limitless blue sky. Though at first an image of such Victorian obviousness seems absurd, it was in fact an entirely apt expression of the scope, opportunity and freedom into which for a few moments I felt caught up. But it was only for a few moments. I quickly became aware that I could not hold the absorbed state which contact with "Vivian" demanded, and very soon had to say reluctantly, "Good-bye, I must drop now."

I hope it is clear that at the time this experience seemed completely normal and the invisible "Vivian" as real as a friend one meets in the street. I felt nothing but delight at learning how magnificently happy he was and how wide the scope he now had for his brilliant inventive mind. This lack of fear is common to many experients.'[17]

'*You have no concepts for these conditions. I can only give you poetic images.*' That was the key comment. It was only too true. Nobody has any concepts for conditions which differ in *kind* from those conveyed through the senses, for one reason because the senses, as Professor H. H. Price has pointed out, reveal only those elements in our surroundings which make for physical survival. Blake told us the same thing long ago. 'This life's five windows of the soul/Distort the heavens from pole to pole . . .' And from this parochial distorted picture has grown language, with its either/or expressions, such as subjective *or* objective, then *or* now, here *or* there, in *or* out, up *or* down. (Blake once wrote in a letter: 'God keep me . . . from supposing Up and Down to be the same thing as Experimentalists suppose.') No wonder that Jean-Paul Sartre called language a 'structure of the external world' and said that 'the poet is outside of language' and that 'instead of knowing things by their names, it seems that one must first have silent contact with them.' No wonder, too, that men have been driven to mathematical models to describe the world of sub-atomic physics, that Eastern mystics say, 'Not this, not that', and that visitors to the unfamiliar aspect of the world opened up by psychedelic drugs can only mutter, 'If you haven't been there, you *can't* understand.' No wonder that, even on the physical level, Professor Richard Gregory has asked: If a space traveller met something entirely new, would he be able to see it?

It was only to Vivian's psychological state, then, that I could relate; to his joy, his sense of scope, of opportunity; one might almost say to the quality of his *relationship* to his environment, but not to that environment itself. I was, as it were, on the level of Einstein's dog − if he had a dog − who could share a fraction of his delight when formulating a new concept, but could not envisage its cause.

If these apparent contacts are not illusory, can one guess at a possible process? May the right hemisphere of the brain, which, as Professor Ornstein wrote, is largely associated with intuition and artistry, provide a misty trail between the conscious self and the deeper and vaster subliminal world? And can there be anything in my feeling that the subliminal world passes without a break into other aspects of being? Such an idea fits in with the sense of the numinous evoked by natural beauty and art – especially by music, the art of pure relationships.

Whatever the explanation of such experiences, I cannot deny that I have them. I shall therefore encourage myself with Professor H. H. Price's remark that it will be the timidity of our hypotheses rather than their extravagance which will provoke the derision of posterity, to record a curious sensory hallucination which took place during the second world war. At the time I did not know what to make of it as the pattern of discarnate relationship which it suggested does not conform to our either/or outlook. That pattern, in fact, seemed as paradoxical as the 'wavicles' of physics. I think, however, that possibly I may now have come upon a hierarchical relationship into which it will fit and which I will describe later.

I had two friends, one an old retired priest, a saintly character whose health had broken down and who lived alone in a cottage in a wood. The other was an equally idealistic old Highland doctor, Hector Munro, who had been a close friend of A.E.'s. I had good evidence that both were gifted with ESP and I innocently assumed that they would be able to 'meet' in what I can only call an inner as well as an outer sense. So I took the doctor to visit the priest. They were carefully polite, but clearly made no real contact. In what seemed to me a rather pathetic attempt to do so the priest took the doctor to see his library, while I sat alone on the floor by the fire wondering why the two did not 'flow together' as I had assumed they would. In front of me there hung a portrait of an ancient sage. As the reasoning side of me was quiescent, I was not at all surprised when he appeared to lean out of the frame and say, 'If those two were to meet in the sense you want them to on your level, they would lose their identity. But they will be able to do so and yet retain it when they reach ours.' (I must repeat that this type of experience seems perfectly natural at the time.)

The experience preceded my meeting with Vivian, so I accepted the sage's information in a childlike fashion and left it at that. But the meeting with Vivian and other more recent experiences, such as the unexpected awareness on my balcony of the physical world as part of of the Whole, have made one question become insistent: do all relationships within the Whole resonate through every aspect of it? For instance, as I asked earlier, do men sometimes unknowingly act out that merging-without-loss-of-individuality of which the old sage spoke? In the West we love to feel ourselves as separate embodied sparks of consciousness, yet most of us delight to inter-relate in physical activities which achieve results that none of us could manage alone. Take membership of a rowing eight or a dance band or the life-enhancing experience I have known myself of playing orchestral or chamber music. Each player is very much himself and gives everything he has. Yet that everything is no more than part of a larger musical whole which can only be created by all the players together. And take intellectual co-operation. A friend told me of a group of undergraduate mathematicians who were given a weekly task of co-operating to produce a joint solution to a very difficult problem. One week a member of the group fell ill before the problem had been issued, but rejoined his companions before it had been solved. Not having heard what it was, he said on arrival, 'I know the answer to this week's problem. It is so and so . . .'

He was right. How had this come about? Had their common interest caused an inner subliminally communicating group to form? In *The Ghost in the Machine* Koestler develops the old view that life must be hierarchically organized. 'The members of a hierarchy,' he writes, 'like the Roman god Janus, all have two faces looking in opposite directions; the face turned towards the subordinate levels is that of a self-contained whole; the face turned upward towards the apex that of a dependent part.'[18] For these Janus-faced subwholes, which occur in all types of hierarchy, he has coined the term holon. Could the absent undergraduate, who knew the answer to a problem not yet solved by his fellows, have been a component holon of a larger one formed by the group as a whole?

I have also to seek a possible explanation for four experiences of apparent greater-than-human discarnate presences, of whom the first two seemed to be linked to particular places. The following description of these two was written before I had tried to find a place for such happenings. The first occurred in 1938, when, my husband having left the Foreign Service, I came home from America, to be shocked by the tragic unemployment throughout the country. Was there any way an ordinary woman could help? To find out I went to lunch at the House of Commons with a friend, an ex-miner M.P. As before, I quote from my record:

'Arriving as usual, too early, I settled down on a bench in the long entrance to Westminster Hall, relaxed and let the world fade out. It was perhaps due to my mood – how could one help? – that I found myself passing . . . into the ambience, the consciousness – what words can one use? – of a profoundly wise and powerful Being who, I felt, was brooding over the Houses of Parliament. In that inner space he towered so high that the actual buildings seemed to be clustered about his feet. Metaphorically speaking. There was no image of him. Nor was I aware of anything like feet. But I was acutely aware that his task, his deep concern, was to influence for good the deliberations of Parliament and also that he thought in terms of long evolving patterns rather than of one particular moment in time.

As usual, I could not hold this experience, nor could I repeat it next time I went to the House. Yet it moved me deeply and I longed to talk of it. But to whom? My husband was in Africa and I knew other people would only smile and say, "Poor thing! A bit eccentric, you know." . . . Then I remembered one person, a saintly old man who lived in a wood . . . He would not laugh at me.

He did not. On the contrary, as soon as I arrived he began spontaneously to talk to another man present about the Angel of the House of Commons. (He was a Christian.) . . . Startled, I blurted out, "Then you have felt it too?" He laughed, "Of course I have," he said. . . . Some years later, when waiting for my younger son in an empty music school at Eton, I once more seemed to pass . . . into the ambience of a great Being. He appeared to have the school in his care, and, like his fellow at Westminster, he created an atmosphere of brooding wisdom and calm. I think the most impressive part of these experiences was this sense of calm, of certainty. They were in no hurry. They knew what they were about. And they made humanity seem like flustered ants.'[19]

At the time, as I said, I had no thought of trying to relate such beings, 'real-seeming' as they were, to 'normality' or even to other kinds of ESP-type experience. Indeed, there was little encouragement to do so, since even one of the kindliest of academics, who had a deep interest in psychical research, laughingly dismissed my impressions of them as silly. My materialist-conditioned side would have liked to agree with him, but the trouble was that those beings induced in me a reverent awe, yet more intense than listening to the finest music. That such as I could have *invented* them was ridiculous. However, nowadays Professor Michael Polanyi can talk of a stratified universe, Koestler of hierarchies of holons, and pioneer physicists allow us to think of the physical world we know as no more than an abstraction from the real world, made by the senses for practical purposes. Perhaps, then, people who experience such towering presences may toy with the idea of them as being superior holons, existing in forms beyond sensory perception, but not beyond a human being's intuitive capacity to relate (like my imaginary Einstein's dog) to their quality and intention, or to represent them to ourselves by symbolic images. I have even wondered, could my two presences be, so to speak, localized holons; could such holons grow greater down the ages through the accretion of discarnate members of a particular church, nation, or any other community, which those members had loved and worked for in this life? A possible minor case could be the Society for Psychical Research. In his great *Lectures on Psychical Research*, Professor C. D. Broad remarked that when certain of its members who were sensitives had the apparent experience of contact with the discarnate, it was always with their upper-class British predecessors in the Society. Was the 'next world' peopled only by upper-class British nineteenth-century psychical researchers? he asked. With all respect, this puzzles me. In 'this world', too, like gravitates to like; Cambridge academics to Cambridge academics, pop singers to pop singers, Marxists to Marxists.

Incidentally, I have realized lately that of the ten friends to whose actual deaths I have reacted at the time, or who seem to have visited me shortly afterwards, eight, in common with me, had taken an interest in psychical research. And they were not among the friends with whom, emotionally, I have been most closely linked.

While I seem merely to react to the situation and wishes of my incarnate friends, but seldom have any impression whether or not they are feeling conscious of me, with the discarnate it can be otherwise. As I have said, on occasion they seem – at close quarters – to take the initiative, either to give symbolic information, or, more often, to indicate action they want taken. But in both cases the contact seems to take place when my reasoning side is quiescent. I will given an extreme example of this as it seems to emphasize that contact with other aspects of reality takes place at a subliminal level and that awareness of such contact then has to emerge as best it can to the conscious level.

In 1969 I was badly shaken by seeing in *The Times* a long obituary of a great friend, Guy Wint, and two days later I found myself answering, out loud, an apparent request of his, *before* I was conscious of his presence. In fact, my attention was only attracted by hearing the sound of my own voice. It is a very curious experience to hear a part of oneself, of which at the level of physical-world experience one is not aware, answering somebody else of whom at that level one is also not aware.

Whether or not with justification I am not competent to judge, but when later on I read the following passage in Dr Grey Walter's Eddington Memorial Lecture on brain rhythms my mind leapt back to this experience of replying to a request before, at surface level, I was aware of its having been made. It again seemed to suggest a lack of barriers between 'physical' and 'ultra-physical' aspects of being. Dr Grey Walter said:

'. . . there is objective evidence that spontaneous impulses to explore and the evocation of imaginary experiences are preceded and accompanied by electric events as clear and substantial as those I have described in relation to interactions with the outside world.' [Note, the *preceded* by . . .]

'It is an eerie experience to discern through an electric machine the genesis of a person's intentions, to predict his decisions before he knows his own mind. Even more impressive, is the experience, when one is oneself harnessed to such a machine, to find that by an effort of will one can influence external events, without movement or overt action, through the impalpable electric surges in one's own brain. Not surprisingly, perhaps, the repeated exercise of such effort requires the attainment of a peculiar state of concentration, a paradoxical compound of detachment and excitement.'[20]

Very tentatively one speculates whether, after the words 'evocation of imaginary experiences' there might be added 'and subconscious interactions of an ESP or psi-in-general type'. At least the paradoxical combination of detachment and excitement has often been described by experients in whom such apparent interactions have reached surface consciousness.

With Mrs Wint's permission I base my description of my experience of a request from her husband on my account written at the time.

Guy Wint and I usually met to work in London. Our main interests in common were the drama and psychical research, including the question of survival. Very occasionally I spent a night with him and his wife in Oxford, but as she was kept very busy looking after her family and their many friends, I tried to be as unobtrusive as possible. I also felt a slight barrier between her and me in spite of her extreme kindness; and I was astonished the other day to learn from her that she had liked me, but looked on me as a formidable figure of whom she was very frightened! I mention this as it may reduce the likelihood that she was the telepathic source of the following experience – although, of course, I cannot be sure she was not.

On the Sunday, two days after Guy's death, I was sitting quietly alone, about to begin work, when, to my great surprise and with no previous sense of his presence, I found I had put my head down on the desk and was answering him out loud with sobbing emotion, 'Oh, *yes* Guy, *yes*, I *will* try! I *will* try!' Then, very startled, I came to myself and realized with distress that I had no idea what I had heard myself promise. On such occasions I ignore my reasoning side and try to behave as my discarnate friends want me to do. It would seem knavish not to. So I tried to pick up what Guy wanted. It seemed to be that I was to make immediate contact with his wife, Freda. This was embarrassing. She was much younger, beautiful, with many friends on the spot, and I saw no reason why she should want to hear more from me than the letter of condolence I had already written. Moreover, being economically minded, I tend not to make long-distance calls except for an urgent practical reason. But on this occasion the pressure was too strong to resist, so I rang up Freda, and, as she seemed pleased, talked about my experience and about Guy. Then I wrote to her and rang again several times during the next three weeks. The result was a letter from her thanking me for my calls and letters. She said she thought that without me and another friend who had done the same thing she would have 'gone off her rocker', because everyone else was tactful and did not mention Guy, whereas the one thing she wanted was to talk about him.

I got the impression that Guy was extremely happy, and subsequently two other friends told Freda that they felt aware of his joy at release from suffering. This may sound heartless on his part, but I tentatively suspect that, if individuals do survive, it is *our* limitations which create the sense of separation between them and us; it is we who *assume* they are gone. To them a valued relationship may not cease to exist at death. In that case, they may look on the death of the body as no more portentous than going to Australia – especially if their relationship to what we call time happens to differ from ours.

At least, as far as I could perceive it, Guy's sole intention, as with Julia and others, was to send help to someone he loved: nothing about his own situation, except that I was able to relate to his state of happiness. In the following experience, on the contrary, the apparent intention, like Vivian's, was to tell me about the situation of a much loved newly dead friend, Professor Sir Cyril Burt. That he should want to do so was natural, since with him, too, I had discussed the question of survival of consciousness after death and had also quoted his views on it in print. But according to Vivian, it will be remembered, *information* about conditions different in *kind* from ours can only come at second-hand, by means of imagery. And this time imagery is what I got. It may also be natural that it was musical rather than visual, since in life Professor Burt had been an audile rather than a visualizer and he was also a good musician. Again I describe the incident from the account which I wrote at the time.

Sir Cyril Burt died in the late afternoon of 10 October 1971, and Dr Charlotte Banks telephoned to tell me so that evening. I had known that he was very ill, but had been given the impression that, even if he did not get better, his departure would be a slowish process. His sudden death was therefore a very severe shock to me, not for his sake, for I had realized that his ageing body would soon hamper his beautiful mind, but because I loved and depended upon him very much. As my husband said to me, 'You have lost your rock.'

The next morning I was no less shaken, and the physical effect, which I have felt before in similar circumstances, was that my body and knees continued to shake and tears poured from my eyes. These were not tears of sorrow, but as if they released my body from pressure it could not otherwise take. After breakfast something impelled – or rather compelled – me to go and play the second movement of Mozart's little piano sonata No. 10, in C major. This surprised me greatly as for years I have not played the piano; my technique has gone, and also stiffness and lack of energy prevent it. Moreover, I felt tired and was very busy in a Martha-like fashion, which made the action the more surprising. My husband came in, astonished, and told me afterwards that he nearly said 'What on earth are you doing?' and then decided not to.

As I always pay careful attention to that kind of 'order' I tried to observe what the movement appeared to convey. It was an impression of calm serenity – the kind of serenity of being at ease in natural surroundings – garden, flowers, woods, water – *peace*. There was a feeling of ordered simplicity – a momentary gentle regretfulness during the second minor theme, and then that second theme ending in the major key in perfect peace. And the key, I afterwards realized, was F major, that of the Pastoral Symphony and Beethoven's fifth violin sonata. I felt intensely that it was *as if* Professor Burt were telling me: 'This is how things are with me.' There is no external evidence, of course, that this was so.

Next I felt, embarrassing as it was so soon after he had died, that I was to telephone Gretl Archer, his devoted friend and secretary, and tell her about the incident. She replied: 'Do you know, whilst under sedation less than three hours before his death in hospital, the professor was playing the piano on his bedtable. I was watching his fingers, trying to find out what he was playing, but couldn't even guess as I had also to look at his face, which had such a blissful expression on it.'

Yesterday, 14 October, I told a little of this to Miss Alison Dobbs, who had brought me a pile of letters between her nephew, the mathematician, Adrian Dobbs, who had died in 1970, and Professor Burt, because I had put them in touch. In one of the letters Adrian wrote that nobody had ever helped him as much as had Professor Burt, and she thought that this would please me. This morning (the next day) came a letter from Miss Dobbs to say that on returning home she had found a small bag of Adrian's more recent notebooks and the first one she opened had the following quotation about Mozart on the first page she looked at. Although the phraseology is not mine, it could not have expressed better what the Mozart slow movement appeared to be telling me about Professor Burt, especially the last lines.

Miss Dobbs' letter ended: 'It did strike me as odd that out of five notebooks, I opened Mozart. That is why I send it at once.' (The quotation was from *The Impossible Adventure*, by A. Gheerbrant.)

'In the music of Mozart there is a strange charm in the widest sense of the word, to which no Indian could remain insensible. On them as on us the music seemed to exercise a soothing influence: it relaxed the body and allowed the soul to expand gratefully. It was sort of oxygen, the very gentlest of balms. It dissipated fears, melancholy and the fatigues of the journey. It solaced our loneliness and gave us comfort in the primitive life we were leading. Above this sombre countryside, eternally closed around its secret, it placed a trembling forest of clear-toned violins, which made the hairs of the skin move as the bluish cassava shoots moved in the wind on the hill slope. Such music did not stiffen the body or clamp down a mask of fear on the faces of those who listened. It opened up the secret places of the heart, it made a thousand hidden voices surge up from the hidden centre of things, a thousand colours, a thousand unsuspected forms.'

My reasoning side would prefer to leave out the two following additions to the Burt–Mozart experience, but it would be dishonest to do so, since I am in no position to assume that they are somewhat coincidental by chance, rather than by discarnate intention or the law of like to like. The first suggests that Adrian Dobbs, a friend whom I had made through our common interest in psychical research and whose aunt had sent me the quotation from his notebooks about Mozart's music, had already made contact with me after his death in 1970. I had had the impression that he wanted me to send a certain message to

Professor C. D. Broad, of whom he had been a close friend at Cambridge. I did so, as can well be imagined, with considerable diffidence, but Professor Broad replied very kindly and at length that the message was apt and arrived while he was working on Adrian's papers.

The second addition is part of a letter written by Mozart himself to his father shortly before the latter's death. It was sent to me by a friend on hearing of my Burt–Mozart experience, and fits in with my compulsion to play a piece of Mozart's music in particular.

'As death, when we come to consider it closely, is the true goal of our existence, I have formed during the last few years much closer relations with this best and truest friend of mankind, so that his image is not only no longer terrifying to me, but is indeed very soothing and consoling. And I thank my God for graciously granting me the opportunity (you know what I mean) of learning that death is the key which unlocks the door to our true happiness. I never lie down at night without reflecting that – young as I am – I may not live to see another day. Yet no one of all my acquaintances could say that in company I am morose or disgruntled.

For this blessing I daily thank my Creator and wish with all my heart that each one of my fellow creatures could enjoy it.'[21]

I need hardly add that the Burt–Mozart incident as a whole stirs up the conflict between my two sides. The reasoning side says, 'Silly overimaginative build-up!' The intuitive side replies, 'If you think that, you're a fool.'

So my problem is: how much is my reasoning side conditioned against acceptance of the idea of communication with the discarnate by a mental climate which insists that the physical world as presented by the senses and their tools is the only real world? On the other hand, how much is my intuitive side conditioned by wishful thinking? I don't mean necessarily the wish for the perpetuation of one's own self-regarding little ego. Many people are free from that form of selfishness; but a number seem to feel 'cribbed, cabined and confined', to long for an extension of consciousness, a wider horizon, the increased scope and opportunity that Vivian so joyfully conveyed. Incidentally, if he and one's other discarnate visitors are illusory, a reason must be found for the usefulness of their sometimes surprising requests.

The conflict between the reasoning and intuitive side of the human psyche may only be resolved when the recent discoveries of physics (and probably, more to come) about the parochialness and illusory nature of the physical world, as presented through the senses have more thoroughly permeated the general mental climate. Most of us still feel as Dr Johnson did when he kicked the stone, for men have always been as immersed in their contemporary mental climate as in the air they breathe. Fortunately that climate slowly changes with new discoveries. If you *know* the earth is flat it makes sense to picture heaven above and hell below. If your age is four (I heard this story lately from a friend) and your mother tells you her swelling body contains a baby given her by your father, it makes sense (with apologies to Freud) to warn him: 'You know that baby you gave mummy? Well, she's eaten it.' How would Francis Bacon have made sense of a TV set? I asked a mathematician friend, who answered, 'Would he have had any alternative to magic?'

However, the struggle to understand may be needed to strengthen our mental muscles. J. B. Oppenheimer says: 'The experience of seeing how our thoughts and our words and our ideas have been confined by the limitation of our experience is salutary . . .' This may encourage ordinary scientific laymen to try to think for themselves, especially as he adds that even the greatest scientists find it hard to struggle out of the cocoon of contemporary thought.

'Kepler who loved spheres, discovered ellipses . . . Einstein . . . proposed the idea of light quanta but he could never reconcile himself to the quantum theory logically built up from this basis. And de Broglie, who discovered that there are waves which are associated with material particles, could never reconcile himself to their interpretation as waves which only represented *information* and not some disturbance in a *corporeal medium*.' [My italics.][22]

If a de Broglie could never rid himself of the intellectual need for a corporeal medium to transmit waves, it may be that an ordinary person, experiencing a momentary apparent visit from a friend existing in a realm for which he has no concept, would be capable of no more than a shared feeling, or of second-hand contact by means of a sensory image. But, if such contacts *via* images do occur, who chooses the image? Vivian said *he* gave me the image of a soaring bird. Rightly or wrongly, I felt as if Burt drove me to play Mozart to indicate his situation. One might guess that those two, being highly intelligent, might at once after death have realized the difficulty of giving information about their new conditions and might have used the images to represent them. In fact, Vivian conveyed as much. It has also been suggested by Professor H. H. Price and others that, without realizing it, the newly dead in general may continue to make mental images resembling their earthly surroundings for their own benefit – or perhaps to suit their expectations. (Such image-making could be analogous to our dreaming.) In my youth I read a nice story, I think by Annie Besant, about a journey she believed she had made on 'the astral plane'. There she saw a woman, newly arrived and on her knees, worshipping a splendidly traditional God the Father, complete with a long white beard on a high white throne. Unfortunately, wrote Mrs Besant, she had forgotten to make his back.

As against this, it may be the psychological type of the experient which determines the image: a visualizer may babble of green fields or an audile hear celestial music. A report suggesting this is recorded by D. Scott Rogo. During a visit to the then Archbishop of York, a Lady C. was sharing a room with a Miss Z. She wrote:

> 'I was sleeping with Miss Z. when I suddenly saw a white figure fly through the room ... I ... called out to Miss Z., "Did you see that?", and at the same time Miss Z. exclaimed, "Did you hear that?". Then I said instantly, "I saw an angel fly through the room", and she said, "I heard an angel singing".'[23]

Rogo also quotes a case which suggests an attempt to represent the inconceivable in terms of an image, which the experient recognizes as being no more than an image. An artist's model, who was also a sensitive, reported that, while in trance, she could hear non-physical music. But the artist commented, 'She is obliged to use the term music; it is the word which for us corresponds most closely to the enchantment which still holds her in strong emotion.' (I, too, once had an experience which may have been faintly comparable, and I deliberately record it to show how demented such incidents can sound, when written down in three dimensional terms. It was of climbing up the 'mountain range' climax of the Chopin A flat Ballade to a place of incredible beauty. Could that have been an image for some condition beyond conception, with which ruminating about the Ballade brought me into contact?)

For simple people things are easier, because they do not bother themselves with such questioning. The other day I read some automatic writing by a widow, which purported to come from her recently departed husband. She wrote, as from him, that after death he had been met by his mother and taken to a cosy cottage where he was thoroughly happy and comfortable. She was immensely cheered. The more sophisticated will say, 'Poor simple soul! It comes from her own subconscious, of course. She's compensating for her loss.' That may very often be true. But dare *I* discount all my experiences in order to make that assumption in every case? In the light of Vivian's statements and of the old sage's description of conditions where the like-minded can merge without losing identity, dare *I* assume that love cannot link two people across the apparent Divide? And if the link is with the wife's subliminal level, perhaps her husband's happy state could only be conveyed to her sense-bound conscious mind through some such humble image. But suppose the widow were of my type, which appears to experience immediate *imageless* linkage with other personalities, incarnate or discarnate. Then she might not need to do automatic writing. She might, at moments, directly feel her husband's calm content and continued love as I seemed directly to feel Vivian's delight at increased opportunity, Guy's and Julia's happiness and Professor Burt's serenity.

I hope that investigators will one day take more interest in the fact that ESP-type impressions are received by different experients in different ways, for it may then turn out that more people than is realised have experiences which may be linked with the discarnate. In the past for instance, because my own, both mundane and otherwise, were usually imageless, I had tried to dismiss them as mere imagination until an outstandingly talented and honest sensitive, Mrs Osborne Leonard, said to me the first time we met, 'I see you do what I do, but I put it out there.' She waved a hand. 'You do it direct.' This illuminating remark gave me the courage not automatically to thrust away such experiences as chance happenings or 'mere imagination'.

The following incident illustrates what I mean by different patterns of reception. I was asked to write my first book about psychical research when very busy and under some stress; yet there was a strong inner pressure – though at the same time *as if* from outside myself – to get on with it. The pressure was especially strong to write in a certain way when I reached the point of trying to envisage the problems which could face the discarnate if they did attempt to communicate with us, as these are indicated in a series of automatic writings known as the Society for Psychical Research's Cross Correspondences. (It seemed to come from 'above and behind' – more or less metaphorically speaking. I am here in trouble with words.) It was a great relief when at last I felt I had written what 'somebody' wanted. Soon afterwards Miss Gertrude (Nancy) Johnson, a fine sensitive who had done a lot of experimental work with the psychical researcher, G. N. M. Tyrrell, came to lunch with me. After lunch, to my surprise – I have never had this impulse before or since – I felt impelled to go and sit on the floor *leaning against her* and read part of what I had written. But I did not mention my experience of pressure. What follows is from my contemporary record.

'I had reached a point which would have been of particular interest to George Tyrrell when Nancy, shaking like a leaf, cried, "Rosalind, Rosalind, there *is* George!"

She was tremendously overcome with emotion and I held both her hands firmly and said, "Now Nancy, calm down. Listen to what he wants." But she was still deeply moved, and kept repeating, "It's George! It's George! just there in front of us", and then, after a few moments, "Now, he's gone!"

For several minutes afterwards she did not seem to be "here" with me. This is a figure of speech, to convey that her consciousness appeared to be focused elsewhere, though she was not in trance. Finally she seemed to refocus and I asked, "Can you tell me what he wanted?"

"He seemed pleased," she said, "it was like when he used to be struggling with a difficult bit of his work and I would say things that helped him clarify his ideas and then he would get it. He would not say much but would look satisfied. He had done what he wanted. He looked like that."

I asked her how she saw him and she said he was sitting on the sofa opposite us. "But that is quite secondary," she added. "What was so much more important to me was that *he* was there. I felt *him*."

"You mean a sense of his presence?" I asked. "Yes, yes, it was *George!*"'

It is, of course, simple enough to say that to be read to about possible communication with the departed would be likely to arouse in Nancy emotional memories of a much-loved friend and guide, memories which were strong enough to induce a self-created hallucination. On the other hand, looked at with no presuppositions either for or against survival, the approving George whom Nancy experienced fitted my previous sense of being pushed to write a difficult passage in a certain way and of having achieved what 'somebody' wanted. And of this pressure I had told Nancy nothing, though she may have picked it up from me telepathically at a subliminal level. But why did *I* not identify George as George when feeling the pressure? One possible answer may lie in my old sage's remark about merging without loss of identity. George's interests were very much those of the Frederic Myers group with whom the Cross Correspondences were concerned, and one can well imagine him merging after death with the holon that group might have formed. Moreover, his friendship with me was much involved with the same interests. Therefore, when I *wrote* the passage which I read to Nancy, I might have been responding to pressure by the Myers group as a holon, whereas when *reading* it, I may well have been insensitively ego-centred, concerned with 'my' book, and not open to any *psi* impressions. But Nancy was George's adopted daughter and the link between them was very strong. Perhaps I should remind any reader that I do not record this incident as evidence for survival, but to compare Nancy's experience, which fitted her relationship with George, and my own, which fitted mine. Still, they were both relationships which one could picture as holding between different aspects of reality.

I now come to two outstanding experiences which I realize may have been working for years beneath the surface to modify my attitude towards the possible existence and also the nature of surviving consciousness. I have tried elsewhere to describe them, but the attempt is inhibiting, not only because the shades of Freud and Skinner loom over one's shoulder, but also because the only words I can find to use seem illogical, over-dramatic and yet absurdly inadequate. For instance, subjective and objective no longer implied opposites, and in an ecstatic yet totally non-possessive sense the poor battered word, love, became the human expression of that harmony of the universe, belief in which, so Einstein told Hans Reichenbach, caused him to find his theory of relativity. In fact, during those experiences the old rhyme "'Tis love that makes the world go round' became a sober scientific statement, and energy and consciousness were two aspects of one reality. In a letter to me, Sir Cyril Burt once put his idea of that reality like this:

'I am convinced that there is only *one* basic order – which appears as logical or mathematical to our cognitive intuition, aesthetic to our emotional intuition, and moral to the volitional or conative. *And* it is essentially numinous.'

Both these experiences were of contact with what I can only call discarnate focus points of that basic order, which, of course, includes consciousness. In human terms their impact was of personal presences, presences so much more 'real', even in memory, than any physical-world contact and so infinitely 'out of my class', that to suggest, as some psychologists have done, that I had imagined them is merely funny. The key word is *quality*. Not, of course, that such contact implies any special quality on the experient's part. 'The Bright Ring of Eternity', like the sun, shines on the just, the unjust and the stupid alike, but all three usually keep their eyes firmly closed. It so happened that, on these occasions, circumstances, which need not be recorded here, tweaked mine slightly open.

These presences differed from the lesser ones of my recently departed friends in that the friends *come to me*. The presences did not 'come' or 'go'. Nor did they seem in any way localized, like the great beings whose concern seemed to be with Westminster Hall and Eton Chapel. The best I can say is that they *were*. They pervaded. This will sound foolishly paradoxical, but as far as I can judge, a vital difference between one's so-called normal state of consciousness and the one in which such experiences occur is that in the second what we call paradoxes are normal. Those presences, for instance, although they were intense focus points of energy and intensely personal, still had neither needs nor boundaries. I could say that they 'disappeared' 'upward' and 'inward' to draw life from the blazing spiritual central core, and at the same time expanded 'downward' and 'outward' to envelope me and all else in it. Yet these little geographical divisive words are silly: disappear, upward, inward, downward, outward, central, core. What could such words mean when core and circumference are one? Especially when the core is everywhere and there is no circumference?

Both presences brought home to me in different ways that one reason for my lack of concepts for even the apparent relatively accessible ultra-physical conditions in which Guy and Vivian functioned was my own egocentricity. The first made itself known as a visible image of celestial joy, beauty and compassion, far, far 'above' me. As I was looking 'up' towards it in adoring humility it switched me round, so to speak, to face 'the other way', thus enabling me to look 'out' with a fraction of its eyes at the infinity of interweaving relationships within the boundless One. The result was astounding, acutely conscious, *I entirely ceased to be aware of myself*. (Paradox again.) For that reason I could *see* the interweaving patterns *as such*, not in relation to *me*. So I could love them – really love them. Perhaps at creative moments artists, poets, musicians, scientists, mathematicians, 'see' in something of that fashion and are thus able to bring the rest of us nearer to being in tune with the central harmony. (I can hardly bear to use these silly little words.)

Of course, for such as I, the vision had to fade. I remember it only at intervals and then, mostly, to think *about* it. I cannot fully relive it. Fifteen years later I had a sharp reminder that this was my own fault. Again a great presence (this time invisible, but into whose ambience I seemed to be lifted by my ecstasy at a moment of extreme natural beauty) made me look through a fraction of its eyes. But this time I had to look down – down – down. And what I saw at the bottom was – me: a little slow-moving feeble object, with all its tiny doors of perception muddied over by egocentricity. Its attention was fixed on itself. No wonder the mud had caked.

So far I have been recording some of my ESP-type experiences as if they were incidents in a journey which might hint at the nature of that journey's end. Is it annihilation, or, as the experiences faintly suggest, an expansion of consciousness? (One remembers that in the physical aspect of reality consciousness has expanded from amoeba to man as he now is. May it not expand further, even here?) While recording them, I found myself, oddly enough for the first time, attempting to relate them, (1) to each other, (2) to communication in daily life, (3) to what, though still widely accepted as the last word, begins to look like yesterday's science, and (4) to what seeps out to the layman about today's physics. This attempt has induced a tentative change of attitude which I will try to explain.

As regards (1), I now realize that, if my experiences are looked upon as examples of relationship, they are strung along a thread which is *continuous* with the sensory interactions of daily life. First come telepathic interactions which, like sensory ones, are a means of relating to living people. Next come interactions with discarnate friends, which resemble telepathic ones with the living, except that in my case (apart from urgent telepathic requests from my husband) those friends sometimes seem to show more active initiative than the living. Thirdly, the old sage from the picture gave me the idea of a still more intimate relationship, the merging of discarnate individuals into groups, yet without loss of their own identity. In 1940 I had never heard of holons, but this seem as not inapt way of describing possible discarnate ones. Finally, come my awed and adoring contacts with what I shall call the great holons, which bodied forth the one harmony – love.

As regards (2) and (3), however real and helpful my experiences feel to me, they 'break the rules' and are therefore unthinkable. 'Fie, Mrs Heywood, go home to your kitchen, for shame!'

But what about (4)? Even if today's physics have not found a home for these unthinkables, they have done so, as we have seen, for others in a fashion which seems to us to make orthodox materialism look rather parochial. The extraordinary changes that are taking place need time to penetrate to the lay world, and as yet make us feel bewildered. The 'week before last', so to speak, we were told that to travel in a train faster than fifteen miles an hour would cause blood to gush from the nose; the 'day before yesterday', that to break the sound barrier would disintegrate an aeroplane, and 'yesterday' that nothing could travel faster than light. In March 1974 came a splendid traveller's tale in the

New Scientist, reporting the pursuit by two physicists of a mysterious particle they call a tachyon, which appears able to do just that. I have wondered, when watching the spokes of a wheel revolving too fast to be visible, or when seeing an ultra-sonic whistle being blown which was silent to me, whether the possible existence of speeds of movement or vibration, beyond the adult human being's senses or imagination, might have something to do with our lack of concepts for conditions in which discarnate consciousness might exist. A few days after reading about the tachyon hunters I was told about a little girl whose mother had been drowned. The day after the disaster her father shut himself up alone with his grief, but she insisted on seeing him. She had some news. 'I've been talking to Mummy,' she said, 'and she says, "Not to worry". She's still with us, but going faster, so that we can't see her.' Nonsense – or out of the mouths of babes? ... After all, in the Here and Now the speed of a praying mantis catching a fly is beyond our perception.

I must confess that, since the admittedly feeble attempts by experients to describe 'impossibly' paradoxical (in our language) happenings are so often laughed at, it is rather agreeable to find physicists pretty well out-stripping us with their paradoxical neutrinos, which, we are told, lack all physical attributes, yet sweep for ever in their billions through our bodies; their positrons, which are said to travel momentarily backward in time, and the capacity shown by their electrons, over and above those quoted by Oppenheimer, to pass through two holes at once. This is a feat, said Sir Cyril Burt, which no ghost has equalled. We are told, too, that matter and energy are identical, that the world of space and time as we experience it does *not* exist and that non-physical fields *do* exist. Finally, without going into reports about the equivalent marvels of the macrocosm, I will quote a physicist's very recent description of diversity within the One. 'What we call an isolated particle is in reality the pro-duct of its interaction with its surroundings. It is therefore impossible to separate any part of the universe from the rest.[24]

So – how can I try to answer the question: What, if anything, do certain experiences of my own suggest to me about the possible nature of life after death?

This tentative attempt to look at those experiences in the light of the concepts of like to like, hierarchies of holons and the paradoxical findings of today's physics, has, whether justifiably or not I don't know, given me somewhat more courage to envisage that my occasional apparent contacts with consciousness functioning in wider aspects of reality may possibly be genuine. There seems less need to distrust such contacts in the light of yesterday's certainties, since yesterday's certainties no longer seem to exist. It is rather as if a prison door were swinging slightly open to disclose what may be occasional glimpses of the Pacific.

Further, the concepts of like to like and of a hierarchy of holons have also suggested to me what seems a thinkable picture of the nature of ultra-physical consciousness. For one thing, they give a pattern into which the old sage's description of discarnate individuals merging with out loss of identity will fit. And it makes sense to suppose that holons might exist of finer quality than the present stage of even the best human beings. To assume that *we* are at the top of the ladder seems rather arrogant. So, too, does the widespread desire for survival after death of the little entities we now are. But the idea that our more co-operative, less self-regarding components could together become a component of a greater discarnate holon suggests a loss of imprisoning egocentricity and an enlargement of consciousness which it is exhilarating to envisage.

Finally, the idea that discarnate holons can build up into greater ones brings those tremendous focus points of consciousness, those great presences, of which I have a few times felt humbly aware, into the continuing pattern. They can even be imagined as the basis of the traditional world-wide belief in gods, angels, devas . . . a belief perhaps resulting from faint glimpses of them mediated through the 'intuitive' right hemisphere of the brain, but laughed at today by the masterful left-hand sequential reasoner. I wrote above of human arrogance. I am too well aware of the arrogance of a non-academic woman in speculating, as I have done, about the nature of man – not to mention the universe! On the other hand, even housewives, like Einstein himself, have to learn by experience. And to hide one's little experiences, for fear of seeming a fool, would be a cowardly act. The other day I came upon a poem by the pre-Socratic philosopher, Xenophanes, translated by Karl Popper. It says what I feel, as I could never do.

The gods did not reveal from the beginning
All things to us, but in the course of time
Through seeking we may learn to know things better.
But as for certain truth, no man has known it,
Nor shall we know it, neither of the gods
Nor yet of all the things of which I speak.
For even if by chance he were to utter
The final truth, he would himself not know it;
For all is but a woven web of guesses.[25]

But Xenophanes was writing of man as he still is, faced by mystery and quality beyond his present comprehension. If he does not destroy himself, may he not, over the aeons, evolve into a more talented guesser and grow some antennae which can sense wider aspects of the woven web of the One?

December 1973

Notes

(1) Michael Polanyi, 'Science and Man', *Nuffield Lecture* (5 February 1970).

(2) E. Schroedinger, *What is Life?* (1969).

(3) Herbert Dingle, *The Scientific Adventure* (1952).

(4) J. B. Oppenheimer, *Science and the Human Understanding* (1966).

(5) Summarized from 'ESP in the Light of Modern Physics' in *Science and ESP*, ed. J. R. Smythies (1967 and 1971).

(6) Since writing the above I have read the following passage in Arthur Koestler's section of *The Challenge of Chance* by Alister Hardy, Robert Harvie and Arthur Koestler (1973), 235: 'The twin tyranny of mechanical causality and strict determinism has come to an end; the universe has acquired a new look, which seems to reflect some ancient archetypal intuitions of unity in diversity, on a higher turn of the spiral. Mach's principal has become an integral part of modern physics, even though it has an odour of mysticism. For it implies, not only that the universe at large influences local events, but that local events have an influence, however small, on the universe at large. As Whitehead has put it, rather dramatically, "there is no possibility of a detached self-contained existance."'

(7) A. Eddington, *The Nature of the Physical World* (1931).

(8) Quoted by A. Vallentin in *Einstein* (1953).

(9) The term ESP is now used by researchers to describe the incoming or perceptive branch of what are popularly called psychic phenomena. The outgoing or active branch includes such apparent phenomena as table-tilting, the little understood forces released by frustration (traditionally and misleadingly called poltergeist activity), and so on. To avoid the superstitions associated with the word psychic, investigators usually speak of the two branches together as *psi* phenomena. *Psi* is a neutral term suggested by the well-known psychologist, Dr Robert Thouless.

(10) Henry Margenau, 'ESP in the Framework of Modern Science' in *Science and ESP*, ed. J. R. Smythies (1967 and 1971), 222.

(11) Quoted by Professor E. R. Dodds in *Supernormal Phenomena in Classical Antiquity* (1973).

(12) The crucial question as regards possible communication with the discarnate is of course: Does the brain generate or transmit consciousness? Orthodox materialists assume the first, but recent evidence has forced such experts as Sir John Eccles, Lord Adrian, the late Professor Sir Cyril Burt, Dr Wilder Penfield and Professors W. H. Thorpe and Gomes, among others, to envisage the second. See, for example, J. C. Eccles, *The Brain and the Unity of Conscious Experience* (1965), J. C. Eccles, ed. *The Brain and the Conscious Experience* (1966) and Cyril Burt, *Journal* S. P. R. (December 1967).

(13) D. H. Lloyd, M.D. (pseudonym), 'Objective Events in the Brain correlating with Psychic Phenomena', in *New Horizons*, journal of the *New Horizons Research Foundation*. Toronto, Vol. 1, No 2 (Summer 1973). Other experiments in the USA by Dr Charles Tart and by Dr Douglas Dean, have also demonstrated that physiological ESP responses to emotional stimulii occur without being accompanied by conscious awareness of the stimuli.

(14) Robert E. Ornstein, 'Left and Right Thinking', in *Psychology Today* (May 1973). See also *The Psychology of Consciousness* by the same author, and an article about him in the *New Scientist* (6 June 1974), 606.

(15) Henri Poincaré. *Mathematical Creation* quoted in *The Creative Process*, ed. Brewster Ghiselin (1952).

(16) Julia was another friend who has appeared to turn up invisibly shortly after she had been killed in an air crash, with insistent instructions as to how I could help her mother. Though they were surprising, when carried out, they worked.

(17) Rosalind Heywood, *The Infinite Hive* (1964, 1967 and 1971) entitled in the USA *ESP, A Personal Memoir*.

(18) A. Koestler, *The Ghost in the Machine* (1967), 45–49.

(19) From *The Infinite Hive*.

(20) Grey Walter, 'Observations on Man, his Frame, his Duties and his Expectations', 1969.

(21) *Mozart's Letters*, trans. Emily Anderson, Vol. 11, p. 907.

(22) J. B. Oppenheimer, *The Flying Trapeze* (1962), 5–6.

(23) D. Scott Rogo, NAD: A Study of some unusual 'Other World' Experiences (1970).

(24) Dr F. Capra, *Main Currents in Modern Thought* (1972).

(25) Quoted in Brian Magee, *Popper* (1973).

14
Whereof one cannot speak . . . ?
Arthur Koestler

●

I

In his *Unpopular Essays*,[1] Bertrand Russell has a telling anecdote:

> 'F. W. H. Myers, whom spiritualism had converted to belief in a future life, questioned a woman who had lately lost her daughter as to what she supposed had become of her soul. The mother replied: "Oh well, I suppose she is enjoying eternal bliss, but I wish you wouldn't talk about such unpleasant subjects" . . .'

This sounds like the perfect paradigm of man's split mind, in which belief and disbelief lead an agonized coexistence. The unpleasantness of dying is a hard, cold fact. On the other hand, not only eternal bliss (or eternal torture), but also the more sophisticated versions of life after death present problems which our minds are incapable of handling: they are far beyond the reasoning faculties of our species (though not, perhaps, of other species on millions of older planets). In computer jargon we would have to say that we are not programmed for the task. Confronted with a task for which it is not programmed, a computer is either reduced to silence, or else it goes haywire. The latter seems to have happened, with distressing repetitiveness, in the most varied civilizations. Faced with the untractable paradox of consciousness emerging from nothingness and returning to nothingness, their minds went haywire and saturated the atmosphere with the ghosts of the dead and other invisible presences who at best were inscrutable, but mostly malevolent, and had to be placated by grotesque rituals, including human sacrifice and the slaughter of heretics. The evidence from anthropology, from ancient and modern history, provide conclusive proof of the paranoid streak endemic in our species, perhaps due to some evolutionary mistake in the construction of its nervous system.

There is, of course, another side to the medal. We remember the old sage who said that philosophy is the history of man's endeavours to come to terms with death. If the word death were absent from our vocabulary, our great works of literature would have remained unwritten, pyramids and cathedrals would not exist, nor works of religious art – and all art is of religious or magic origin. The pathology and creativity of the human mind are two sides of the same medal, coined by the same mint-master. A cynical observer from outer space might ask whether this need be so, whether the glories of one side are worth the horrors of the other. Hegel thought that ours is the best of all possible worlds; one wonders whether the praying mantis would share this opinion while paying the price for the glories of procreation. Or whether the poor wretch strangled on the *vile garrotte* would find consolation in the thought that Goya was to immortalize him. Does this redress the equation between the glory and the pathology? Our cynical alien would rather conclude that this planet is ruled and ravaged by a freak species, an ill-conceived experiment of the mint-master.

According to the theories of Paul MacLean, which are finding growing support among neurophysiologists, the unprecentedly rapid expansion in the course of the last five hundred thousand years of the human neocortex resulted in faulty co-ordination between this philogenetically new acquisition – the 'thinking cap' which governs rational thought – and the archaic structures of the brain, which we share with reptiles and lower mammals, and which govern our emotional reactions. This evolutionary discord is said to have resulted in a state of 'schizophysiology', a split between reason and emotion which is endemic in the human condition. Emotion is the older and more powerful partner in the divided household, and whenever there is conflict, the reasoning half of the brain is compelled to provide spurious rationalizations for the senior partner's urges and whims. This is why some paranoid delusions appear so consistent and compelling – madness yet with method in it – including the weirdest notions concerning after-life. The neocortex may repeat its dreary syllogisms: 'all men must die, Socrates is a man, ergo, et cetera', but the old brain which occupies the larger part of our skulls passionately rejects the notion of personal non-existence: unable to make a categorical distinction between the ego and the world, the end of the ego means to it the end of the world – which is obviously unthinkable. Accordingly, the old brain considers survival as self-evident, while its

timid and pedantic junior partner is given the task of filling the
post-mortem void with some science-fiction scenario. Given un-
restricted scope for fantasy, it is surprising what a poor job it made of that
scenario. The Pit, Gehenna, Hades, Sheol recur with monotonous
regularity like the dreary stage-props in Gothic horror-thrillers; while
the celestial habitats seem designed to make the dead wish to die from
boredom. I take no pleasure in blasphemy; my point is the poverty
of man's imagination even if given an infinite playground.

I have mentioned science fiction: it provides a chastening lesson. Its
heroes, thousands of years ahead of us, sail to distant galaxies through
hyper-space faster than the speed of light, but their thoughts, feelings,
and vocabulary are limited to the narrow range of the present. The
rugged astronaut landing on the third planet of Aldebaran behaves in
the same way as he would in a drugstore in Minnesota: the Milky Way
has become an extension of Main Street. Its inhabitants may be genius
lizards communicating by radar-guided telepathy, yet we could not care
less: curiosity is tickled for a few pages, but they are too strange to be
true, and we soon get bored. Our imagination is narrowly limited: we
cannot project ourselves into the distant future, not even into the distant
past: the figure of an Egyptian schoolmaster under the Eighteenth
Dynasty is only a shadowy silhouette; we are unable to breathe life into
it. Hence the failure of the historical novel. Every culture is an island;
it communicates with other islands, but knows only itself; and the
islands of the living are severed from the Atlantis of the dead.

II

But this severance need not be total and complete. 'The more detailed
pictures of life after death are,' wrote Renée Haynes, 'the less acceptable
they seem to be.' Obviously, we have to move in the opposite direction:
away from pictures and details, from 'misplaced concreteness', as
Whitehead called it. This implies clearing the lumber room of the
accumulated visual and verbal junk, the graven images and verbal
imprints, the whole paranoid phantasmagoria. After all, the Iconoclasts
of the Middle Ages were a deeply religious movement which could have
been inspired by Whitehead's caveat.

After the spring cleaning the air may become healthier and more
transparent. Atlantis may now appear even more remote, but at the
same time a more sober approach may suggest itself. I am referring to
recent advances in parapsychology and *avant-garde* physics, which,
though not directly concerned with the question, seem to provide the
only *objective* clues to it. (The *subjective* approach of the mystic is com-

plementary to it as yin is to yang, but lies outside the scope of this chapter.)

Two contributors to this volume (Renée Haynes and Rosalind Heywood) have already alluded to the mind-boggling paradoxa of contemporary physics, and I have written about them elsewhere at some length.[2] Here I shall confine myself to a brief recapitulation of the philosophically more relevant points, where the boundaries between physics and metaphysics become indistinguishable.

III

By the end of the 1920s, Einstein, de Broglie, Schrödinger, and Heisenberg had effectively de-materialized matter. What appears to us as solid mass, m, was shown to be the equivalent of a very high concentration of energy, E; and the simple equation $E = mc^2$ (where c is the speed of light – perhaps the only mathematical formula which ever caught the public imagination) was validated by the thermo-nuclear bomb and by less dramatic methods of laboratory research. The latter produced conclusive evidence that the so-called elementary constituents of matter, such as electrons, protons, neutrons, etc., behaved, according to circumstances, as massive particles or as unsubstantial waves. 'The electon', de Broglie proclaimed, 'is at the same time a corpuscle and a wave.'[3] This dualism is fundamental to modern physics, and is known as the Principle of Complementarity. In Heisenberg's words: 'These two frames of reference mutually exclude each other, but they also complement each other, and only the juxtaposition of these incompatible frames provides an exhaustive view of the appearances of phenomena...'[4] In another place he makes a remark which lets the cat out of the bag, as it were: 'What [we] call 'Complementarity' agrees very neatly with the Cartesian dualism of matter and mind.'

Another giant of modern physics, Wolfgang Pauli, expressed the same idea:

'The general problem of the relationship between mind and body, between the inward and the outward, cannot be said to have been solved. Modern science has perhaps brought us nearer to a more satisfactory understanding of this relationship by introducing the concept of complementarity into physics itself.'[5]

One might add to these quotations almost any amount of similar pronouncements by the pioneers of contemporary physics. It is evident that they regarded the parallel between the two types of complementarity – body/mind and corpuscle/wave – as more than a superficial analogy. It is, in fact, a very deep analogy, but in order to appreciate what it implies, we must try to get some inkling of what the physicist means by the 'waves' which constitute matter. Commonsense, that treacherous counsellor, tells us that to produce a wave, *there must be something that waves* – a vibrating piano-string, or undulating water, or air in motion. But the whole conception of matter-waves excludes by definition any medium with material attributes as a carrier or substratum of the wave. Thus we are faced with the task of imagining the vibration of a string but without the string, or the grin of the Cheshire cat but without the cat – another task for which we are not 'programmed'. We may, however, derive some comfort from the analogy between the two complementarities. The contents of consciousness that pass through the mind, from the perception of colour to thoughts and images, are un-substantial 'airy nothings', yet they are somehow linked to the material brain, as the unsubstantial 'waves' and 'fields' of physics are somehow linked to the material aspects of the sub-atomic particles. This is what Jeans had in mind when he wrote his famous *pronunciamento* : that physicists were virtually unanimous in moving away from the materialistic view of reality because 'the universe is beginning to look more like a great thought than like a great machine.'[6]

That was written in 1937. By that time solid matter had quasi-evaporated from the physicists' laboratories, was transformed into patterns of concentrated energy, and ultimately dissolved into the stresses and warps in the curvature of space. Parallel to this vanishing act, our concepts of space, time, and causality, to which the computers in our cranium were programmed, turned out to be totally inadequate when applied to events on the sub-atomic or supra-galactic scale. 'Atoms are not *things*,' Heisenberg wrote. 'When we get down to the atomic level, the objective world in space and time no longer exists.'[7]

Nor does strict causality and rigid determinism apply on that level. The Principle of Indeterminacy is as fundamental to modern physics as Newton's Laws of Motion were to classical mechanics. It implies that the universe at any given moment is in a quasi-undecided state, and that its state in the next moment is to some extent indeterminate, or 'free'. Thus if an ideal photographer with an ideal camera took a picture of the total universe at any given moment, that picture would be to some extent fuzzy because of the indeterminate state of its ultimate constituents.*

Thus for the last fifty years it has become a commonplace among

---

* It can be shown that however short the exposure-time, the Indeterminacy Principle will still blur the picture.

physicists that the strictly deterministic, mechanistic world-view can no longer be upheld; it has become a Victorian anachronism (although behaviourist psychology and large sections of the educated public still cling to it). The nineteenth-century model of the universe as a mechanical clockwork is a shambles; and since, with the advent of relativity and quantum theory, the concept of matter itself has been de-materialized, materialism can no longer claim to be a scientific philosophy.

What are the alternatives?

IV

I have quoted some of the giants (all of them Nobel laureates) who, in the first half of our century (more exactly in its first three decades), jointly dismantled the rigid clockwork and attempted to replace it by a more sophisticated model, sufficiently flexible to accommodate logical paradoxes and ideas previously considered unthinkable. In the half century which has passed since the revolution of the 1920s, countless new discoveries were made – by radio telescopes scanning the skies, and in the bubble chambers keeping track of sub-atomic events – but no satisfactory model and no coherent philosophy has yet emerged comparable to that of classical, Newtonian physics. One might describe these years as one of the periods of 'creative anarchy' which repeatedly occur in the history of science when the old concepts have become obsolete and the breakthrough leading to a new synthesis is not yet in sight. The last such interregnum in cosmology lasted nearly a century and a half, from the publication of Copernicus' *De Revolutionibus* in 1541 to that of Newton's *Principiae* in 1684. Owing to the acceleration of history – which includes the history of ideas – the present phase of creative anarchy will probably be much shorter, and when the new synthesis arrives we shall marvel at our previous blindness. At the time of writing theoretical physics itself seems to be in a bubble-chamber, with the weirdest hypotheses criss-crossing each other's tracks. However, one can detect certain general trends. Firstly, there is agreement that the 'model' of the universe can only be an abstract, mathematical one, forsaking any attempt at visual representation, because we are only capable of representing and visualizing phenomena in three-dimensional (3-d) space, moving along a single time axis from cause to effect, whereas a true model of micro- and macro-events would require more, and possibly (according to some) an unlimited number of dimensions where causes and effects are tangled in Gordian knots. When contemporary physicists nevertheless act in defiance of the taboo against making graven images of atom or cosmos, they seem to do so with tongue in the cheek.

Thus, according to John A. Wheeler, professor of physics at Princeton University and a leading figure in *avant-garde* physics, the geometry itself of three-dimensional space 'fluctuates violently at small distances'. He then draws this surrealistic picture:

'The space of quantum geometrodynamics can be compared to a carpet of foam spread over a slowly undulating landscape ... The continual microscopic changes in the carpet of foam as new bubbles appear and old ones disappear symbolize the quantum fluctuations in the geometry ...'[8]

This turbulent sea of bubbling foam is meant to represent – or rather, symbolize – Wheeler's concept of super-space (his italics):

'The stage on which the space of the universe moves is certainly not space itself. Nobody can be a stage for himself; he has to have a larger arena in which to move. The arena in which space does its changing is not even the space-time of Einstein, for space-time is the history of space changing with time. The arena must be a larger object: *superspace* ... It is not endowed with three or four dimensions – it's endowed with an *infinite* number of dimensions. Any single point in superspace represents an entire, three-dimensional world.'[9]

Superspace, or hyper-space, has been an old standby of science fiction, together with the concept of parallel universes and reversed or multi-dimensional time. Now, thanks to radio-telescopes and atom-smashers, they are acquiring academic respectability. The stranger the hard experimental data, the more surrealistic the theories devised to account for them. Professor Feynman of Caltech interpreted the tracks of positrons in the bubble-chamber as evidence that these particles travelled over short distances backward in time, and instead of being laughed out of court he got the Nobel Prize in 1965.

Wheeler's superspace has some remarkable features; one of them is multiple connectivity. This means, to put it into simple – and simplified – language that regions which in our homespun 3-d space are far apart, may be temporarily brought into direct contact through tunnels or 'holes' in superspace. They are called wormholes. The universe is supposed to be criss-crossed with these wormholes, which appear and disappear in immensely rapid fluctuations, resulting in ever-changing patterns – a cosmic kaleidoscope shaken by an invisible hand.

(Incidentally, these wormholes in the microscopic foam should not be confused with the astronomer's Black Holes in the sky, also first postulated by Wheeler. Black Holes are regions in the universe into which the mass of a burnt-out star which has suffered gravitational collapse is sucked to be annihilated – or to emerge in a different universe in super-space. Fantastic as this may sound, at the time of writing (July 1975) several Black Holes have been tentatively identified by astronomers; and the search for more is being actively pursued in numerous observatories.)

V

The wings of analogy are notoriously treacherous, but nevertheless useful for short flights, or rather hops, provided we always remember that metaphor is not proof.

Bearing this warning in mind, there are obvious analogies between modern science and para-science, modern physics and metaphysics. The first we met was the apparent affinity between the two basic principles of complementarity: particle/wave and body/mind. We may now ask the further question: if matter can transform its mass into radiation and thus become pure 'disembodied' energy, is it still absurd to speak of discarnate mental energy? More precisely: is such talk still as absurd as it may have sounded fifty years ago, before the revolution in physics dethroned matter and taught us that atoms are not 'things'? And is it still legitimate to jeer at the term 'mind-stuff' (coined by Eddington) as unscientific when a physicist can describe the universe as a bubble-bath in superspace? Dr I. J. Good of *The Scientist Speculates*[10] fame went even further: 'Matter is aethereal and mind is the solid rock . . . It is but a short step to the assumption that all minds are part of a single system . . .'[11] Is is still justifiable to deny the possibility of telepathic signals, when physicists accept action-at-a-distance in various forms, from gravity to wormholes, to the so-called 'Einstein–Podolsky–Rosen (EPR) paradox'?*

Similar questions can be asked, based on analogies which are not conclusive but strongly suggestive, about other categories of para-psychological phenomena, including psychokinesis and isolated flashes of precognition, where the direction of time's arrow seems to be reversed; but this would require excursions into even more abstruse and technical regions of theoretical physics. The point to retain is that phenomena which half a century ago seemed to defy the laws of nature

---

* Broadly speaking, this famous experiment designed by Einstein indicates that if two electrons have been bounced off each other and fly off in different directions, interference with either of them will influence the other, however far apart they may be. Cf. *The Challenge of Chance*, p. 228.

now appear less offensive because those laws are no longer regarded as strictly valid; and the weird theories advanced to account for those phenomena now appear less preposterous because the theories advanced by physicists are even more weird and insulting to naïve commonsense. The universe of classical physics, consisting of hard little billiard balls bouncing about in strict obedience to the laws of mechanics, has been replaced by the indeterminate quantum foam; its sharp contours have become fuzzy, its structure softened, its laws made more tolerant and permissive. An object flying through the air without physical cause, as so often reported in Poltergeist phenomena, is no longer considered to offend the laws of nature, only the laws of probability. And these laws, which have replaced causality in modern science, are not physical laws in the strict sense. They *work* – as every physicist, insurance company or roulette operator can testify; but nobody can explain how and why they work. The greatest mathematician of our time, John von Neumann, called them 'black magic'. We can leave it at that.

VI

One aspect of modern science appears to be particularly relevant to our subject: the trend towards a new conception of holism. It was actually initiated at the turn of the century by 'Mach's Principle' which states that the inertial properties of terrestrial matter are determined by the total mass of the universe around us. Here again there is no satisfactory explanation as to *how* this influence is exerted; yet Mach's Principle (as re-formulated by Einstein) occupies a key position in modern cosmology. Its metaphysical implications are fundamental – for it follows from it not only that the universe as a whole influences local, terrestrial events, but also that local events have an influence, however small, on the universe as a whole. Philosophically minded physicists are acutely aware of these implications – some to their satisfaction, others to their discontent. Bertrand Russell flippantly remarked that Mach's Principle 'savours of astrology',[12] while Henry Morgenau, professor of physics at Yale, made this thoughtful comment:

'Inertia is not intrinsic in the body; it is induced by the circumstance that the body is surrounded by the whole universe ... We know of no physical effect conveying this action; very few people worry about a physical agency transmitting it. As far as I can see, Mach's principle is as mysterious as your unexplained psychic phenomena, and its formulation seems to me almost as obscure ...'[13]

If we turn from macro- to microcosm, we find similar 'holistic' developments. Thus Heisenberg: 'The system which is treated by the methods of quantum mechanics is in fact a part of a much bigger system (eventually the whole world).'[14] There are no independent parts, functioning in splendid isolation from the rest of the universe. Rather, 'only if the whole universe is included in the object of scientific knowledge can the qualifying condition "for an isolated system" be satisfied.'[15] Or, the physicist Dr F. Capra: 'What we call an isolated particle is in reality the product of its interaction with its surroundings. It is therefore impossible to separate any part of the universe from the rest.[16] And lastly, Professor David Bohm of Birkbeck College, University of London (his italics):

> 'It is generally acknowledged that the quantum theory has many strikingly novel features . . . However, there has been too little emphasis on what is, in our view, the most fundamentally different new feature of all, i.e. the intimate interconnection of different systems that are not in spatial contact. This has been especially clearly revealed through the . . . well-known experiments of Einstein, Podolsky and Rosen . . .
>
> 'Recently interest in this question has been stimulated by the work of Bell, who obtained precise mathematical criteria, distinguishing the experimental consequences of this feature of "quantum interconnectedness of distant systems" . . . Thus, one is led to a new notion of *unbroken wholeness* which denies the classical idea of analysability of the world into separately and independently existent parts . . .'[17]

These quotes (which could be multiplied indefinitely) do not reflect solo voices, but rather a chorus of eminent physicists who are aware of the revolutionary implications of their research. The overall picture that emerges is reminiscent of the philosophical creed of the Hypocratics – 'There is one common flow, all things are in sympathy' – shared by the Pythagoreans and Neo-Platonists, and summed up by Pico della Mirandola, the fifteenth-century Platonist (whose writings inspired Kepler in his search for the planetary laws): 'Firstly there is the unity of things whereby each thing is at one with itself. Secondly there is the unity whereby one creature is united with the others and all parts of the world constitute one world.'[18]

The majority of contemporary physicists would underwrite these lines. In a remarkable recent book, *La Gnose de Princeton*, subtitled *Des Savants à la Recherche d'une Religion*,[19] Professor Raymond Ruyer drew attention to the quasi-mystical conclusions towards which the physical theories of the 'gnostics of Princeton' tend to converse.* But it is a sober mysticism, born in the laboratory. The medieval mystic talked of 'sympathies', 'correspondences', of the All-One, of the part being contained in the whole, yet in some sense also containing the whole. The 'gnosis of Princeton' has a paradigm or metaphor for every one of these statements.

One of the most striking of these paradigms is the hologram†. I shall not attempt to explain how it works, but its principle is a method of photography (without lens) which records the interference patterns of a split laser beam on a transparent photographic plate. When this is again illuminated by laser light, a sharp three-dimensional image of the photographed object is seen. But the uncanny property of a hologram is that if you cut off a piece of it and illuminate it by the laser beam, the *whole* photographed object will still be visible – only it will be less and less sharp the smaller the fragment cut off from the plate. Thus each part of the hologram potentially contains all the information describing the whole, although the information becomes more summary the smaller the part. Details will be lost, but the *Gestalt* – the configuration of the whole – is preserved. The metaphors one can derive from the principle of holography are quite dizzy-making. Some neurophysiologists believe that it provides a model for the storage of memories in the brain. The mystic would say that it confirms what he always knew that 'everything hangs together', that the part can contain the whole, that microcosm reflects macrocosm and is reflected by it.

But if this is demonstrably true of material phenomena, there is no valid reason to prevent us from applying these insights to mental phenomena as well – to draw parallels to Mach's principle, to the EPR paradox, the wormholes in superspace and so on, which obliterate the assumed barriers between individual minds. If in the world of matter 'everything hangs together', we may expect that this also holds for the complementary world of mind; and (to quote Gould again) 'it is but a short step to the assumption that all minds are part of a single system.'

This indeed was the opinion of one of the greatest among the founding fathers of modern physics, Erwin Schrödinger, whose wave equation of the electron – the formula of the 'matter-wave' – represents a decisive

---

* Gell-Mann borrowed for his theory of elementary particles the Buddhist term 'the eightfold way'; he was rewarded by the discovery of the omega-minus particle, which the theory predicted and the Nobel Prize in 1969. Other terms used in the technical jargon of quantum physics include 'quark', 'strangeness' and 'Charm'. Behind the school-boyish humour there is the awed awareness of mystery.

† Invented by Denis Gabor, Nobel Prize 1971.

turning point in the history of science.* Schrödinger's interests were divided between physics and philosophy, which may perhaps explain why he was able to see the mystical implications of the matter-wave equivalence, expressed in his equation, more clearly than his colleagues; and he had the courage to state them publicly and unequivocally in his lectures and books. (In this respect he anticipated the 'gnostics of Princeton' by several decades).

One of Schrödinger's most important papers has the title 'What is an Elementary Particle?' Immediately below, the sub-title of the first section states the relevant part of the answer: 'A Particle is Not an Individual'. Here are a few extracts from the paper (summarizing the conclusions, and omitting the technical arguments on which they are based):

'Atomism in its latest form is called quantum mechanics. It has extended its range to comprise, besides ordinary matter, all kinds of radiation, including light – in brief, all forms of energy, ordinary matter being one of them. In the present form of the theory the 'atoms' are electrons, protons, photons, mesons, etc. The generic name is elementary particle, or merely particle ...

This essay deals with the elementary particle, more particularly with a certain feature that this concept has acquired – or rather lost – in quantum mechanics. I mean this: that the elementary particle is not an individual; it cannot be identified, it lacks "sameness" [personal identity]. The fact is known to every physicist, but is rarely given any prominence in surveys readable by non-specialists ... The particle, as we shall see, is not an identifiable individual ...

No doubt the notion of individuality of pieces of matter dates from time immemorial ... Science has taken it over as a matter of course. It has refined it so as safely to embrace all cases of apparent disappearance of matter ...'

He then gives the example of a log burning away; scientists from Democritus to Dalton never doubted –

'that an atom which was originally present in the block of wood is afterwards either in the ashes or in the smoke. In the new turn of atomism that began with the papers of Heisenberg and of de Broglie in 1925 such an attitude has to be abandoned. This is the most startling revelation emerging from the ensuing development, and the

* He shared the Nobel Prize with Heisenberg in 1931.

feature which in the long run is bound to have the most important consequences. If we wish to retain atomism we are forced by observed facts to deny the ultimate constituents of matter the character of identifiable individuals. Up to recently, atomists of all ages, for all 1 know, had transferred that characteristic from visible and palpable pieces of matter to the atoms, which they could not see or touch or observe singly. Now ... we must deny the particle the dignity of being an absolutely identifiable individual ... An atom lacks the most primitive property we associate with a piece of matter in ordinary life. Some philosophers of the past, if the case could be put to them, would say that the modern atom consists of no stuff at all but is pure shape ...'[20]

Schrödinger the physicist had the main share in the demolition of the concept of matter (though he modestly gave priority to de Broglie and Heisenberg); Schrödinger the philosopher was both terrified and elated by what he had done. The elementary particles, the supposed 'building blocks' of the universe, had lost their identity, turned out as consisting of 'no stuff at all' but only pure shape – in other words, those building blocks were a mirage, an illusion, the veil of Maya. The next step almost forcibly led him to regard the presumed individual separateness of *minds* as equally illusory:

'There is obviously only one alternative, namely the unification of minds or consciousnesses. Their multiplicity is only apparent, in truth there is only one mind. This is the doctrine of the Upanishads. And not only of the Upanishads ... Let me quote as an example outside the Upanishads an Islamic-Persian mystic of the thirteenth century, Aziz Nasafi:

"On the death of any living creature the spirit returns to the spiritual world, the body to the bodily world. In this however only the bodies are subject to change. The spiritual world is one single spirit who stands like unto a light behind the bodily world and who, when any single creature comes into being, shines through it as through a window. According to the kind and size of the window less or more light enters the world. The light itself however remains unchanged."'[21]

There was no inner conflict between Schrödinger the physicist and Schrödinger the metaphysician. The two aspects of his thought were interdependent, complementary. Thus, after commenting on the passage from Nasafi quoted above, he continues:

'Still, it must be said that to Western thought this doctrine has little appeal, it is unpalatable, it is dubbed fantastic, unscientific. Well, so it is, because our science – Greek science – is based on objectivation, whereby it has cut itself off from an adequate understanding of the subject of Cognizance, of the mind. But I do believe that this is precisely the point where our present way of thinking does need to be amended, perhaps by a bit of blood-transfusion from Eastern thought. That will not be easy, we must beware of blunders – blood-transfusion always needs great precautions to prevent clotting. We do not wish to lose the logical precision that our scientific thought has reached, and that is unparalleled anywhere at any epoch.'[22]

Elsewhere, he makes it clear what he considers to be the 'blunders' and 'clotting' in Eastern mysticism: the doctrine of the transmigration of souls. Taking that away, 'one has to renounce the alleged justice in world-events, which cannot be defended anyway. What remains is the beautiful conception of unity and absolute interconnectedness, of which Schopenhauer said that it was his consolation in life and would be his consolation in dying.'

Schrödinger's own formulation of that conception is found in various passages of his books; for instance, in the closing pages of his classic *What is Life?*, a work which became a landmark in biophysics (and which introduced the new concept of negentropy):

'From the great Upanishads the recognition ATHMAN = BRAHMAN (the personal self equals the omnipresent, all-comprehending eternal self) was in Indian thought considered ... to represent the quintessence of deepest insight into the happenings of the world ... Consciousness is a singular of which the plural is unknown; there *is* only one thing and what seems to be a plurality is merely a series of different aspects of this one thing, produced by a deception (the Indian MAYA); the same illusion is produced in a gallery of mirrors ...'[23]

Quantum physics turned out to be a gallery of mirrors in which the elementary particles are reflected, although they have no real identity; and personal consciousness appears as an equally deceptive entity, like the fragment of a hologram, contained in the whole and containing a miniature version of the whole. Its essence – its supra-individual component – is indestructible and timeless, only its deceptive individuality is tied to the body in life and death, i.e. subject to time. Commenting in this context on the profound changes which the concept of time has undergone in modern physics, Schrödinger concluded his fifth Tarner Lecture in Trinity College, Oxford, 1956, with the memorable words:

'To my view the "statistical theory of time" has an even stronger bearing on the philosophy of time than the theory of relativity. The latter, however revolutionary, leaves untouched the unidirectional flow of time, which it presupposes, while the statistical theory constructs it from the order of the events. This means a liberation from the tyranny of old Chronos ... But some of you, I am sure will call this mysticism. So with all due acknowledgement to the fact that physical theory is at all times relative, in that it depends on certain basic assumptions, we may, or so I believe, assert that physical theory in its present stage strongly suggests the indestructibility of Mind by Time.'[24]

Equally memorable is this passage, written in the last year of his life:

'For me personally all this is *maya*, although a very lawful and interesting *maya*. The eternal element within myself (to use straight medieval language) is hardly affected by it. But this is a matter of opinion.'[25]

VII

Parapsychologists have adopted the term 'psi-field' for psychic interactions, as a complement to the physicist's gravitational, electromagnetic etc. fields. The late Professor Sir Cyril Burt commented:

'There can be no antecedent improbability which forbids us postulating yet another system and yet another type of interaction, awaiting more intensive investigation – a psychic universe consisting of events or entities linked by psychic interactions, obeying laws of their own and interpenetrating the physical universe and partly overlapping, much as the various interactions already discovered and recognized overlap each other.'[26]

It seems reasonable to assume that some of the basic insights gained by modern physics are – *mutatis mutandis* – also applicable to the psychic field which is complementary to it, as mind is to body, corpuscle is to wave. Perhaps the most profound of these insights is the rediscovery, on a higher turn of the spiral, of the Pythagorean (and Vedantic) concept of cosmic unity, where 'everything hangs together', as distant regions are connected by Mach's principle or by superspace. If we apply this principle to the psi-realm, we arrive at some sort of Eddingtonian 'mind stuff', complementary to Wheeler's carpet of quantum foam. The bubbles in it which appear and disappear represent individual consciousness, emerging from and vanishing into the universal froth. If this sounds wildly speculative, let us always remember that we are dealing with analogies derived from the theories of highly respectable physicists; and after all, sauce for the gander is sauce for the goose.

Reciprocal to this neo-holistic view of matter and mind is the reduced autonomy of the parts. 'Atoms are not individuals' – they have no personal identity. By analogy, individual minds are not truly, or entirely, 'self-contained selfs'. They interact with their environment and with other minds by both sensory and extrasensory communication. The latter is presumably mediated by the psi-field, or psychic aether – whatever you like to call it. It is reflected in a passage in Whately Carington's Myers Memorial Lecture, given in 1935:

'Telepathy takes place because there is an underlying unity of consciousness beneath and beyond the level of cleavage and separation enforced by our temporary segregation into bodies. If we go down far enough we come to levels common to all, and this is the universal consciousness by virtue of which we are veritably all members one of another. After death, consciousness – I think – persists but not in the localized and delimited way that our observation of physical bodies and their reactions has led us to expect.'[27]

Thirty years later, Frank Spedding gave another memorable lecture to the Society for Psychical Research in which he carried Carington's metaphor one step further:

'We can picture the living world as an archipelago of millions of little islands, each representing an individual conscious entity. Immediately below the surface lies the individual sub-consciousness ... Beneath this again the land joins up and in this stratum there is a collective subconscious where ideas and thoughts from one individual subconscious mind are transmitted to another individual subconscious mind and if these turn up in the conscious mind we get the phenomenon of telepathy ... We can no more picture the *modus operandi* of our subconscious mind than we can form a mental picture of an electron ... At birth the island of consciousness appears as a tiny speck and at death it disappears beneath the waters. I would include the whole of life in this analogy.'[28]

VIII

Assuming, then, the existence of such a psychic substratum out of which individual consciousnesses are formed and into which they dissolve again after three score years and ten – how does the solid brain fit into this picture? It must be admitted that it does not fit at all as long as we remain captives of that materialist philosophy which proclaimed – as Burt ironically phrased it – that the chemistry of the brain 'generates consciousness uch as the liver generates bile. How the motions of particles could possibly "generate" this "insubstantial pageant" [of images and ideas] remained a mystery.'[29]

This feeling of mystery was also shared by eminent neurophysiologists, like Sir Charles Sherrington, and neurosurgeons like Wilder Penfield. both of whom propounded a modified Cartesian dualism of brain and mind, where mind was the controlling agency. 'To declare that these two things are one does not make them so,' wrote Penfield. And Sherrington: 'That our being should consist of *two* fundamental elements offers, I suppose, no greater inherent improbability than that it should rest on one only . . . We have to regard the relation of mind to brain as still not merely unsolved, but still devoid of a basis of its very beginning.'[30]

If we reject both naïve materialism and rigid Cartesian dualism, the principle of complementarity offers a more promising approach.* Mind is not generated by the brain, but associated with the brain. The nature of this association is one of the oldest problems of philosophy; I shall only mention here one hypothesis, which was originated by Henri Bergson and taken up by various writers on extrasensory perception. In this hypothesis the brain acts as a protective filter for consciousness. Life would be impossible to live if we were to pay attention to the millions of stimuli constantly bombarding our senses, to the 'blooming, buzzing multitude of sensations', as William James called it. Hence the nervous system, and above all the brain, function as a hierarchy of filtering and classifying mechanisms which eliminate a large proportion of the sensory input as irrelevant 'noise' and abstract the relevant information which requires attention and action. On our hypothesis, this filtering and computing arrangement at the same time also shields consciousness from the buzzing multitude of *extra*-sensory messages, images and impressions floating around in the psychic aether in which part of our individual consciousness is immersed.

The 'filter' hypothesis could also account for the apparent capricious-

* For a more detailed discussion of this approach, see *The Ghost in the Machine*, Chapter 14.

ness and relative rarity of parapsychological phenomena. This opinion was shared by the Wykeham Professor of Logic at Oxford, H. H. Price, who wrote:

'It looks as if telepathically received impressions have some difficulty in crossing the threshold and manifesting themselves in consciousness. There seems to be some barrier or repressive mechanism which tends to shut them out from consciousness, a barrier which is rather difficult to pass, and they make use of all sorts of devices for overcoming it. Sometimes they make use of the muscular mechanisms of the body, and emerge in the form of automatic speech or writing. Sometimes they emerge in the form of dreams, sometimes as visual or auditory hallucinations. And often they can only emerge in a distorted and symbolic form ... It is a plausible guess that many of our everyday thoughts and emotions are telepathic or partly telepathic in origin, but are not recognized to be so because they are so much distorted and mixed with other mental contents in crossing the threshold of consciousness.'[31]

IX

We thus arrive at an overall view of individual consciousness as a kind of holographic fragment of cosmic consciousness – a fragment temporarily attaching itself to a body with its filtering and computing apparatus and eventually returning to, and dissolving in, the all-pervading mind-stuff. About the first process we know a little; about the second nothing at all. But the first may contain some clues to the second.

Freud and Piaget, among others, have emphasized the fact that the new-born infant does not differentiate between ego and environment. It is aware of events, but not of itself as a separate entity. It lives in a state of mental symbiosis with the outer world, an extension of the biological symbiosis in the womb. The universe is focused on the self, and the self *is* the universe – a condition which Piaget called 'protoplasmic' or 'symbiotic' consciousness. Vestiges of it may survive in sympathetic magic, and in that self-transcending 'oceanic feeling' which the mystic and the artist strive to recapture at a higher level of development, a higher turn of the spiral.

Thus the small child knows as yet no firm boundaries between self and not-self, and Piaget's classic studies have shown that the formation of that boundary is a gradual process, spread over several years, until the child becomes fully conscious of its own, separate, personal identity; or to put it differently, until its symbiotic consciousness is channelled into ego-consciousness and learns to operate the computer inside its still soft skull.

Is there any symmetrical relationship between the emergence of individual consciousness in the newborn and the process of its dissolution in death? We can make a thought-experiment in which the direction of time's arrow is reversed, as in a film played backwards. In this sequence, as the child reverts to infancy, its consciousness of personal identity would gradually dissolve and become extinct with its return into the womb. Just before that return it would go through the traumatic experience of being reduced to silence, stopping breathing and feeding. In the womb it would continue to shrink in size while its tissues de-differentiate into the fertilized egg, and eventually, after another traumatic event, into two germ-cells. Yet we cannot say at what exact point the growing foetus acquires reactivity and the rudiments of sentience or 'mind'; nor at what point it loses it in the reversed sequence. And if we switch from ontogeny to philogeny (of which the former is a summary recapitulation), we are again unable to draw a line where consciousness makes its appearance on the evolutionary ladder. Ethologists who spend their lives observing animals – from mammals to birds to insects – refuse to draw such a line, while neurophysiologists talk of spinal consciousness in lower organisms and biologists of the protoplasmic consciousness of protozoans.* Bergson even asserted that 'the unconsciousness of a falling stone is something different from the unconsciousness of a growing cabbage.' After the arrogant materialism of the last century, the vanguard of physicists and biologists seems to be moving towards some form of pan-psychism.

At first sight there is not much comfort to be derived from our reversed film sequence. Birth is a dramatic break in the individual's development, but it merely marks the transition from one form of organic existence to another, whereas death is a transition from organic to anorganic. As far as bodily processes are concerned, there is no symmetry between pre-natal and post-mortem development. The point of playing the film backwards was merely to remind ourselves that individual consciousness is not an all-or-nothing phenomenon, but a matter of degrees, starting from an undifferentiated state of 'protoplasmic' awareness, attaching itself to a developing organism, and

---

* Such as the *foraminifera* which construct microscopic houses out of spicules of dead sponges – houses which Sir Alister Hardy calls 'marvels of engineering skill, as if built to a plan'. Yet those single-celled creatures have no nervous system.

becoming gradually individualized; and – so our hypothesis runs – after detaching itself from the dying organism, becoming de-individualized, also gradually, in the post-mortem phase. But de-individualization is not meant here to equal extinction. It means merging into the cosmic consciousness – the island vanishing below the surface to join the sunken continent – or Athman joining Brahman – whichever image you choose.

The emphasis is on the gradualness of the merging process. It is admittedly difficult to reconcile with the fact that at the moment of death (even if it was approached gradually through senescence and coma) the complementary partnership between the mind-stuff and the body is brusquely abolished. How then can some vestiges of the psyche continue to function for some time? Carrington's theory suggests that the essential component of the psyche, that which is part of and submerged in the universal psi-field, always retained some autonomy, never became welded to one particular body. It always communicated by extrasensory signals which penetrated the filtering and computing apparatus; now that those protective devices of the body are no longer needed, the gradual dissolution of the alone into the all-one – into Nirvana or the mystic's 'white light' – can proceed unimpeded.

Some radio-receivers display a curious habit: after you have switched off the apparatus, the music continues, faintly, for a few seconds before it fades away; or a voice briefly persists like a ghostly echo. The physicist's explanation is actually quite simple, but the effect is rather puzzling, and may serve as a metaphor for the relatively well-attested cases (such as the famous cross-correspondences) where communications from the recently dead are received by the living. On the hypothesis of the gradual extinction of the individual aspect of the psyche, such signals would be due to vestiges of a personality still clinging to the discarnate mind-stuff – like the ghost-voice coming from the turned-off radio receiver. The general insipidity of these communications and the infantilism often manifested in the physical phenomena produced during seances would indicate the progressive decline of these vestiges of personal consciousness – as in our film played backward – from adulthood to infancy before being reabsorbed in the universal womb. It is true that some apparitions – assuming that not all are hallucinations – are not of the 'recently' dead but seem to have originated centuries ago. But time has become an ambiguous entity in modern science, and emotional 'hang-ups' may retard the process of de-personalization.

To invoke yet another metaphor – what else can one do when faced with the unutterable? – compare this process with the flow of a river into the ocean. As it approaches the estuary, the river becomes tidal, is periodically invaded by the ocean – the mystics' intimations of eternity. On the other hand, even after leaving its solid banks, the river carries deposits for miles past its point of entry into the ocean, muddying its clear waters with vestiges of the dry land, until it loses itself and the last traces of its origin. But this does not mean that the river has been annihilated. It has only been freed of the mud that clung to it, and regained its transparency. It has become identified with the sea, spread over it, omnipresent, every drop catching a spark of the sun. The curtain has not fallen; it has been raised.

X

This outlook, however subjective and vague, is at least sufficiently definite to exclude belief in personal immortality – warts and all. At the same time the hypothesis of a cosmic psi-field is no more fantastic than the physicist's superspace replete with quantum foam, and even has some affinities with it. Carrying speculation one last step further, we might assume that the cosmic mind-stuff evolves as the material universe evolves, and that it contains some form of historical record of the creative achievement of intelligent life not only on this planet, but on others as well. Our astrophysicists now tell us that there are between a hundred and a thousand million potentially life-supporting planets in our galaxy alone; and some of these are so much older than the earth that the evolutionary stage reached by their inhabitants must compare to man as man compares to the amoeba. Science fiction is much too parochial to convey even an inkling of such forms of existence. 'Reality' wrote J. B. S. Haldane, 'is not only more fantastic than we think, but also much more fantastic than anything we can imagine.' Perhaps when we are no longer entangled in the veil of Maya we shall catch a glimpse of it.

Notes

(1) Bertrand Russell, *Unpopular Essays* (1950), p. 141.
(2) *The Roots of Coincidence* (1972) and *The Challenge of Chance* (with Sir A. Hardy and R. Harvie) (1973).
(3) Quoted by Heisenberg, *Der Teil und das Ganze* (1969), pp. 101f.
(4) Heisenberg, *op. cit.*, p. 113.
(5) Pauli, 'Der Einfluss Archetypischer Vorstellungen auf die Bildung Naturwissenschaftlicher Theorien bei Kepler' in Jung-Pauli, *Naturerklärung und Psyche. Studien aus dem C. G. Jung-Institut, Zürich, IV* (1952), p. 164.

(6) Sir James Jeans, *The Mysterious Universe* (1937), 122f.

(7) *Op. cit.*, 51.

(8) 'Superspace and the Nature of Quantum Geometrodynamics', in *Batelle Rencontres* (1967), 246.

(9) Quoted by Laurence B. Chase, 'The Black Hole of the Universe', *University, A Princeton Quarterly* (Summer 1972).

(10) *The Scientist Speculates – An Anthology of Partly Baked Ideas*, I. J. Good, ed. (1962).

(11) Parascience Research Journal, Vol 1, No. 2 (February 1975), p. 5.

(12) Quoted by D. W. Sciama, *The Unity of the Universe* (1959), 99.

(13) In *Science and ESP*, J. R. Smythies, ed. (1967), 218.

(14) *Op. cit.*

(15) F. S. C. Northrop in his Introduction to Heisenberg's *Physics and Philosophy* (1959).

(16) *Main Currents in Modern Thought* (September–October 1972).

(17) D. Bohm and B. Hiley, 'On the Intuitive Understanding of Non-Locality as Implied by Quantum Theory' (preprint, Birkbeck College, Univ. of London, 1974).

(18) Pico della Mirandola, *Opera Omnia* (1557), p. 40.

(19) Paris 1974.

(20) In Erwin Schrödinger, *Science, Theory and Man* (1957), 193f.

(21) Erwin Schrödinger, *Mind and Matter* (1958), 53–4.

(22) ibid., pp. 54–5.

(23) *What Is Life?* (1944), 88–90.

(24) *Mind and Matter, op. cit.*, 86–7.

(25) *Meine Weltansicht* (1961), 108.

(26) In *The Scientist Speculates, op. cit.*, 86.

(27) 'The Meaning of Survival' (Soc. for Psychical Research, 1935).

(28) 'Concepts of Survival', in *J. Soc. for Psychical Research*, Vol. 48, No. 763 (March 1975), 15–16.

(29) 'Psychology and Psychical Research'. The Seventeenth Frederick W. H. Myers Memorial Lecture (Soc. for Psychical Research, 1968), 34–5.

(30) *Integrative Action of the Nervous System* (1906).

(31) Quoted by Adrian Dobbs, 'The Feasibility of a Physical Theory of ESP', in *Science and ESP, op. cit.*, p. 239.

Index

•